ILLUSIONS OF OPPORTUNITY

ILLUSIONS OF OPPORTUNITY

Employee Expectations and Workplace Inequality

SONIA OSPINA

ILR PRESS *an imprint of*

CORNELL UNIVERSITY PRESS | Ithaca and London

First published 1996 by Cornell University Press.

Printed in the United States of America

♾ The paper in this book meets the minimum requirements of the American National Standard for Information Sciences— Permanence of Paper for Printed Library Materials, ANSI Z39.48-1984.

Library of Congress Cataloging-in-Publication Data

Ospina, Sonia Margarita, 1955–
     Illusions of opportunity : employee expectations and workplace inequality / Sonia Ospina.
     p.   cm.
   Includes bibliographical references and index.
   ₁ ISBN 0-87546-356-8 (alk. paper). — ISBN 0-87546-357-6 (alk. paper)
   1. Discrimination in employment—United States.   I. Title.
HD4903.5.U58085   1996
331.13′3′0973—dc20   95-44709

To all working women and men who struggle to make sense of their work lives.

To my parents and siblings, who helped me make sense of the world as I was growing up.

To my husband and son, who help me make sense of my present and future.

The American society proclaims the worth of every human being. All citizens are guaranteed equal justice and equal political rights. . . . As American citizens, we are all members of the same club. Yet at the same time, our institutions say "find a job or go hungry," "succeed or suffer." They prod us to get ahead of our neighbors economically after telling us to stay in line socially. They award prizes that allow the big winners to feed their pets better than the losers can feed their children. Such is the double standard of a capitalist democracy, professing and pursuing an egalitarian political and social system and simultaneously generating gaping disparities in economic well-being.

(Okun 1975:1)

We believe implicitly that everyone has the right to a rewarding, satisfying job. Opportunity, we believe, is the great satisfier; it is in our cultures and in our dispositions. . . . Why isn't it more fully developed and represented in our theories and measures?

(Schneider, Gunnassen, and Wheeler 1992:65)

Contents

viii
Contents

Tables and Figures

Tables

Figures

Preface

While feelings of frustration in our work settings sometimes stem from personal sources, a pervasive, daily sense of disenchantment may arise from more systemic causes. Yet despite the serious intellectual effort underlying most research on work attitudes, findings based on traditional social science models do not seem to offer much insight into these causes. These models ignore how the invisible ceilings, walls, and floors that create organizational inequality affect work experiences. By ignoring this phenomenon, social science may also help replicate the same forces it attempts to understand.

We find ways to deal with our daily work frustrations. Yet despite these efforts, we continually experience a subtle sense of being "on guard," as if we had to protect ourselves from our own supervisors and employers. The feeling stems from the presence of unequal distributions of power, resources, and decision-making capability in organizations, which in turn reflect a machinery that labels, classifies, and sorts individuals into particular slots. Such categorizations define who we are and where we ultimately stand in the larger social system. Once we accept a zero-sum game as part of our work life—when we essentially shrug our shoulders, convinced there is nothing we can do—we feel cheated. We have a basic sense that we *deserve more*. By accepting participation in a distributive system that classifies people into fixed categories, we are robbed of some of our own integrity as human beings.

As a consequence, many of us spend a considerable portion of our productive lives postponing the "good" feelings and the "good" times, waiting for the weekend and for our much planned and anticipated vacation, while barely tolerating our seven- to eight-hour work days. Indeed, such postponing may be one reason why things remain the same despite our recognizing that they could be not only different but better. In an era when we almost desperately search for meaning in our lives, we nevertheless take for granted arrangements that in one way or another make life less enjoyable than it could be. And work is one of the areas in which we most urgently must challenge this state of affairs. Indeed, when work ceases to be a source of personal validation, when jobs do not provide meaning in our lives, when our work slots define who we are (rather than our inherent humanness defining our work), then it is time for us to question our existing workplace arrangements and the frameworks that allow us to accept them.

I initially observed these discrepancies between people's expectations and work experiences in a setting unfamiliar to me. At that time I was interested in solving a research puzzle about work morale in a public organization, and I spent long months observing people and jobs, structures and processes, verbal and written discourses. I studied the codified information provided by personnel records as well as the subtle cues observed during everyday interaction among employees. I also used every written formal and informal document I could locate. The findings were fascinating—and disconcerting. When I discussed them, people invariably said, "I've experienced that too. It's good to see I'm not alone."

While this book is in part a product of that project, it also reflects my thinking about related issues during the years following the data collection. In particular, *Illusions of Opportunity* incorporates new ideas I developed while teaching graduate courses in organizational theory, public management, and human resource management. These courses are designed for students who have been or will become managers and policy analysts in public and nonprofit organizations. From my students I have heard many stories similar to those I am recounting here. And I have observed such patterns in other agencies where I have participated as a researcher, consultant, or adviser to students doing field projects.

Our society makes a strong formal argument about the value of equality of opportunity, yet we do not seem to question hard enough the social arrangements that make equality difficult to implement. I hope that the ideas presented here will be a small contribution toward breaking that cycle. Thus, as readers identify with parts of the stories told and, perhaps, say to themselves, "I knew that," I invite them to rethink the implications and responsibilities behind their reaction—as managers, as employees, as social scientists, and as individuals who care about the human condition.

Employees and managers from the organization studied, colleagues and mentors from the original research project, present colleagues (including my lifetime partner), students at the master's and Ph.D. levels, and organizations I have advised since have all contributed considerably to the way I frame and understand the issues I have written about in this book. Even though they have no responsibility for the ideas and content, my intellectual debt to each is enormous. Particular thanks go to Richard Williams and Ernesto Archila for intellectual and emotional support; Fran Benson and Barbara Feinberg for developmental and editorial guidance; Patricia Roos, Steve Cole, Mark Granovetter, Dennis Young, Tom Sexton, and Elizabeth Durbin for substantive feedback on earlier stages and drafts of the project; Amy Schwartz, Sandra Decker, Ellen Schall, Zouleyma Escala, Yrthia Dinzey, Juliet Offori-Mankata, Gina McCaskill, Rick Delaney, Allan Kraus, Saudamini Siegrest, Elizabeth Kolodnay, Serena Soo-hoo, and Mary Sanders for all types of help and support throughout the process; the New York University Research Challenge Fund and the Rudin Junior Faculty Fellowship of the Samuel and May Rudin Foundation for financial support. Selected portions of the data analyzed in this book have been used in articles published by the following journals: *Business and Economic Review* (Ospina 1991), *Public Productivity and Management Review* (1992a), and *Review of Public Personnel Administration* (1992b). This material appears here by permission of the publishers.

SONIA OSPINA

New York City

PART I

THE PROBLEM: A PERVASIVE GAP

Introduction: The Promise of Opportunity and the Experience of Inequality

Organizations are stratified systems that rank individuals within a hierarchical social order. They are also part of a culture whose very foundations are built upon the ideal of equality. As such, organizations endorse an institutional discourse of equal opportunity and merit while simultaneously sanctioning organizational practices that produce inequality. This contradiction colors daily life for most people at work; it largely influences employee perceptions and reactions to the workplace.

The combination of ingrained beliefs about merit and actual experiences of inequality produces a subtle but real gap between what people expect from work and what they actually get out of it. Employees must engage daily in individual and collective attempts to make sense of this discrepancy and to resolve the cognitive dissonance it may produce. Both the nature and degree of these efforts represent critical ingredients of an organization's climate and general work environment. Yet, those who study work attitudes have been, for the most part, blind to this discrepancy. They have ignored its role in influencing affective reactions such as dissatisfaction, resentment, or disengagement, as well as satisfaction, enthusiasm, and organizational commitment.

The Gap

Attention to the contradiction between the ideals and the realities of equality is not new. Several scholars have studied it in their effort to understand public opinion. McClosky and Zaller (1984) relate the discrepancy to value conflicts caused by the coexistence of two opposing traditions of belief, capitalism and democracy. At the heart of the American ethos, they argue, lies the contradiction itself: "While most Americans favor a competitive, private economy in which the

3

most enterprising and industrious individuals receive the greatest income, they also want a democratic society in which everyone can earn a decent living and has an equal chance to realize his or her full human potential" (p. 292). Verba and Orren (1985) link it in turn to a schism people in the United States experience between the economic and the political spheres of social action. Kluegel and Smith (1986) frame it as a clash produced by the coexistence of values of the dominant ideology of opportunity and merit on the one hand, and strong doubts about the justice of economic inequality on the other. These authors argue that the contrast between a prevalent, stable, dominant ideology and emerging challenging beliefs produces inconsistencies, fluctuations, and contradictions in U.S. public opinion.

In their empirical study of beliefs about equality among leaders, Verba and Orren (1985) highlight the pervasiveness of the contradiction by describing its various configurations. They identify, for example, one gap between economic reality and the economic ideal of equal opportunity, another gap between political reality and the political ideal of equality of results, and yet a third gap between the conflicting ideals of equality of results and equality of opportunity. They emphasize the complexity of the contradiction by identifying four distinct tensions between "competing ideals of equality (opportunity versus result), competing units of comparison (individual versus group equality), competing standards of judgement (reality versus ideal), and competing domains (politics versus economics)" (p. 250). The combination of these polarities, they argue, "set[s] the tone and color[s] the content of American beliefs about equality" (p. 20).

Yet discussions of the discrepancies underlying the American ethos have traditionally used a macro level of analysis. Exploring how the broader contradictions manifest themselves at the level of social interaction represents an equally relevant agenda. Moving down to the micro level of social inquiry, the problem for those interested in organizational life becomes how this contradiction gets played out in the workplace. This question becomes even more interesting once we acknowledge the critical role organizations play in social life. Organizations are the chief means whereby the most important ideologies sustaining the present social system—technocracy, meritocracy, and bureaucracy—translate into social practices. How do working people reconcile the cognitive gaps produced by contradictions in social ideologies and practices? How are these discrepancies addressed at the level of daily interaction, and how do they affect employee interpretations of work? These are some of the questions framing the story told in this book.

The Story

This book explores the pervasiveness of the basic contradiction outlined above. It examines the effects of the contradiction on work attitudes by focusing on a large public organization—here identified only as the Public Services Agency (PSA)—in a major city. The aim is to provide a detailed account of how a group of employees made sense of the contradictory signals produced by their work experience. Through this case I examine how work was officially defined (by a civil service system "guaranteeing" equality and merit), how this official definition translated into real work arrangements (characterized by patterns of opportunity and unequal outcomes), and how people in three different career ladders—operators, analysts, and clerical employees—responded to the inconsistent effects of the system's implementation.

Studies have already shown that individuals' positions within a job structure play an important role in shaping responses to the job, to co-workers, and to the organization at large (Kanter 1977). Here I argue that these responses are also influenced by the contradiction between the actual experience of organizational processes (along with the unequal outcomes associated with them) and expectations molded by the broader ideologies of merit and fairness in the workplace. The diversity of employment arrangements and opportunities typical of the present work environment make the contradiction even more apparent to employees today. This awareness in turn shapes their participation as organizational citizens. Waving the banner of merit, stratified work systems promise equality for all, but they deliver special protection to some at the expense of others. Although these opportunity dynamics represent a ubiquitous social force influencing work attitudes in contemporary organizations, they have received very little attention in the traditional literature.

The book's main contribution to the study of organizations is its effort to move beyond the traditional—and often narrow—ways of thinking that characterize research on workplace attitudes. An interest in the relationship between employee attitudes and workplace inequality requires viewing the organization as *a stratified social system embedded in a broader system of stratification*. When this is done, *opportunity* emerges as a significant ingredient of work life, one that deserves more attention than scholars have afforded thus far (Muchinsky 1987; Schneider, Gunnarson, and Wheeler 1992).

This view of organizations also challenges traditional notions of opportunity. Studies of workplace inequality suggest that the competition over organizational rewards does not take place on a level playing field. In his study of a corporate hierarchy Rosenbaum (1984) documents workplace mobility tournaments that eliminate losers early on and place winners in advantageous positions for future competition. These organizational "chains of opportunity" are well documented in the stratification literature (White 1970; Murphy 1988). Rather than generic opportunity, employees encounter patterned opportunity in the workplace (Kanter 1977; Baron, Davis-Blake, and Bielby 1986). Employees may not be fully cognizant of these dynamics but their consequences are very real. They directly influence the social context in which employees process information to interpret their work experience.

The framework underlying my argument connects opportunity structures to perceptions of justice, and those two factors to work attitudes, in a single causal model, as follows: *opportunity structures → perceptions of justice → work attitudes.*[1] The model highlights the relevance of social context in shaping employee responses to work. Consistent with the model, this book is built on a conscious attempt to integrate three separate research traditions into the same framework. I have relied on the organizational stratification tradition to explore the first component of the model (opportunity structures); on the organizational justice and social psychology traditions to develop the second component (perceptions of justice); and, finally, on the organizational behavior tradition to explore the links to the third element (work attitudes). Even though knowledge from each field was vital to the story, theories of social stratification provided the unifying thread to weave the argument that challenges the research tradition on work attitudes.

The presentation of the argument follows the same logic. After formulating the problem and describing the organizational setting in Part I ("The Problem: A Pervasive Gap"), in Part II ("Realities: Documenting Patterns of Opportunity") I analyze opportunity structures for three groups of employees. I also identify the basic organizational forces that helped shape these structures in the context of PSA. Part III ("Perceptions: Experiencing Workplace Inequality") explores the links between opportunity structures and employee cognitive maps. It focuses on how perceptions of justice affected PSA employees' interpretations of their work. Finally, in Part IV ("Reactions: The Social Context of Work Attitudes") I establish an empirical link between those opportunity-colored perceptions and work attitudes such as dissatisfaction and resentment.

As the story unfolds, it becomes apparent that employee cognition was influenced by a powerful discrepancy between expectations and experiences. Employee expectations stemmed from misleading images, that is, illusions of opportunity derived from the broader ideology of merit. Their work experiences, in contrast, were permeated by recurrent instances of organizational inequality, derived from the actual implementation of employment practices. Definitions of organizational reality that emerged from individual and collective efforts to cope with organizational inequality gave meaning to the daily work experience of each occupational group. Both illusions and realities of opportunity were part of the cognitive structure employees used to interpret and respond to their work.

PSA employees experienced unequal opportunities in a presumably merit-oriented system. They then strove to make sense of the reward distribution process in ways that would resolve this discrepancy. For example, employees involved in separate opportunity structures endorsed different and competing definitions of merit in support of the most favorable mode of reward distribution. They also tried to affect discussions about "merit criteria" in ways that would justify both their right to organizational rewards and their claim to being deserving organizational citizens.

The dynamics generated by these cognitive attempts to resolve the contradictions between realities and images ultimately affected the organizational climate, promoting low morale and increasing the potential for group and interpersonal conflict. There was also a "boomerang effect," when this conflict and low morale negatively influenced the work attitudes of other PSA employees in all career ladders.

I do not claim that the processes studied in PSA are typical of every organization. I do argue, however, that the effect of opportunity on work attitudes in this one organization illustrates mechanisms and dynamics of resource distribution that are typical of most stratified work systems characterized by hierarchical arrangements. As will become clear, contradictions within contemporary work arrangements may be exacerbated in public organizations, where work is colored by the formal ideology of the "merit system" (as its followers call the civil service system). The discrepancies between expectations and experiences are highlighted, and issues of distributive justice become more transparent, in an organizational context that formally espouses the right of equal opportunity under the law. Yet similar issues arise, under different terms, in any organization characterized by hierarchical work arrangements of the type described in this case.

The Analytical Strategy

The empirical findings reported here are based on the study of patterns of association between work attitudes and individual, job, and contextual factors (including opportunity) in a particular organizational setting. The case study relied on both quantitative and qualitative modes of inquiry. Primary data were gathered using participant observation, semi-structured interviews with selected personnel (PSA employees and managers), unobtrusive analysis of written material about the organization, and a questionnaire about perceptions of work and satisfaction. The latter targeted a cross-section of employees working in the three career ladders. The unobtrusive study of opportunity included a careful analysis of personnel files and other agency artifacts such as written administrative procedures regarding promotion, evaluation, and the merit system; agency job descriptions; civil service documents; payroll rosters; and other PSA forms and reports.[2]

The qualitative examination of opportunity structures and employee perceptions was complemented with a quantitative analysis of the link between opportunity related factors and work attitudes (with an emphasis on job satisfaction). Multivariate models helped assess variations in opportunity and in job satisfaction within and across the three career ladders. The goal was to explore how individual, job and organizational variables affected satisfaction, *given the participation of employees in specific opportunity structures*.[3] This analysis confirmed that patterns of opportunity typical of each structural context influenced employee satisfaction in each ladder. "Thick descriptions" derived from observation, interviews and document analysis added texture to interpret these findings.[4] The Appendix describes the methodology for the original research project.

The Public Nature of PSA

Contemporary American public bureaucracies generate many of the employment opportunities available to members of almost all occupational groups. The study of work attitudes in these bureaucracies is therefore both legitimate and widely applicable.[5] Exploring the impact of stratification processes and outcomes on work attitudes of public employees is a valid intellectual exercise in itself. I would argue, however, that the story of PSA provides insights into the reality of the workplace regardless of the sector.

The civil service system can be viewed as the public version of a type of employment relationship characterized by employee protection from market competition. But this form also exists in the private sector. In many industries internal labor markets (ILMs) have become typical ways of organizing work.[6] An increasingly common type is the corporatist model found in many large private organizations in the United States and Japan (Lincoln and Kalleberg 1990). The public version of this ideal type is known in the literature as "the bureaucratic labor market," perhaps to differentiate it from similar types occurring in other sectors and industries (DiPrete 1989).

That PSA is a public agency, does not limit this study's potential usefulness to public management only. What is generalizable about the story of PSA is the pervasiveness of employee efforts to make sense of their job experiences in a stratified work system. Indeed, sooner or later virtually all employees have a personal confrontation with this contradiction: the system distributes rewards according to an individual's title and rank and at the same time espouses a discourse of equality of opportunity based on merit. Although the ideology highlights the inherent equal worth and dignity of each individual human being, the patterns of opportunity produce a reality that promotes irrelevant feelings of superiority-inferiority, unnecessary status differences, artificial superordinate-subordinate relations, and the neglect of the needs and interests of some members of the organizational community (Deutsch 1985).

As long as work is arranged under systems that create invidious distinctions among human beings, organizational life in public and private settings alike will continue to be built around this fundamental contradiction.[7] Very few employees in this country are exempt from experiencing it in one way or another. Many more will become exposed to it as their own vulnerabilities become evident in today's competitive environment. When retrenchment or reorganization efforts touch them, as seems highly probable in the present economic context (Osterman 1988), they will have to confront it.[8]

Exploring the Nature
and Impact of the Gap

The impending shift from a manufacturing to an information and service-based economy in the United States suggests that work will become increasingly dependent on the willingness of employees to commit themselves to an organization's mission. Increased employee-client interactions in service delivery and labor-intensive information technologies illustrate the relevance of positive employee attitudes and behaviors. The shift may also represent a historical conjuncture in which old ways of organizing are questioned and replaced by newer and more flexible "organic" designs. In this context, attention to employees' cognitive and affective reactions to their work becomes a critical prerequisite of organizational effectiveness and successful change (Beer et al. 1985).[1]

Within this environment of increased competition, a preoccupation with the allocation and distribution of resources (including jobs and people) necessarily heightens concerns with distributive justice in the workplace, even among people who may have had no interest in the subject before. Heightened uncertainty triggers a generalized attention to fairness in the workplace. Organizational justice has, in fact, become a relevant consideration for managers because it helps shape employee responses to work (Cropanzano 1993). The acceptance of this phenomenon as part of the managerial agenda is illustrated by the first paragraph of a management book on the topic:

> Justice matters when actions or decisions by people within organizations potentially benefit or harm the interests of some individuals or groups in a differential manner. Concerns for justice may also be invoked when actions or outcomes violate people's expectations concerning "the ways things happen" or "the way things are supposed to be." (Sheppard, Lewicki, and Minton 1992:ix)

Since competition for scarce organizational rewards is typical of hierarchical work arrangements, it is clear that justice will matter most of the time. Furthermore, increased competition in the contemporary work environment challenges the existing distributive order, and this in turn raises people's sensitivity to issues of justice. These realities cannot be excluded from social science's search for a better understanding of work. The contradiction between opportunity expectations and the experience of inequality may, in fact, illuminate work attitudes in today's highly volatile work environment. The two sides of the contradiction—reality and image—provide a background against which to improve our understanding.

Realities: Inequality and the Contemporary Organization of Work

Organizations are the place where people experience stratified work arrangements at a personal level. Indeed, many processes of social selection and allocation that result in unequal social positions in the larger social structure take place within the micro world of the organization (Baron and Bielby 1980; Baron 1984).[2] A person's attainment of a given socioeconomic position can be conceptualized as a function of several social forces. One can imagine at least four levels of reality, from the interaction of forces in the larger socioeconomic system down to the interaction of individuals within an organization. These levels can be represented as concentric circles surrounding an individual employee. The levels are structural and institutional contexts that interact with one another and, in so doing, affect the individual's work experience (see Figure 1).

Each structural level itself represents a type of stratified system with a life of its own. The outer circle, representing the most macro level, includes the economic forces generated by specific social systems (capitalism, industrialism). Moving inward, the next circle represents the level of sectorial labor markets (industry, services, government). Next are occupational and craft labor markets. Finally, the innermost circle represents the organizational labor market. The employment relationship is enacted within organizational job progressions. Embedded within these, the job represents the realm where individuals experience the social impact of the other structural levels.[3]

Studies in the organizational stratification tradition have documented that the work environment is characterized by separate employment contracts for particular "types" of employees within the same organization or industry (Rosenbaum 1984; Baron, Davis-Blake, and Bielby 1986; DiPrete 1989). While some arrangements are a function of the classic rules of supply and demand in the broader labor market, others are based on nonmarket institutional forces affecting the organization. Consider the new form of work organization proliferating in countries as different as the United States and Japan. Confronted with the

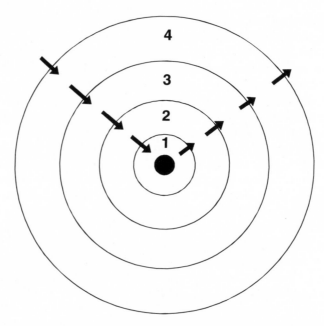

Figure 1. Structural and institutional levels affecting individual attainment. • = individual and job; 1 = organizational and internal labor market; 2 = occupational and craft labor market; 3 = labor market economic sectors; 4 = other economic forces. Graphic by David Grossman.

imperative to maximize commitment, a firm will seek to promote among employees a serious personal investment in the firm's future through the development of internal labor markets. In this type of arrangement a highly structured, formalized apparatus provides legitimacy to the rules for reward distribution.[4] However, its implementation has resulted in the coexistence of a core of permanent employees and an adjacent group of workers holding temporary jobs. The temporary workers constitute an expendable work force whose exclusion from the permanent employment system is reflected in low wages, few benefits, and little job security (Pfeffer and Baron 1988; Lincoln and Kalleberg 1990).[5]

Clusters and progressions of jobs within the same firm may therefore be defined by logics as different as market competition and welfare corporatism. Working conditions, criteria for recruitment and hiring, terms of compensation, criteria for promotion, and prospects for on-the-job training may in fact vary from one career ladder to the next within the same organization—a condition that scholars refer to as heterogeneity in the organization of work (Althauser 1987). Phrases describing equivalent realities include "internal labor markets" (Doeringer and Piore 1971; Osterman 1984a and b), "segmented labor markets"

(Gordon, Edwards, and Reich 1982), or "tiered job structures" (DiPrete 1989), depending on the author and the perspective used.

Students of these phenomena have concluded that the opportunity to demonstrate one's merit and thus to gain access to organizational rewards may not be equally distributed. Indeed, one's chances of success are likely to vary according to one's location within particular work arrangements. The latter define the terms of the employment contract. Inequality results from the institutionalization of the employment relationship in jobs and clusters that respond to the technical and social imperatives of the contemporary organization of work. Individual attainment takes place in these organizational contexts, where opportunity is socially structured and unequally distributed. The images of opportunity that people bring to their jobs do not acknowledge this reality, however. Whereas employees enter the organization with certain expectations about their opportunities, they find themselves participating in work arrangements that allocate opportunities and rewards unequally.

Images: Equality, Opportunity and Merit

The combination of the idea of opportunity and the belief in an inherently just world yields the formula most commonly used to interpret social reality in the United States: what one gets out of life is one's own doing, and nothing can stop a person genuinely committed to the pursuit of success. Using a 1980 survey of the beliefs and attitudes about inequality in Americans aged eighteen or over, Kluegel and Smith document the strength of what they call the "dominant stratification ideology" and its stability over the previous three decades (1986:5). This ideology, they argue, has three basic premises, which most Americans accept: there is plenty of opportunity for economic advancement based on hard work; individuals are personally responsible for their own economic fate; and unequal distributions of economic rewards are generally appropriate and fair. The authors argue that people accept this ideology even though they have doubts about the justice of economic inequality.[6] These doubts are largely responsible for the inconsistencies found in people's opinions about inequality, although the evidence suggests that acceptance of the ideology is still pervasive.[7]

The notion of "deserving" as a focal organizing theme of people's lives (Reis 1984) is illustrated by the generalized belief in an inherently just world, one in which people generally get what they deserve (Greenberg and Cohen 1982; Kluegel and Smith 1986).[8] Consider two independent studies of working-class families striving to survive during the late 1970s and early 1980s. They describe how respondents attributed their precarious economic condition to choices made earlier in life, including factors such as quitting school early. As parents, these couples strongly urged their children to try to take control of their fate and to avoid repeating their mistakes (Rubin 1976; Halle 1984). Other studies show that many social groups, the unemployed for example, have similar responses with respect to their sense of deserving (Lane 1986).

At a more general level, data from the National Opinion Research Center (NORC) show that during the 1970s more than two-thirds of the public believed that "hard work is most important in getting ahead" while less than one-tenth believed that "luck or help from others is most important" (Lane 1986). The pervasiveness of these beliefs in America can be further illustrated by the absence of change over time. A comparison of nine NORC surveys spanning fifteen years yields only a two-point change in the percentage of people who believe that individual effort explains success. In 1973 65 percent of the public believed that "people get ahead by their own hard work" and 10 percent attributed success to "lucky breaks or help from other people". In 1988 the same question yielded a distribution of 67 percent believing in hard work and 12 percent in luck (Mayer 1992:90). Even more striking is a comparison between two AIPO (American Institute of Public Opinion, Gallup) surveys, one from 1939 and the other from 1970, in which first 80 percent and then 86 percent of the respondents attributed success largely to ability, compared to 16 percent and 8 percent who attributed it to luck (Mayer 1992).[9]

In another instance, a survey was made of two groups of adolescents who attended the same local high school in 1924 and 1977, an interval of fifty years. This study illustrates an enduring belief in personal responsibility for success or failure in this country. Forty-seven percent of both groups said it was true that "it is entirely the fault of the man himself if he cannot succeed" (sic) (McClosky and Zaller 1984). By 1988, 38 percent of the adults answering a Gallup poll attributed poverty to lack of effort and another 17 percent said it was both lack of effort and circumstances beyond control (Gallup 1989).

Both the self-congratulatory attitude of those who feel they have attained what they deserve and the direct or indirect self-blaming attitude of those who feel they are responsible for not having succeeded reflect a strongly ingrained ideology of merit in the mind of the average American worker. The hegemony of these beliefs is consistent with a pattern of thinking rooted—both historically and ideologi-cally—in the market system that predominates in Western societies, particularly in the United States. The emphasis on fair competition within a free market makes "merit as competence" the prevailing definition of success, in contrast to personal origins.

The values underlying these beliefs represent a particular way of understanding the world that is no more than three or four hundred years old. Their philosophical roots can be found in the doctrines of the Enlightenment and in the documents that legitimated the major political upheavals accompanying the transition from the feudal aristocratic to the capitalist democratic systems, including the French Revolution and the decolonization of the Americas (Wallerstein 1988).

The ideas that sustained the democratic revolutions of the eighteenth and nineteenth centuries also contrasted "particularism" and "universalism" as two distinct sets of value systems about the rights and obligations of individuals. Consistent with this was the distinction between ascription and achievement. The emergent value system rejected particularism and ascription while embracing universalism and achievement, under the distributive slogan "to each according to his or her merit (contribution)" (Deutsch 1985).

This switch represented a clear preference for a justice of earned deserts, based on the principle of equity, which fits well with market competition. The assumption was that a "free market" for labor impartially sets the market price for different qualities and quantities of labor. The "invisible hand" of the market ensures that those with greater contributions to make, based on their ability, effort, or talent, will in fact be directed toward the most difficult and important positions, thereby benefiting society at large. This notion of proportionality between inputs (contributions) and outputs (rewards) represents the dominant distributive justice principle in the United States, taking precedence over the principles of need or equality.

Deutsch (1985) claims that the pervasiveness of this principle stems from the tendency of economic values to spread through different arenas in a market society. The equity principle implicitly assumes that economic rationality and financial values are appropriate in all types of social relationships and in different areas of social life. As individual worth becomes equated with economic utility, price tags are assigned to different levels of usefulness in society. Once work is defined as a transaction, individualistic and competitive work environments mirror and reinforce the dominant equity principle.

Since it assumes that the market follows natural laws and market outcomes are inevitable, this value system emphasizes individual agency. The self is credited or blamed for one's fate in a competition where the best inevitably thrive.[10] This belief helps explain why in this country self-esteem derives to a large extent from market transactions that define a person's place in the structure, and why productive work has become a centerpiece of life (Lane 1986, 1991). It also helps explain why justice in the distribution of resources and rewards is based on a commitment to provide equal opportunities so that individuals can achieve based on their merit.[11]

Of course, such beliefs are neither universal nor necessarily endorsed by all members of the American society.[12] But historical analysis of the norms of equity and equality do indicate that market-based systems tend to foster values such as instrumentalism, individualism, and competition, which favor an equity principle of justice, while other types of social organization may promote the values of communalism, collectivism, and cooperation more consistent with an equality principle of justice (Lane 1986; Sampson 1983).

Dominant meanings assigned to equality, opportunity, and merit as criteria for allocating social rewards have also changed over time (McClosky and Zaller 1984; Verba and Orren 1985). The Puritan ideal of "equality of the elect" was linked to "God-given grace." In the Revolutionary War period the criterion for virtue changed to the more secular notion of "intellectual talent." Such ability legitimized, in the eyes of the Constitution's framers, the existence of a "natural aristocracy" (Bell 1973). In the nineteenth century, an anti-elitist view of society related merit to "personal effort and ingenuity." At the turn of this century, the definition switched toward a Darwinian conception of native intelligence as "objectively" measured by IQ and other psychometric techniques (Tyack 1974; Spring 1985). In the late twentieth century, with the advent of the so-called postindustrial society, a new definition of merit highlights the ownership of technical skills, usually acquired through or demonstrated by the possession of higher education credentials (Collins 1979). While the definitions have changed over time, they have done so incrementally, one on top of the other, creating an amorphous concept that people can shape to use as they see fit.

Meanwhile, the popular culture clings to the notion of merit as competence, which represents today the most accepted form of social ranking. Indeed, if there is a consensus in the American ethos, it is around the idea that something other than personal characteristics should define where a person ends up in the competition for success. Yet, depending on the structural location, and on the type of cultural capital held by the person making the claim, one particular definition of merit may become more legitimate than another in a particular social context.

The precarious agreement on the legitimacy of merit is based on the tacit assumption that as long as the starting point and the general rules of social competition are fair, anything goes. Americans in general feel comfortable with the idea of a hierarchical society, one in which some have more than others, so long as they believe that people get to the top on their own, through fair competition. What this society cherishes most is the notion of equality before the law, which, in theory, results in the opportunity for individuals to prove their merit.[13]

The U.S. version of equality can be characterized, therefore, as a demand for equal treatment in the conditions and processes that allow people to participate in competitions, rather than as a demand for equal distribution of outcomes. Moreover, the underlying principle of distribution is still that of proportionality, or equity, which is not egalitarian to the extent that it allots different amounts of benefits or burdens to different members of a group (Oppenheim 1980). In this sense, the demand for equality in this country may very well represent "a demand for an equal right and opportunity to become unequal" (Taylor 1991:62).[14] This paradox represents, in fact, the background of the contradiction to be examined in this book.

The Paradox Mirrored within the Organization

The intellectual roots of the modern definition of merit as competence and its connection to the generalized sense of justice in the United States point to the construct of the "rational-legal bureaucracy" defined by Max Weber's study of organizations at the turn of the century. This "ideal type" had become, by the mid-twentieth century, the most typical and the most legitimate form of organizing the workplace. Today's questioning of the model by scholars and managers alike may represent the beginning of another historical transformation of similar proportions (Maccoby 1988; Barzelay 1992). Yet the values underlying the bureaucratic model still provide the most cogent understanding of the way employees apply the notion of "deserving" as they make sense of the experience of work in modern organizations. These values also help sustain the illusions of opportunity employees hold as they enter a given workplace.

Bureaucracy's superiority over previously dominant forms of organization lies in its direct contribution to protect organizational members from the whims of individual "masters." Universalistic criteria secured continuity and stability and reduced ambiguity in the employment relationship. This contrasted with the particularistic organizational forms of feudalism, early capitalism, and slavery, where relations were personalized and highly idiosyncratic. Bureaucracy's protective nature is illustrated by three clusters of features: its definition of the structure and function of work, its means of rewarding effort in the workplace, and its protection of individuals in organizations (Perrow 1986).

First, bureaucracy is built upon a hierarchy of offices, on specialized training and expertise, and on the specification of limited areas of competency, responsibility, and authority for each organizational member. This specialization and coordination of tasks facilitates control over individual performance. Jobs represent areas of competency associated with different salaries and status, according to the function they play in a hierarchical division of labor. These assumptions provide the pillar of traditional human resource management systems, which focus on job evaluation and classification schemes.

The second feature of bureaucracy deals with rewards. Bureaucracy ensures the creation of fixed salaries graded by rank, the clear separation between the organization's and the person's private affairs and property, and the notion of careers constructed on promotions according to seniority or achievement. That rewards are attached to the *job* not the person permits the creation of external standards of merit, independent of personal qualities. The impersonality of the system helps to separate ascribed from achieved criteria to assign rewards.

The third characteristic of bureaucracy is the protection of individual rights and the prevention of the arbitrary use of power typical of earlier organizational forms. This includes limits on a superior's authority over subordinates and the right to appeal decisions and formulate grievances—features emphasizing universalistic criteria.

The first cluster of bureaucratic attributes (structure and function of work) lay the structural ground for collective action. They help institutionalize rules that protect individuals. The second and third clusters (rewards and protections) provide important ideological boundaries to frame the experience of work. They help sanction permissible behavior by introducing issues of merit, equity, and fairness.

These traits are thus clearly connected to modern variations of the psychological contract and to contemporary definitions of employment. In the same way, they are linked to the sense of "deserving" that employees attach to performance. The strength of these links illustrates the connection between bureaucratic ideology and the technocratic and meritocratic ideologies. The three share a preoccupation with efficiency, universalism, and achievement associated with instrumental rationality. Technocracy and meritocracy work as ideologies at the institutional level of society. The theory of bureaucracy helps convert them into social practices at the organizational level. These belief systems reinforce each other and are directly experienced by the average individual, who spends a large portion of his or her life in organizations. Most of us have been born in a hospital, educated in a school, and hired to work in a private, public, or non-profit agency.

At the core of these three notions lies an acceptance of the belief that inequality is necessary for effective social organization. Even though in theory bureaucracy equalizes people by placing the emphasis on jobs, in practice it classifies them by assigning different worth to different jobs. Differences in worth are expressed in monetary values (salaries associated with jobs) and in statuses (the perks and deferences associated with jobs). Equity becomes a means to justify morally the rights and obligations tied to the superior-subordinate relationship (McClintock and Keil 1982). Rewards are tied to the degree of compliance with duties and obligations, thus rationalizing the possibility of unequal results in the distribution of resources. The system then justifies inequalities in the name of economic rationality. It allows those benefiting from the distribution of power to feel that they deserve to be where they are, and it restrains the discontent of those who are not benefiting by sending the signal that they are where they deserve to be.[15]

By depersonalizing work (depersonalizing it in a positive sense) bureaucracies have promoted the use of universalistic values to ensure a more predictable and stable social interaction between subordinates and bosses. At the base of this interaction, however, is a value system that assumes hierarchical distinctions and deference to authority. And "immediacy of response" and a "suspension of judgement" are expected from subordinates toward persons in the upper echelons of the hierarchy (Argyriades 1991).[16]

The technocratic view of production (and its accompanying meritocratic view of hiring) thus reinforces the belief that bureaucracy represents the *best* technical solution to organization, and that it is best because the movement of people through it is based on universalism and achievement (Bowles and Gintis 1976; Tyack 1974). Since hierarchy would seem to be legitimated by Science and Reason, individuals internalize the authority of superiors over inferiors and accept their own position in the structure. Indeed, the authoritarianism of bureaucratic hierarchies and the resulting inequality of incomes and status are viewed as legitimate consequences of "neutral" organizational arrangements. In this context, justice and fairness become equated with objectivity and efficiency, and this serves as the basis for compliance and acceptance of the social and organizational status quo.

This discussion suggests that "merit" is more than the mere possession of technical knowledge or competence. It also includes a person's willingness to use his or her cultural and technical capital for the sake of the organization and at the request of its managers. Such compliance is, however, a hard request to make on employees and workers who have always assumed that having a "voice" and actively participating are a citizen's right and duty. Here we confront a historic irony in which the expansion of bureaucratic discourse, with its capacity to regulate ever larger chunks of individual life in the name of rationality, comes into contradiction with the claims of a liberal democratic discourse designed to protect individual agency (Ferguson 1984).

This contradiction is the source of the gap between expectations and realities. As Chapter 1 suggested, this gap mirrors a broader contradiction, one which colors belief systems in this country. At its heart, as McClosky and Zaller (1984) argue, is the conflict between the values underlying the two dominant belief systems of capitalism and democracy. Capitalism values individuals according to their contributions to production, whereas democracy advocates the equality of all; capitalism emphasizes a reward system that encourages individual competition and promotes unequal distributions, whereas democracy emphasizes the protection of all individuals and consideration of their needs regardless of their contributions; finally, capitalism endorses the fairness of market competition, whereas democracy upholds the right of popular majorities to override market forces for the collective good. McClosky and Zaller argue that these conflicting values have shaped ideological divisions and help explain swings in the national mood.

This contradiction also forms the basis of many tensions found today within bureaucracies. One manifestation, for example, is people's love-hate relationship with this type of organization: they criticize it when it works against their interests but demand it when other organizational practices are unfavorable to them. Such ambivalence will only intensify as the bureaucratic form is reinvented or replaced by new forms of organization emerging in an increasingly competitive environment. Whatever forms appear, their designers will still face the problem of how to protect employees from the potential arbitrary use of power within organizations (Perrow 1986).

The Intellectual Project: Exploring the Impact on Work Attitudes

The stratified nature of work systems cannot be ignored in the search for systematic explanations of employee reactions to work. In his classic statement about work behavior, Hirschman (1970) suggests that employees' reactions to their work experience can follow one of three behavioral patterns: exit, voice, or loyalty. Part of the cognitive dynamics leading employees to make these choices is a search to validate the sense of deserving, given a zero-sum competitive reward system.

Despite their contributions, very few existing theories have seriously considered the implications of this argument. Most research on organizational behavior and organizational justice seems to be based instead on traditional assumptions about merit and opportunity. This research takes for granted inequalities produced by stratification, and it ignores systemic contradictions in its explanations of attitudes, behavior, and interaction at work. This represents a blind spot in both scholarly and popular views of work attitudes.

Once organizations are understood as stratified systems, at least three aspects of organizations will be seen to influence work attitudes: the actual process of resource distribution and its outcomes, employees' perceptions of these, and the social context that defines how employees make sense of their experience. The premise of this approach is that opportunity structures affect work attitudes, but only as mediated by people's self-evaluations in social contexts characterized by varying degrees of inequality. These contexts consist of interrelated forces—personal and structural, subjective and objective, micro and macro—that affect social interaction and cognition. Understanding this complexity demands drawing knowledge from several areas of organizational studies.

In particular, three formal perspectives on the study of work shed light on the way employees address work contradictions and their effect on work attitudes: the organizational behavior tradition in the study of attitudes, the organizational justice tradition within social psychology, and the stratification tradition in the study of the organizational determinants of inequality. A critical application of these traditions can strengthen them ever while questioning their reticence in acknowledging inequality and in linking it to work attitudes.

The Dialogue with the Organizational Behavior Tradition

Expectancy theorists in the need-satisfaction approach to work attitudes (Vroom 1964; Stone 1992) have focused in particular on the gap between what employees want and what they get. This gap is produced by the contrast between broad human needs and a narrow range of job attributes offered to fulfill them. The organizational behavior (OB) tradition conceptualizes the gap strictly in psychological terms, predicting that it will widen or shrink depending on the internal predispositions of the person involved. I conceptualize the discrepancy differently. The gap between expectations of opportunity and the reality of inequality stems from a stratified work system, and it is thus less dependent on psychological traits than on organizational situations. The extent of the discrepancy is a function of the cognitive dissonance that occurs in situations characterized by high uncertainty when there are transparent violations of the principle of justice in the distribution of organizational resources. The need-satisfaction gap therefore provides both the base to understand the problem and important knowledge of individual reactions to help frame it. But we can improve on it by framing the gap within a broader social context, one that includes the impact of organizational structure.

At first glance, the proposed approach is more in line with the work of structuralist scholars working in the job redesign tradition of organizational behavior. These scholars suggest that an organizational reality may acquire different meanings in different structural contexts (Oldham and Hackman 1981). These scholars use mediation models to link work attitudes (such as job satisfaction) to structural factors (such as work function) and to individual factors (such as occupational status). They have demonstrated, for example, that, other things being equal, occupational status may affect job satisfaction differently, depending on whether the workers are blue-collar or white-collar. The claim is that occupational status, however it is defined, moderates the relationship between individual traits, job attributes, and job satisfaction (Mustari 1992).

What is not clear from these models, however, is the social meaning of this mediating role. The processes by which occupational status actually affects job satisfaction are a black box within the structural models of the OB tradition. The same applies to other "individual" attributes considered in the literature. For example, the impact of race and gender on job satisfaction may be better understood by focusing on structural obstacles such as placement in "opportunity-deflated ladders" or participation in job-segregated clusters. These "individual" attributes may be less important in defining a person's psychological makeup than in defining "who they are" in a given social context, although theoretically job placement should have been influenced exclusively by merit considerations.

In this sense the relationship between individual, structural, and attitudinal variables is much more complex than the structuralist OB tradition has assumed. It is here that the "cognitive revolution" emphasizing the intersubjective nature of social reality can enrich explanations of work attitudes. The information processing school within the OB tradition has been suggesting this since the late 1970s (Salancik and Pfeffer 1978), but it has produced only a limited amount of empirical work. It is in another area of organizational inquiry that issues of cognition have been most successfully incorporated into the empirical study of work attitudes. Not surprisingly, given the conceptual link between work attitudes and inequality, this is the area of organizational justice.

The Contributions of the Organizational Justice Tradition

The literature on organizational justice draws on insights from cognitive psychology to study what produces a sense of justice or injustice in the workplace. As important as it is to study the structural basis of opportunity, it is equally critical to study how perceptions are molded within specific organizational settings. This is the only way to identify the institutional factors that shape employees' definitions of a job and its rewards, as well as their own sense of what they deserve.

The organizational justice literature acknowledges that work perceptions are tempered by generalized social beliefs about merit and justice. Employees expect their employer to fulfill certain moral obligations consistent with dominant principles of distributive justice. Definitions of "deserving" and merit underlie employees' psychological contracts and color their cognitive maps at work. These cognitive maps, or "schemata," provide meaningful ways to judge reality (Salancik and Pfeffer 1978; Folger 1987; Bartuneck and Moch 1987). The notions of "counterfactual thinking" and "cognitive dissonance," coined by cognitive psychologists, are critical to this discussion (Murningham 1993). Cognitive dissonance is a mental mechanism that equips individuals with the ability to think "imaginable alternatives" to existing states of affairs. Workers can, in their minds, undo an existing outcome of the reward distribution process and visualize different levels of favorable outcomes. These are called "referent outcomes" (Folger 1993). If the envisioned alternative does not coincide with the reality, the person will experience some degree of cognitive dissonance; the result will be a negative reaction to the outcome.[17]

Cognitive psychologists also suggest that positive or negative reactions to the outcomes of resource distribution are linked to factors such as the nature of the outcome (positive or negative), the agent that produced the outcome, the characteristics of the process itself, and the normative standards used to understand its legitimacy (Folger 1984, 1993). These factors point to the social nature of the mechanisms by which people interpret their experiences at work. Indeed, reference groups and socially relevant definitions of reality provide helpful contextual information for interpreting the outcomes of resource distribution.

Thus subjective constructions of work, including referent outcomes, do not spring exclusively from individual experiences or from the psychology of each individual employee. Reference groups and socially relevant comparison categories, for example, emerge from the structural designs that inform acceptable behavior and individual action in organizations. That these designs also produce unequal processes and outcomes in resource distribution is a critical factor in daily social interactions at work. Even when employees are not totally aware of them, patterns of inequality may still influence their affective reactions in the workplace. An important contribution of social cognition to organizational behavior research is the notion that people may not be aware of the cognitive processing occurring at all times, because information processing may be conscious or unconscious, controlled or automatic (Ilgen, Major, and Tower 1994). As a pervasive reality of the workplace, organizational inequality is always part of the social setting within which employees process information. That this reality is relatively invisible does not deny its potential influence on people's lives. The organizational justice tradition's blindness to the impact of this systemic inequality has limited the potential application of the theories of social cognition to our understanding of work attitudes.

Enter Organizational Stratification Research

If one takes seriously recent insights about the dynamics of organizational stratification, one needs to search for an explanatory model that incorporates the subtle yet very real manifestations of the organization of work. These include heterogeneous work arrangements, opportunity structures, and career ladders viewed as the structural contexts in which jobs are embedded. The conceptions of distributive justice associated with these structures, and the definitions of merit used to make sense of them, would also become important. As well, this theory would have to consider how these factors can motivate employees either to accept or to question inherently unequal work arrangements.

Central to this way of thinking is the stratification tradition interest in the macro dynamics of legitimation and its role in shaping employee responses to organizational interaction. As will become increasingly evident in the next chapters, the conceptual lens of stratification theory greatly enhances the knowledge provided by traditional models of work attitudes. Research findings about the organizational determinants of inequality suggest, however, that we should also focus on the micro level of jobs and job progressions and on the intermediate level of the organizational reward system.

The intellectual project of this book hence consists in broadening the narrow focus of the three traditions. Expectancy theory and the organizational justice tradition emphasize employee perceptions of their job experience. These approaches must also consider the actual conditions of stratification in which those experiences occur. The organizational stratification tradition focuses on "objective" opportunity structures. The knowledge it provides about the organizational determinants of inequality can benefit from a systematic investigation of employees' expectations, perceptions, and interpretations of inequality—how they experience it subjectively. By taking advantage of the best from each tradition, this book aims to reflect more accurately the complexity of organizational reality.

The Organizational Setting

PSA is one of many bureaucracies under mayoral authority in a large metropolitan area.[1] Based on the size of its employee population and the amount of public funds it uses, it is a fairly large organization. At the time of the study, PSA had a budget of approximately $396 million. It employed about 12,800 persons, which accounted for 6 percent of the entire city work force. Its employees represented a wide array of white- and blue-collar occupations, including skilled craft workers, manual laborers, administrative employees, programmers and computer analysts, engineers, architects, and lawyers.[2] Three important occupational groups among these were the operators, the clerical employees, and the analysts.

Operators, analysts, and clerical employees performed different functions in the organization. At the heart of PSA were those who performed production tasks and rendered services to the public. This group I have labeled "operators"; they represented the operating core of the organization. In contrast, clerical employees represented part of the support staff of the organization; their jobs were designed to assist people in the core. Finally, the analysts were part of the growing technostructure of PSA. Removed from the operating core itself, analysts helped design, plan, change, or train those who participated directly in the work flow (Mintzberg 1979, 1989).

How typical was PSA compared to other public agencies in the same municipality? The answer to this question may vary according to the criteria of comparison. For our purposes, the employment structure is a relevant standard of comparison, because it represents a critical determinant of the opportunity dynamics among employees in various career ladders. Of the twenty largest city agencies including PSA, seven had either identical or very similar employment structures to that of PSA. Taken together, these eight agencies accounted for 80 percent of city employment. Of the eight, three had identical structures to that described for PSA.[3] They were characterized by the existence of a rigid distinction between employees monopolizing operations and those providing technical and administrative support.[4] In addition, at least four other agencies had similar, although not identical, employment structures. These, too, separated professionals from administrators, but in a less rigid way.[5]

Since 80 percent of all city employees participated in employment structures identical or similar to PSA's, the reader should be convinced that the work experience of PSA employees was fairly typical for this city, both in relative and in absolute terms.

An Overview of PSA

PSA had five decentralized departments, each headed by an executive-level manager. Two were responsible for direct production tasks, while the other three provided services to support these operations. At the heart of this structure was the Operations Department, coordinating the basic organizational task and housing 68 percent of all agency employees. While all departments were fairly hierarchical, the support units were more flexible and flat, and the production units were more rigid and bureaucratic.

Consistent with this design, PSA had many work facilities distributed throughout the city. Its organizational culture reflected this geographical dispersion, as people referred to their workplace as either the "main office" or the "field." The latter stood for the locations dispersed around the city where equipment was housed and where most blue-collar production workers reported for work. In contrast, business-dressed employees performed their white-collar work in the relatively corporate-like and clean environment of the main office. The headquarters were located in the downtown municipal government area in several well-maintained locations. The largest was a ten-story building which housed support services such as personnel, budget and payroll, management analysis, and of course the commissioner's office.

Information flowed back and forth between headquarters and various lower-level jurisdictions in the field—the boroughs, the districts, and the sections. Each borough had a supervisor and an assistant, who were directly accountable to the main office. With their display of computers, carpets, and coffee machines, borough offices seemed more like branches of the main office than field stations. The significant difference, and an important cultural icon, was the large bulletin board that showed the location and schedule for the machinery and personnel in each subunit, according to its geographic and administrative jurisdiction.[6]

Further down in the production line were fifty-nine district offices dispersed through out the city. Sometimes located close to the borough offices, they functioned as independent entities. They represented life in the field in a more striking way. A consultant in PSA described the district garages as "high-roofed, cavernous buildings, large because of the huge [machinery] they house." The same source offered the following portrait of the district workplace:

> As one enters the garage, off to one side and sometimes up a flight of stairs, is the district office. The district super . . . is responsible for the supervisors in the field and for the district generally. He has his own office. Within the garage, there is usually another office for other supervisory personnel—garage supervisor, perhaps section supervisors and support staff, including clerical workers. . . . On the wall is the district's Board, where each [operator] is listed with the assignment of the day. . . . The garage office is a bustling place, especially at 7 or 8 AM, just before and after roll call. The desks are cluttered, phones ring, and there is an atmosphere similar to offices anywhere. (Source: internal report)

These work sites each had a locker room, showers, and a lunch room that was also used for playing cards during breaks. Furniture was sparse, with a few old tables and chairs.

The third field level, the section office, was staffed by a team of workers and a supervisor. While some teams met in the district garages, others met in small offices furnished with only a desk and a phone. The section office was distant from the district office and all the higher levels.

PSA enjoyed an excellent reputation as a highly innovative agency. Labor-management relations were good, and public funds were used rationally and efficiently. The agency had consolidated its present structure after separating from a parent agency in the 1960s. In the 1970s, the agency's employee population grew significantly. After the separation the public considered the agency sloppy and wasteful of public resources. The agency also had a bad reputation for poor performance and low worker morale. Then the process of expansion reversed in the 1980s, in part because of the city's fiscal problems and in part because of strong new leaders who promoted important changes in the main operation. Labor and management worked together to run the operation more efficiently and with fewer people. A reduction in the number of operators and an improvement in performance made PSA a model among other municipal agencies. By the late eighties PSA had developed a work environment characterized by innovative approaches to the delivery of public services. One drawback in this transformation was its strong attention to the operators (workers delivering the services); less attention was paid to the working conditions of the administration and support employees.

Ironically, PSA's innovations also led to the creation of new administrative and support positions at both the managerial and premanagerial levels. The introduction of computers and management information systems accelerated the growth of specialized staff employees. As PSA started monitoring performance to improve productivity, analytical functions—usually requiring professional training—gained relevance. In addition, trained clerical employees were needed to keep the work flow and its documentation running smoothly at the new level. ·

This growth also resulted in the uneven development of the administrative and support career ladders, the structure of which grew slowly as different occupational groups entered PSA. The employment conditions of the new jobs did not necessarily respond to a single, consistent logic that mirrored the development of the production jobs. Instead, their growth was to a large extent a function of the historical circumstances marking their creation and of the political clout of their incumbents during their evolution (Rich 1982).

PSA's Employment Structure

In addition to the field/headquarters dichotomy, PSA employees could be classified into two large groups, line and staff, according to the relationship of their tasks to production. Seventy percent of PSA's personnel were line employees responsible for production tasks. The organization of these employees placed much emphasis on differences in rank, and members had direct authority over operations. The other 30 percent were staff employees who either performed supportive clerical tasks and services or supplied technical advice to line officials. Operators were line employees, while analysts and clerical employees were staff.

Line and staff employees interacted daily to keep the organization running smoothly. The organizational culture stressed the importance of good relationships between the two groups and rewarded behavior that was consistent with this value. For example, task forces or policy-making committees would usually include individuals of both types. Yet, the same culture sanctioned practices and policies that suggested clear differences between the two groups. For example, headquarters offices tended to be made up entirely of individuals from either one or the other group. Most of the staff offices had very few line employees, except at the managerial level. In addition, most members with some authority in the headquarters-based Operations Department had field experience as line operators.

The line and staff groups also differed in terms of their social and work experiences. Line operators shared a strong tradition of participation in family and social events through employee organizations and clubs. The staff employees had tried organizing their own associations around ethnic lines, professional interests, or other common backgrounds, but—despite their participation in large and more impersonal labor unions—staff employees had not acquired the strength or cohesion provided by the operators' organizations.

Operators usually shared a European ancestry and were often neighbors at home. They were all men, which means that even since the separation from its parent, agency production tasks had been carried out within a male-oriented culture. Operators who became managers had "grown up" together on the job. As they moved to the main office they assumed the demeanor and behavior appropriate to their position, but the male-dominant culture remained pervasive.[7] This was apparent, for example, in the large number of male managers occupying line positions at headquarters. Staff employees, on the other hand, represented a more diverse set of individuals. They included women and a larger number of people of color. As a group, they varied in terms of educational attainment.

The demographic composition of employees in the agency at the time of the study provides further evidence of diversity. In terms of race/ethnicity, 71 percent of the employees were white, 20 percent were African-American, and 8 percent were Latino, Asian-American, or other. In terms of sex, 92 percent of PSA employees were men.[8] A similarly skewed representation existed for the other three city agencies with employment structures identical to PSA's. This suggests that PSA's demographic distribution—and the experiences derived from it—were typical of at least one-third of the city's work force.

The Internal Organization of Work

Typically blue-collar in nature, operator work consisted of light and heavy manual work in the field. Among the assignments these workers performed at the entry and intermediate levels were lifting heavy loads, driving and operating heavy equipment, transporting equipment and loads from one location to another, performing miscellaneous tasks in garages, and helping to maintain the vehicles. As they moved up the ladder and into district and headquarters offices, operators engaged in more administrative tasks, even though these were always closely connected to the agency's core operation. For example, supervisors oversaw the work at district and borough levels, engaged in budget activities, participated in labor-management committees, performed manpower activities, and implemented general operational and administrative procedures.

PSA clerical employees performed varied tasks with different levels of complexity, such as general office duties, humanpower planning, the organization and coordination of office activities, and assistance in the management of data related to personnel, payroll, and accounting. Examples of simple clerical tasks performed in PSA included office errand work, typing, transcribing, operating a switchboard, performing computation work on records, and assisting in various administrative tasks. More complex tasks included maintaining time and personnel records and field logs, preparing field reports, requisitioning supplies and maintaining inventories, typing, and operating automated office equipment.

Analysts in turn were responsible for projecting and monitoring productivity by analyzing performance indicators and operation statistics. They performed humanpower and human resources analysis, managed information and data systems, diagnosed managerial problems and proposed solutions to them, and helped prepare the agency budget.[9]

Analysts and clerical employees in PSA considered themselves white-collar employees who belonged to the staff group. In contrast, operators viewed themselves as blue-collar line employees. The three occupational types were found in all units, jurisdictions, and levels of PSA's organizational structure. Each type, however, had its own career ladder and its own route for possible success at PSA.

PSA's Job Structure

At the time of the study there were approximately 275 job titles at PSA.[10] These derived their meaning from their location in an implicit social scale constructed from the experience of work:

> A fixed job cannot be defined merely by a title or set of skills however specific. It must be referred to a set of counterpart jobs with which it has regular, prescribed relations; each of them is defined similarly so that a fixed job is defined relative to a whole structure of persons and positions in the social structure. (White 1970:4)

Each job title occupied by an operator, clerical employee, or analyst was part of a ladder defining the terms of employment for incumbents. These definitions in turn shaped the way employees identified themselves and their places within the organization. Career ladders provided the structural and social context in which this social ranking took place (Rosenbaum 1984).

The institutional basis of the job structure in PSA was the civil service merit system (Fox 1993).[11] Job titles in PSA—as in many other government agencies—were codified according to civil service status. They were either unclassified (exempt) or classified. Exempt titles were filled by political appointments (for example, the commissioner). Classified titles were filled by employees who qualified through a competitive examination or met some other clearly specified requirement. Competitive jobs were part of job progressions linking lower with higher titles. Grade levels determined salaries and status through which employees with permanent status moved. An examination was required to enter these jobs. At the time of the study, 87 percent of the employees in PSA had civil service titles. There were also a few noncompetitive titles whose employees did not require examinations but could not be promoted to other jobs (McKinney's Consolidated Laws 1983). Located at different levels of the job structure, they did not correspond to any job progression. But their job security was equivalent to that of permanent employees. These represented 3 percent of PSA's employees.[12] The additional 10 percent worked outside civil service rules.

Civil service competitive job clusters had diverse internal structures and were regulated differently, according to the labor market they tapped. For example, jobs in several skilled craft career ladders derived their rules and regulations from markets in the private sector. In the same way, professional jobs (lawyers, computer programmers, analysts) were sensitive to the dynamics of larger occupational labor markets in both the private and the public sectors. In contrast, clerical jobs were normally dependent upon the dynamics of the public sector labor market. Finally, the operator cluster, an occupational group unique to PSA, was dependent upon rules and regulations defined exclusively for them.

Studies of career lines and progressions have demonstrated that formal structure and behavioral structure do not necessarily (and do not usually) coincide (Blau 1963; DiPrete 1987). Hence, official documents are not entirely reliable for reconstructing job ladders. Drawing a realistic picture of career ladders in a given organization requires assessing the degree of congruence between the formally designed and the realized career trajectories. The career ladders for the clerical and operator groups were almost identical to the officially prescribed system. On the other hand, the analyst ladder varied significantly from the official version. It included, for example, noncompetitive titles that did not belong to the formal classification but that management used to place analysts.[13]

Figures 2, 3, and 4 show the structure of the operator, the clerical and the analyst ladders respectively.

The most salient attribute of the operator career ladder was its simplicity (Figure 2). There were no horizontal movements and the upward path was straightforward. An operator would enter the ladder and could move to the first supervisory position after one year. At the intermediate level he would supervise operators in the field. He could then move to the second supervisory position, at the district level. This represented a premanagerial title, a job in which the incumbent supervised supervisors. In this level there were several grades through which employees could move. Then they could enter management and work at overseeing general operations at the district, borough, and headquarters levels. Within management they could move upward to reach the highest executive positions in the agency.

The clerical ladder (Figure 3) was similar in structure to the operator ladder, but it was more complex. In this ladder employees have several possible points of entry, depending on their skills. An employee could start at either of two levels. One employee might move directly to a supervisory title, while another might first have been an office aide or shop clerk. Employees from other adjacent ladders could move to a supervisory position. The PAA supervisory position had several salary levels before management. The move from premanagerial positions into management was the same for all, however.

The term "ladder" or "progression" must be used loosely for the analyst cluster of jobs (Figure 4). As in the clerical ladder, there were several short ladders at the base. For example an employee could enter the agency as a staff analyst, move up to the supervisory position of associate staff analyst, and then enter

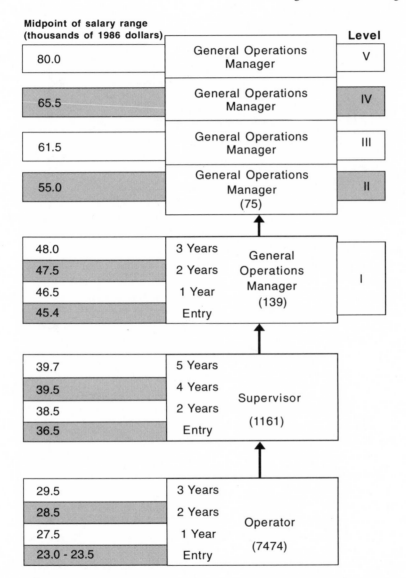

Midpoint of salary range (thousands of 1986 dollars)

Salary	Tenure	Title	Level
80.0		General Operations Manager	V
65.5		General Operations Manager	IV
61.5		General Operations Manager	III
55.0		General Operations Manager (75)	II
48.0	3 Years	General Operations Manager (139)	I
47.5	2 Years		
46.5	1 Year		
45.4	Entry		
39.7	5 Years	Supervisor (1161)	
39.5	4 Years		
38.5	2 Years		
36.5	Entry		
29.5	3 Years	Operator (7474)	
28.5	2 Years		
27.5	1 Year		
23.0 - 23.5	Entry		

Figure 2. Operator career ladder. Numbers in parentheses indicate incumbents at time of study. Graphic by David Grossman.

management.[14] In practice, however, few analysts followed a formal route; many jumped from title to title and from ladder to ladder in an idiosyncratic manner. While it is possible to talk about "entry," "intermediate," "premanagerial" (or supervisory), and "managerial" levels for different types of

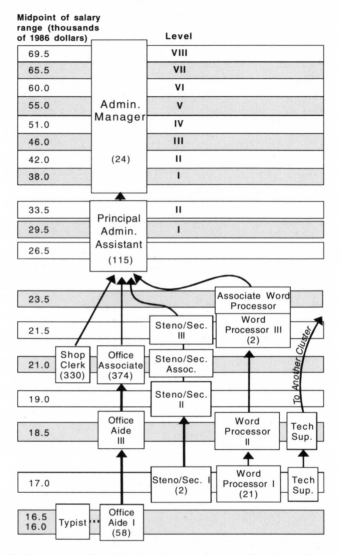

Figure 3. Clerical career ladder. Numbers in parentheses indicate incumbents at time of study. Graphic by David Grossman.

analyst jobs, employees entered the agency at any level, according to their experience and educational credentials.

In a totally bureaucratic system, that is, in an ideal-type civil service system (as outlined by Weber and endorsed by the unions), rational-legal rules are intended to replace subjectivity with "purely objective considerations" in the decision-

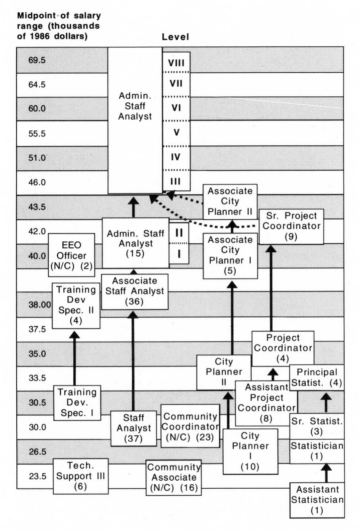

Figure 4. Analyst career ladder. Numbers in parentheses indicate incumbents at time of study. Dotted arrows indicate informal career path. N/C = Non-competitive title. Graphic by David Grossman.

making process. "Objective" criteria are supposed to establish uniformity among public servants "without regard for persons." One possible consequence of such bureaucratization is, in Weber's words, the "leveling of status honor" (Weber 1978:975), which guarantees equal treatment for all employees regardless of membership in particular social groups. This leads to the question of why there were differences in the three ladders, since all were in theory regulated by the civil service system. Although a full answer to this question is outside of the scope of this book, a brief overview of the institutional environment of PSA will help place the descriptions presented here in perspective.

The Institutional Environment of PSA:
Civil Service and the Unions

Bureaucracies represent one important link in the chain of actions constituting the policy-making process. Bureaucracies are tools for implementing public policy, and their nature and structure are directly linked to the political authority which emanates from the democratic context of government. For this same reason, elements of institutional design—such as the separation of powers, intergovernmental relations across federal, state, and local levels, or issues of "democratic constitutionalism"—impose limits on bureaucratic organizations and affect the experience of those who work there (Kelman 1987; Thompson 1990; Wilson 1989; Brock 1984).

Civil Service as a "Merit System"

Critics of bureaucracy suggest that civil service systems stifle an organization's attempts to become more flexible and adaptive to their environments (Savas and Ginsburg 1973; Barzelay 1992). They recommend alternative ways of ensuring the use of merit principles in public employment. Accordingly, many local municipalities and counties across the country have chosen not to use formal civil service systems as the basis of their personnel management practices. For example, by 1989, out of a sample of 1,246 local jurisdictions, 35.9 percent of the cities and 43.7 percent of the counties had built merit principles into their personnel policies without implementing a civil service system (Fox 1993).[15] While many large cities do use civil service, this employment model is more dominant in the state and federal governments. Here the civil service represents an important institutional response to the demands of public personnel management, in particular in large jurisdictions and bureaucracies.

One can define the civil service system as a formal model for regulating public employment on a merit basis. In essence, this model comprises a set of personnel and administrative practices based on accepted professional standards (Lefkowitz 1985). There is nothing unique in its definition of "merit," which can be found in any state-of-the-art personnel system in the public or private sectors. There are, however, representational and structural features of the civil service system that add an important connotation to "merit" in the context of civil service law.

First, public personnel management must respond to several different and sometimes conflicting goals and values, all of which are important and desirable (Klinger and Nalbandian 1985).[16] Of particular relevance are the values of representation, accountability, responsibility, and responsiveness. To ensure these qualities, public managers must consider external standards of action, standards of professional and technical competence, and standards from the perspective of those being served (Fox 1993).[17]

The degree of centralization required to protect these standards represents perhaps one of the greatest differences between a private and a public merit system (Daley 1990b; Saltzstein 1990; Klinger 1990). Managers in private sector organizations have a relatively large amount of control over their personnel decisions. Not so in civil service. Checks and balances are in place to ensure standards, to avoid the use of political loyalty as the basis of employment, and to promote equal access for minorities. Hence, authority over public personnel matters is fragmented and diffused, and managers are constrained by external actors and institutions (Brock 1984; Thompson 1990). Moreover, internal work arrangements are designed to protect individuals from these and other external influences. They promote progressive movement through the ranks on the basis of objective standards of merit linked to jobs. In a professionally operated public organization, the values and principles of merit translate into formalized and predictable human resource management policies, practices, and techniques.

Six criteria can assess the quality of an organization's merit system, be it civil-service based or not (Fox 1993:9).[18] These are:

1. Recruiting, selecting, and advancing employees on the basis of their relative ability, knowledge, and skills, including open consideration of qualified applicants for initial appointment
2. Providing equitable and adequate compensation
3. Training employees, as needed, to assure high-quality performance
4. Retaining employees on the basis of the adequacy of their performance, correcting inadequate performance, and separating employees whose inadequate performance cannot be corrected
5. Assuring fair treatment of applicants and employees in all aspects of personnel administration without regard to political affiliation, race, color, national origin, sex, religious creed, age, or handicap and with proper regard for their privacy and constitutional rights as citizens
6. Assuring that employees are protected against political coercion and are prohibited from using their official authority for the purpose of interfering with or affecting the result of an election or a nomination for office.

These principles of merit represent the most relevant norms of professionalism in public personnel policy. The list suggests that merit can be associated with the use of standards such as ability, knowledge, skills, and performance; but it also conveys the need for measures of equity, fairness, and protection from political and personal abuse. The variety of goals allows different groups to adopt different definitions of merit according to their interests.

No phenomenon shows this possibility clearer than the civil service reform movement. In this arena multiple definitions of merit have been debated in the name of administrative efficiency. Beneath the struggle for efficiency lies also a struggle for control over public employment. This has shaped the form and content of the merit system at the federal, state, and local levels (DiPrete 1989; Rich 1982). At the municipal level interest groups such as reformers, unions, parties, state legislatures, and public employees have played a role in defining the terms of the debate. They all have contributed to shape the civil service system, which in turn has influenced employment in PSA and in many other municipal agencies today (Rich 1982; Gottfried 1988).

Two groups have played a critical role at the local level in giving merit the "rubbery" consistency required to protect their conflicting interests (Rich 1982). One group consists of "reformers" (initially representing the wealthy, later on sectors of the middle class), and the other, organized labor. Each proposed a definition of "merit" that legitimized their own position on the future shape of employment.

The Role of the Reformers

The civil service reform movement of the nineteenth century was a struggle against the spoils system or party patronage under which appointments were used as rewards for party services.[19] Reformers linked this politicized employment relationship with inefficiencies in local government that, in their minds, required drastic solutions (Van Riper 1958).[20] But there was more at stake in this crusade.

At the local level, nineteenth-century reformers on the U.S. east coast represented a patrician class. Their political power was being eroded by industrialists and by the immigrant-supported political machines. Hence they framed personnel reform as a way of cleansing city government of corrupting influences. Assuming an anti–political party position, they appealed to city officials' sense of morality. Since these patricians were not interested in middle or high positions in government, they could link the movement to the abstract "humanitarian" principles of equality, justice, and freedom, and to the values of Christianity. To this end, they proposed "merit" as a moral imperative that would purify local government and make it more efficient. They proposed, for example, "vertical recruitment" as the way to professionalize the service by motivating the low-ranking employees to move up on their own effort and merit (Rich 1982).

Early twentieth-century local reformers, on the other hand, represented a middle-class group that viewed government as a potential source of employment.

Their version of civil service reform downplayed morality. Instead, it focused on the role of enhanced managerial control to address problems that partisan politics and the fragmentation of administrative authority had produced in public organizations. Influenced by Taylorism and the principles of scientific management, these reformers proposed that politics be separated from local government administration, that an autonomous managerial class of professionals be created, and that new managerial techniques be introduced into the bureaucracy (Fox 1993).

Consistently, they also wanted to replace the notion of vertical recruitment by a horizontal recruitment system. In this system a college education would be required for city managers. Reformers argued that this would lead to hiring the "best" people at all levels of the hierarchy. Another important innovation was a tracking system that put a ceiling on the career mobility of lower-ranking civil servants and recruited high-level administrators from the outside. These dynamics did not occur only at the local levels of government. DiPrete (1989) documents a similar movement in the federal system: a new tiered personnel system separated administrative from clerical jobs and made it virtually impossible to move from one to the other.

The Role of Employees

Employees, both as individuals and as associations, represented another important force in the process of civil service reform. Employees did not just passively accept changes in employment conditions. Civil servants resisted Taylorism as much as factory workers did, and this had an effect on the ways in which merit systems were finally implemented (Rich 1982). Over the years, employee associations played a fundamental role in pursuing pay and benefits legislation, rule changes, and job reallocations and classifications, to the point of instituting "a unique system of employee participation in the crucial aspects of the employment relationship" (Lefkowitz 1985:56).

Some scholars believe, however, that by pushing for civil service enforcement, unions and professional associations may have contributed to the erosion of the principle of equity in representation. Specifically, unions agreed to the imposition of educational requirements, that barred employment for a substantial portion of the population. By aligning with a meritocratic discourse that excluded applicants not possessing educational credentials, both municipal civil service systems and the unions and associations that supported them may have fostered social inequality (Gottfried 1988).

There is no agreement in the literature about the degree of influence unions have had in establishing formal merit systems and shaping employment conditions. The lack of consensus may reflect the variation of this influence across jurisdictions and geographical areas.[21] There are three possible interpretations of the relationship between unions and merit systems. One argues that as unions

grew, merit systems declined (Fox 1993).[22] A second argues that as merit standards declined, employees became dissatisfied, and this contributed to the rise of
unionism (Lefkowitz 1985).[23] And yet a third contends that the two institutions
have coexisted and shaped each other (Spero and Capozzola 1973).

The third position represents the official view of organized labor. Position
classification systems based on duties and responsibilities, all meticulously described, and compensation plans based on the principle of "equal pay for equal
work" are, in this view, important tools to protect workers from the arbitrary
whims of management. Indeed, many public employee unions have strongly
supported the civil service under the assumption that it limits the discretion of
managers in important decision-making areas. That is why organized employees
"have lobbied for laws, litigated against their employers and petitioned administrative bodies. They recognized the value of getting public employment civil
service rights legislation passed decades before Congress enacted the National
Labor Relations Act for private sector employees" (Lefkowitz 1985:56). Proponents of this position insist that the unilateral rule making of the traditional civil
service system needs to be replaced by the bilateral mechanisms of collective
bargaining (Fox 1993). They therefore stress the importance of union involvement in civil service reform.

This view is well represented today in many municipalities with active labor
movements. Many public unions firmly believe that principles of merit must be
protected and enforced through a strong merit system. They believe that part of
their mission is to make sure that the city personnel system and city agencies
comply with the system. A major union leader expressed this as follows:

> [The Union] advocates the merit system at all levels of government and the promo-
> tion of civil service legislation and career service in government as one of the
> objectives stated in its constitution. But civil service laws and rules were found too
> broad to care for the day-to-day problems of employees. Even a good civil service
> system must be policed through the collective bargaining process. (Spero and
> Capozzola 1973:208)

Municipal unions have tried to retain the protective features of the merit
system and at the same time to advocate for the right to bargain over personnel
functions such as position classification, wage administration, and grievances.
Some argue this has been done to the point of eroding the authority and discretion of agency managers (Rich 1982).

The study of PSA supports the view that unions and merit systems coexist and
strengthen each other. In the case of PSA, strong unions tended to protect the
merit system by monitoring its enforcement. These dynamics had an undeniable
effect on the employment conditions in the different career ladders. Employees
who belonged to traditionally strong unions enjoyed working environments

characterized by a high degree of civil service enforcement and by the formalization of rules and regulations in human resource management functions. Employees not represented by strong unions were generally subjected to a more flexible
enforcement of civil service law.

This is, then, the institutional context in which employees worked and interacted with each other in PSA. Having completed now an overview of the organizational setting and its institutional environment, I turn, in Part II, to some of the
work consequences resulting from the variations in civil service enforcement
described in this chapter. I will examine their effect on the work experience of
operators, clericals, and analysts in Parts III and IV.

REALITIES: DOCUMENTING PATTERNS OF OPPORTUNITY

CHAPTER FOUR

Processes: Moving Up, Getting Paid, and Learning from Work

In its modern usage, the term *opportunity* refers to a "favorable or advantageous combination of circumstances that presents an individual with the chance to choose among valued alternatives" (Schneider, Gunnarson, and Wheeler 1992:54). The availability of alternatives includes both present and future options. L. Miller,[1] a civil servant occupying the clerical supervisory title of principal administrative associate, described her opportunities in PSA as follows:

> After twelve and a half years in PSA, I have taken and passed five promotional exams. I have received several merit increases and have gotten yearly contract salary increases. In terms of position in the hierarchy, I am at an equivalent level with an operator supervisor who will have needed only one exam and promotion to get to that position, even if it has taken the same time. In terms of salary, however, I am at the equivalent level with the entry-level title in the operator career ladder. (Source: personal interview)

Miller went on to indicate that these differences extended to fringe benefits and other employment conditions. For example, she described how, given a possible conflict in choices about overtime schedules, operator supervisors had priority over clerical employees of the same status. She also explained that overtime rates were different for both types of supervisors, despite the fact that they might work shoulder to shoulder in the same unit and toward the same objectives. Finally, she observed that clerical employees, unlike operators, did not receive substantive automatic salary adjustments during their first couple of years of work at PSA.

Miller also explained some of the reasons behind the difference between her promotions and those of operators of the same rank. The timing of upward movement for civil servants depended greatly on factors such as the frequency of the exams offered, the size of the lists drawn, and of course, the position of the employee on the list. Not all of these factors, she argued, could be controlled by the employee. Moreover, the degree of control seemed to vary from ladder to ladder in ways that were not totally consistent with the ideal predictability promised by the civil service. For example, in the operator ladder tests were scheduled and administered in an orderly manner, and they usually had a steady format. Despite its hierarchy, this career ladder constantly had openings at the bottom, and upward movement was fairly steady. In contrast, the timing of tests in the clerical ladder had been much more unpredictable and unstable in the last few years.

Miller's descriptions illustrate some of the practical differences between the prospects of clerical employees and operators at PSA. More generally, they illustrate the effect of heterogeneous work arrangements on employees of similar status in different career ladders. As will become clear in the following three chapters, these anecdotal differences were typical of the structure of employment in PSA. Rewards such as promotions, compensation adjustments, and the provision of means for personal growth in the job varied from one career ladder to another.[2]

Studying Opportunity Structures and Organizational Reward Systems

Over the years, stratification scholars have used a wide variety of units of observation to measure organizational opportunity. They have studied careers and career lines (Spilerman 1977), vacancy chains and pulls (White 1970; Stewman 1975; Tuma 1976), organizational demography (Pfeffer 1983), networks (Granovetter 1985a; Ibarra 1993), career ladders and job structures (Reskin and Hartman 1986; Peterson-Hardt and Pearlman 1979), occupational or industry labor markets (Baron, Davis-Blake, and Bielby 1986; Tomaskovic-Devey 1993; Stafford 1989), personnel selection systems (Rosembaum 1984), and organizational labor markets (DiPrete 1989; Baron, Mittman, and Newman 1991).

Such a variety of approaches should not come as a surprise, given that the notion of opportunity is complex: it includes more than one dimension of work and it operates at more than one level of analysis. The conceptual connection among all these possible targets of study becomes clear if one visualizes them as concentric circles with the work experience at their center, each circle representing a different level of interaction (see Figure 1, Chapter 1). Opportunity may connote prospects in a job, a career ladder, an organization, an occupation, or the broader labor market, depending on one's level of analysis.

The methodological options to measure and document patterns of opportunity are equally numerous. Techniques range from intensive qualitative observations of people embedded in structures (Kelsall 1955; Kanter 1984; Osterman 1984b) to precise quantititive stochastic models of mobility (Stewman and Konda 1983) and compensation processes (Pfeffer and Langton 1988). Finally, some scholars have chosen to combine thick descriptions and quantitative tests in their research (Doeringer and Piore 1971; Lincoln and Kalleberg 1990).

The reader thus will benefit from a brief description of the framework I use to study opportunity. The road map presented below is the product of an eclectic combination of "methodological tricks" learned from my exploration of the stratification literature. My goal was to document opportunity rather than explain it. Hence I have deliberately chosen not to espouse any single approach.[3] Instead, I use words, numbers, and visual displays to provide a broad picture of opportunity patterns and their effects on individuals in PSA.

Underlying Assumptions: Opportunity as Personal Experience and as Structural Reality

Job rewards are "characteristics associated with work that provide benefits and utilities to the individual . . . [and are] obtained contingent on continued work performance" (Kalleberg and Griffin 1980:739). Hence, the primary unit of analysis for understanding organizational opportunity is the job, understood as a relational construct. Each position in the organization is part of a larger network of jobs with particular rules that govern employment relationships. The specific terms of an employment relationship are a function of a job's location within the network (White 1970). A cluster of jobs sharing similar characteristics provides the context for the distribution of rewards. It also specifies the conditions for employee performance (Rosenbaum 1984; Kanter 1977).

Moreover, the initial placement of persons in particular chains of jobs already represents a tracking device which steers individuals into predetermined routes (Kelsall 1955; White 1970; Kanter 1977, 1984; Tuma 1976; Rosenbaum 1984; Granovetter 1985c; Baron, Davis-Blake, and Bielby 1986; DiPrete 1989). Employees therefore experience work-related opportunity from participating in specific organizational career ladders. These organizational paths may or may not cross at all, and the quality of work life may vary consistently from one ladder to another. Systematic differences in access to rewards constitute what the organizational stratification literature has called *opportunity structures* within organizations (Kanter 1977; Baron 1984; Lincoln and Kalleberg 1990).

Rosenbaum (1984) has made explicit the "structural" component of opportunity by studying how careers unfolded for a cohort of employees. In his view, opportunity structures can be thought of as a series of implicit competitions for rewards within an organization. He calls this the "tournament model" of career selection. The contests progressively differentiate the cohort, each time further delineating a person's opportunities for future attainments. As individuals move into specific "branches" of what looks like an opportunity "decision tree," their options become more and more limited. As they progress through the system, they encounter a complex mix of factors that ultimately determine who will get what and when. This mix is the organization's reward system itself.

Reward Systems: Organizational Tools to Distribute Opportunity

Organizational rewards have been traditionally associated with upward mobility and to a lesser degree with earnings. Yet as managers well know, employees respond to different incentives and are often willing to make trade-offs. A useful definition of opportunity will be one that considers both its personal and structural aspects and acknowledges the different kinds of incentives employees may expect.

Three Dimensions of Opportunity. Like the abstract notion of opportunity, the concrete idea of a reward system conveys both an organizational and a personal reality. The organizational side refers to the personnel and human resource management processes used to distribute awards (through promotion policies and practices, for example). The personal side refers to individual experiences in the formal competition for resource distribution (when, for example, one gains higher status and compensation through upward job mobility). With this in mind, the three dimensions of opportunity can be broadly defined as follows:

1. *Opportunity for promotion/mobility*: prospects of upward movement and status advancement in the organization
2. *Opportunity for compensation/earnings*: prospects of attaining monetary rewards and other material benefits associated with jobs, such as salary, salary increases, and fringe benefits
3. *Opportunity for job challenge/personal growth*: prospects of learning through the formal and informal development of work-related skills

Taken together, these dimensions constitute the core of the reward system. They give meaning to the social context of work.[4] Paraphrasing Rosenbaum (1984), the opportunities offered by the reward system determine not only the types of incentives to which an individual must respond but also how individuals prepare for the future and how others in the organization treat them. They influence, for example, how much a supervisor is willing to invest in an employee. By reflecting what is formally and actually valued in a given organization, the reward system highlights the keys to success. Individuals can use these signals to judge whether they will be able to satisfy their personal needs, accomplish their career expectations, and fulfil their dreams within an organization.

Three Strategies to Document Patterns of Opportunity. At least three strategies can be used to document patterns of opportunity within an organization. First, evidence of opportunity can be found from exploring the organizational mechanisms used to distribute highly desired rewards. How did promotion, compensation, and job challenge take place in PSA? What organizational activities and actors were involved in these processes? How were the administrative systems utilized to accomplish the task of reward distribution? This first strategy generates qualitative information about the logic of organizational processes but does not document their consequences.

The obvious consequences of job allocations and resource distributions are a second important source of evidence. The strategy here would be, for example, to compare the three career ladders for obvious differences in their structures, their monetary and social values (as assigned through the reward system), and their demographic compositions (the social attributes of people assigned to each ladder). Although such evidence does not help clarify the nature of the allocation process, it does document the end product of the dynamics of opportunity in PSA.

An investigation of the ultimate outcomes of these processes as they affect individuals yields a third set of evidence. The aim here is to document how the emerging patterns enacted through the reward system affect the individual attainment of employees. Simple quantitative models produce evidence for this type of assessment.

From an analysis of these processes, outputs, and outcomes I have produced a portrait of PSA's opportunity structures and its reward system. This portrait is presented in the next three chapters. How promotions, compensation, and job challenge contributed to patterns of opportunity in PSA is the subject of the rest of this chapter. Chapter 5 describes the actual products and outcomes of these practices, and Chapter 6 follows with an analysis of the broader organizational and institutional forces that affected opportunity in PSA. Taken together, the chapters of Part II delineate PSA's formal structure of incentives, the administrative setup that managers used to operationalize it, the actual formal and informal human resource practices derived from the structure and its administration, and the effects of these dynamics on people's chances for success. It will be seen that unequal patterns of opportunity existed within PSA—a finding that replicates the results of previous empirical studies of organizational stratification in public and private settings.

Moving Up

The experience of moving up in PSA varied for employees in the three ladders. Each ladder had different criteria for promotion and different opportunities for advancement. Consider these three work histories of PSA managers:

Operator Manager A was sixty-three years old. He entered the agency as a worker in 1948 at the age of twenty-five, earning a salary of $3340. Between 1948 and 1960 he moved up several grade levels in the same title. In 1961, after fourteen years in the agency, he became a supervisor. He was functionally transferred to the new agency when PSA was restructured. In 1979, after thirty-one years of service, he became a manager. During his tenure he was transferred ten times. (Source: personnel files)

Clerical Manager B was sixty years old. He had entered PSA in 1946, at the age of twenty, as a provisional clerk earing a salary of $1560. Three years later he became a civil servant. In 1955 he got his first promotion. In 1967, after twenty-one years of service, he became a supervisor. In the same year he took a leave of absence from this title and got a provisional appointment in a higher grade of the same job title. In 1977, after thirty-one years of service, he became a manager. When the agency became independent he was functionally transferred to the new PSA, and in 1979 he was reclassified to his present managerial level. He had three transfers during his years of service. (Source: personnel files)

Analyst Manager C worked in PSA as a summer intern during his last year of school in a masters degree program. The following fall and spring he worked part-time as a provisional employee, under the clerical title of office associate. When he finished his degree he was hired full-time with the title of statistician. A year later he became manager of the unit, under the noncompetitive title of community coordinator. He has worked in PSA for *two years*. (Source: personal interview)

These histories illustrate some of the idiosyncracies of climbing PSA in different ladders. Manager A followed the path prescribed formally by the system, as was typical for most operators. Manager B, like many clerical employees, participated in some ad hoc practices that took him outside the system at several points in the process. Manager C, in contrast, followed a fast yet idiosyncratic, unpredictable, and erratic career path, as did some other analysts.

Managers A, B, and C represented the three predominant mechanisms for promotion in PSA: (1) the typical civil service route; (2) provisional appointments following the ideal-type route; and (3) isolated or unpredictable moves. Such mechanisms further reinforced the existing structural differences between line and staff employees. Operators always used the civil service path, while analysts seldom did. Clerical employees used both types of promotions, but the civil service route was more common, especially at the lower levels of the ladder.

Civil Service Promotions

Managers A and B were the two oldest civil servants in PSA. Their histories offer excellent examples of typical civil service careers in PSA. Except for the number of transfers, the stories were similar.[5] Both employees started in their twenties, moved up slowly, were transferred to the present agency from the parent agency, and achieved a managerial position after many years of service. In addition, neither had arrived at the highest levels of the hierarchy despite their long tenure in PSA.

Nevertheless, important distinctions existed. For example, the time of arrival to the first supervisory position was strikingly different. The clerical manager reached a position of authority after investing twenty-one years in the agency, while the operator manager took only fourteen years. All in all, the operator spent 66 percent of his service as either a supervisor or a manager, while the clerical spent 48 percent. The advantage of being a supervisor translated into differences in earnings, since supervisors and managers received higher salary increases than employees at lower levels. These differences had to do with career ladder variations in the criteria used to promote permanent employees.

Advancement via the legal path normally required passing competitive promotional exams for entry-level positions in each title. The requirement then changed to a combination of the evaluation of performance and the assessment of training, experience, special skills, and (if needed) seniority for the higher levels within the same title. For example, an employee could be promoted to principal administrative associate level I, the supervisory title in the clerical ladder, by taking an exam. To move up to level II of the same title, the preceding list of criteria would be applied. In theory, this person would only need to take another examination to move to the managerial title in the ladder.

Using the legal way to move up varied significantly across ladders. All promotions in the operator ladder took place uniformly.[6] Many but not all clerical employees also followed this pattern. Few analysts used the legal way, however. For example, out of four promotions taking place in the clerical ladder during a randomly selected month, three had only slight deviations from the ideal type path. In two cases, employees skipped a premanagerial level as they moved to supervisory positions. In contrast, no analytical employee was promoted following the regular route during the same month.[7]

Civil service represented the most important mechanism to move up for the operators. While all operator managers had permanent status, only 7 percent of staff managers did.[8] The strict enforcement of civil service status for operators is further illustrated by the fact that 100 percent of the line managers were recruited from within, while only 69 percent of the managers from other ladders were. This means that the mobility pattern offered to all operators existed for only one-third of the staff cases.[9] Moreover, a detailed study of the work histories of the few permanent managers who did move up in the staff ladders revealed that only half of them followed the typical civil service route within PSA. Others had transferred into the agency with managerial titles, and one had reached the administrative title through a historical accident rather than by following the prescribed career path.[10]

The predictability of the operator system is highlighted by comparing the cases of two operator managers who moved up the ranks in sixteen years. Both P. and S. Smith, who happened to be twins, entered PSA in the same cohort with the same salary, had the same salary adjustments year after year, advanced to supervisors and to managerial positions the same year, and had, by the time of the study, the exact same salaries! This similarity forces one to wonder how they managed to keep the same pace during the first three levels of the ladder. There were, in fact, some interesting differences, which may help understand their movement. P. was assigned to a special task force in the Operations Unit at the moment of entry. He had five transfers thoughout his career while his brother had only two. P. had received $5000 more than his brother when he was promoted to the first managerial position, even though in the next upgrading step their salary leveled out.

These differences suggest that transfers and participation in task forces played a role in career opportunities. An interesting question is how S., who lacked the same visibility in the agency, managed to keep up with his brother's pace. It is possible that the successful brother used his personal contacts to "pull" his sibling along while he himself was moving up.

Networking played an important role in the formula for career success in PSA, even within the operator ladder. In an interview, an influential operator manager in PSA proudly explained his career success as the result of combining hard, serious work and networking. Other managers were as good or better than him, he admitted, but he had made a constant effort to become visible as he was moving up. He had missed no opportunity to be noticed. He had also been active in the fraternal organization, which frequently offered parties and benevolence events for operators and their families.[11]

In sum, the chances of using the legal route to a successful career as a civil servant in the agency—that is, of eventually reaching a managerial position by following the rules of the civil service system—were unequally distributed within PSA. They were slimmer for employees in the analytic and clerical career ladders.[12] The small number of clerical civil servants in managerial positions indicates that the legal way did not offer the best chances for members of this group to make it to the top.[13]

Provisional Promotions

The competitive titles were often filled by persons who had not taken an examination. When civil service lists were unavailable for a given title, anyone who met the minimum qualifications for the job could be appointed on a temporary basis. These people were called "provisionals" because in theory they were hired until a list of "permanent" civil servants appeared. A union manual lists the most common reasons to appoint provisionals: (1) if turnover in a job category is high, or if there are more newly created positions than eligible people to fill them; (2) if tests for some positions are given infrequently and a current list does not exist for a vacancy; (3) if a general city-wide list for a promotional title does not exist, and there are vacancies for such a position. Provisionals were not expected to stay in the positions more than three months. In practice, they often kept this status for years, vulnerable to being discharged at any moment.[14] This status was very rare in the operator ladder, although it was a common occurrence in the clerical and the analytical ladders.

Sometimes provisionals who were promoted to new titles kept the same civil service status. For example, during the month reviewed, a provisional analyst was promoted from a statistician to an associate city planner with a salary increase of $6,474. Sometimes civil servants who held permanent positions got promoted to a higher job in the same ladder under a provisional status. People called these employees "step-ups." Manager B, whose work history was reviewed earlier, used this practice twice during his career. Step-ups would request a leave of absence from the lower permanent title before accepting the higher provisional position. The case of a fast-track clerical employee further confirms the usefulness of the step-up mechanism for movement into management:

> V. Jung started in 1980 as a provisional office aide (lowest title in the clerical career ladder). Two years later he was promoted to a provisional supervisory position. He moved to a managerial position one year later. In those six years, he took the civil service test and entered the system as a permanent typist to move later to the permanent supervisory position he had held until then as a provisional. Today he is on leave of absence without pay from this title and acts as a provisional manager. (Source: personnel files)

Jung had an undergraduate degree in business administration. In general when provisionals brought credentials to the job, they would not follow the typical path up the ladder as Jung did. Instead they would enter directly into supervisory or managerial positions. Jung must have received his degree while he was working his way up the system. Judging by the speed of his movement, the payoff in the investment was high. The mobility he achieved in six years was equivalent to what normally would take an average of sixteen years for other clerical civil servants following the formal route.

Examples of less drastic step-up movements appeared during the month reviewed. A clerical employee moved from permanent office aide to provisional office associate, with a salary increase of $3,131. Another went from permanent office associate to the supervisory title in the same series and then immediately got a leave of absence to accept a provisional managerial position.

This practice was so common that it was tracked in PSA documents such as personnel action forms and personnel files. These documents reported both the real salary increases for the provisional title and the proportional increases for the permanent title. The history of an analyst manager transferring into PSA from another city agency exemplifies this practice:

> T. Jones entered PSA as an associate staff analyst (a civil service supervisory level title) with a salary of $24,947. He immediately took a leave of absence without pay to accept the provisional title of administrative manager (level II) with a salary of $37,000. Between 1982 and 1986 his personnel file reported simultaneous salary adjustments as follows: in the civil service title the salary increased to $44,246. In the provisional title it increased to $56,429. (Source: personnel files)

The yearly salary increases for this employee were $4,825 for the permanent position and $5,037 for the provisional one. After the last adjustment, the difference between his formal and his real salaries amounted to $12,183. Note also that Jones's movements included a change in career progression from analytical to clerical, a change of status from nonmanagerial to managerial, a change in civil service status from permanent to provisional, and finally a jump in the formal career progression skipping the first managerial level. These erratic jumps were characteristic of analysts trying to build their career at PSA.

Jones step-up experience was typical for many analysts. These employees were able to step up to higher positions because there was no legal attachment to the civil service system. There was, however, some risk associated with these moves. Step-ups could be "bumped" down whenever a civil service list appeared. In fact, keeping track of a dual career in the action form had the important function of minimizing the extent of the risk. Jones could loose his provisional job if he was displaced by a civil service list or, for that matter, by budget cuts. If this happened, he could fall back into his permanent title. The practice of increasing the "formal" salary was therefore necessary to ensure financial security if the bump took place.

In many cases, documents conveyed the image of an invisible hand trying to protect an employee's losses by making new arrangements when changes were imminent:

> R. Gibson entered the agency in 1979 as an office aide with a salary of $7,000. In 1983 she was promoted to permanent office associate with a salary of $15,543. A year later she got a provisional promotion to principal administrative assistant with a salary increase of $4,568. Then in 1985 she

was bumped back to office associate. She was immediately reclassified in the word processor series to buffer the loss in salary. In 1986 she was again promoted to supervisor on a provisional basis, with a salary increase of $5,800. Three months later she was reassigned to word processor III but retained her new salary. (Source: personnel files)

Notice that Gibson's permanent title was always office associate, but other provisional titles were created to ensure there would be no loss of salary. A mentor of Gibson's was probably behind these attempts to buffer the trauma of a bump. Managerial and supervisory employees tended to have enough standing to protect themselves from such drastic changes. But the outcomes were not always positive:

M. Heart moved up the clerical ladder, starting as a shop clerk and reaching the highest supervisory position nine years later. Two years later he was promoted to a provisional managerial title in the same series, with a salary of $27,500. Within the next two years his salary increased by $5,000. Then he was reassigned to his permanent supervisory title with a salary decrease of $6,070. (Source: personnel files)

If employees were on good terms with supervisors and managers, or if for any reason they were in a position to bargain, a fall down the ladder would not represent a financial loss. This, however, would depend on the circumstances and the good will of those with the discretion to decide. Negative decisions, when they occurred, were easily justified by citing the law. Among those work histories that were reviewed, most negative outcomes happened in the clerical ladder; there were none among the analyst careers. Furthermore, the bumping process occurred more often at the lower levels of the hierarchy, where step-ups lacked bargaining power to prevent the negative consequences of the fall.

The pervasive use of the step-up practice in the clerical ladder suggests that civil service enforcement could, in fact, have a negative effect on some of its incumbents. Indeed, the opportunity advantages produced by the tight enforcement of rules in the operator ladder did not translate directly into the clerical context. On the other hand, the lax enforcement of the law may have benefitted provisional employees in the analyst ladder. Incumbents of this progression tended to follow idiosyncratic career paths.

Unpredictable Moves

As an example of an unpredictable path, consider Manager C, whose work history was reviewed earlier. Within the course of two years he changed status from intern to part-time employee, to provisional employee, and finally to manager in a noncompetitive title. In a personal interview he explained this fast movement as a function of having worked in positions where he could meet a variety of people in different areas of PSA. As an analyst who participated in projects of interest to PSA, he met high-level decision makers who were in a position to value his work. This way, he got exposure and visibility early in his career. He claimed that other analysts, such as those working in budget areas, were "buried" and therefore had fewer opportunities for mobility.

Erratic moves in the analyst ladder were a function of the need to find shelters for provisional employees when civil service lists came up for the titles they were occupying. PSA work histories were full of cases in which analysts' titles changed without any parallel increase in salary or other personnel action. Some of these changes represented jumps in career ladders. For example, one analyst was moved within three years from senior project coordinator to estimator mechanic to project coordinator. Another moved within the same time from assistant superintendent of construction to assistant project coordinator to superintendent of construction. These titles belonged to different formal progressions. One of these moves, the first analyst's move from senior project coordinator to project coordinator, was downward. These moves were not accompanied by salary changes nor did they bring about differences in the work performed.

Movement patterns sometimes hid managerial efforts to influence compensation levels indirectly. A change of title could immediately allow a salary increase for the employee, with no change in the work performed. This practice could therefore replace a potential promotion, which would be harder to get through the formal system. Moving to a title from a different career ladder represented in practice a "real" promotion, because it was associated with more money, higher organizational status, and sometimes a change in the quality of work. For example, an employee was promoted from provisional office associate to provisional assistant accountant, with an immediate salary increase of $5,000. Another analyst was promoted from statistician to assistant community coordinator and to executive assistant (a managerial title) within a year and a half, with a salary increase of almost $10,000 in the process.

Another common practice consisted in placing provisional analysts in noncompetitive titles. From the point of view of management these positions were excellent shelters because they did not require an entry exam, they did not entail the bumping risk, and they provided job security and stable compensation. At the time of the study approximately 50 percent of the incumbents of the noncompetitive titles of community coordinator and community associate were provisional employees performing analytical tasks unrelated to community relations. Placement in these titles, however, could affect promotion prospects:

> In 1983, D. Coleman entered the agency as an analyst. She was placed in the noncompetitive title of community coordinator. After less than a year she started supervising three persons. Since the nature of her title did not allow

a promotion, she received instead a merit increase. Two years later she became responsible for another project, and she received another merit increase. When the task force in which she participated recommended the creation of a new unit, she was asked to head it. She was hoping to become a manager. (Source: personal interview)

Promotion to manager would result in a move from a noncompetitive to a competitive title. But her present title was not part of a job progression and had not been designed to lead into management. The new managerial position required approval from the mayor's office. This was a long and complicated process. Civil service law demanded that the new position be advertised, that resumes be reviewed, that candidates be interviewed, and that forms be filled explaining the reasons why candidates were rejected. Coleman seized her new responsibilities under the belief that she would soon be promoted. She was thrilled because moving into management also represented a 15 percent increase in her salary, compared to the 7 percent merit increases she had gotten before. After six months, however, her case was still unresolved. In conversation, she characterized her situation as being in an organizational "limbo." When she received an offer from another city agency, she decided to leave.

This case illustrates some interesting traits in the flexible employment relationship analysts enjoyed. It shows how they could gain exposure through special projects and how the content of a job title could vary to fit the analyst occupying it. It also uncovers, however, some of the human resource practices that created uncertainty and produced unequal chances for analysts. PSA staged a formal recruitment process for a position that was already occupied. This was not an isolated instance. Indeed, members of PSA's Equal Employment Opportunity Office reported similar maneuvers in the selection process of other staff employees. These included delaying hires, trying to change the qualifications for certain positions, or building in job characteristics as "special requirements." An idiosyncratic mix of skills favoring one specific candidate thereby reduced the possibility of identifying others within a broader pool. Other studies of civil service systems in the same municipality document similar practices across agencies (Rich 1982; Gottfried 1988).[15] Finally, Coleman's story is also a reminder that the managerial discretion attained by these juggling efforts can easily backfire.[16] The uncertainty associated with these games was a source of some strain for employees in the analyst career ladder.

Getting Paid

Stratification scholars have been able to document significant degrees of empirical inequality by studying earning differences both across and within jobs, groups, organizations, occupations, and industries (Wright and Perrone 1977;

Beck, Horan, and Tolbert 1978; Pfeffer and Ross 1980; Rosenbaum 1984; Elbaun 1984; Pfeffer and Langton 1988; Tomaskovic-Devey 1993). Most of these studies highlight the importance of the openness of the employment relationship to market forces in explaining wage inequality. This applies both to private contexts (Sorensen and Kalleberg 1981) and to public ones (Borjas 1980). Data suggest that the more protected jobs are, the more likely it is that they will have financial advantages. Compensation patterns in PSA were consistent with the literature.

PSA compensation practices offered advantages to the operators in ways consistent with the promotion advantages described in the previous section. Setting aside other human capital variables, being an operator seemed to have the strongest positive effect on the prospects or expectations for good remuneration over time. Similarly, being a clerical employee seemed to produce the opposite effect. For analysts, the economic disadvantages appeared to be related more to the uncertainty of the distribution process than to the size of the portions. Nevertheless, being a staff employee seemed in general to penalize a person in his or her ability to improve financially in PSA.

Mechanisms for Salary Increases

There were three ways to improve one's salary at PSA: automatic contractual increases, merit increases, and promotion raises. Salary changes recorded in the work histories and action forms showed very different allocation patterns in the operator, clerical, and analyst ladders. While the timing and proportion of the increases for nonmanagerial operators were automatic and regular over time, those for clerical and analyst employees were erratic (except for cost-of-living adjustments in the case of clerical titles).

Contract-based increases included cost-of-living adjustments, experience differentials, and longevity. These depended less on individual efforts than on the bargaining capacity of the union negotiating the contract. The operator career ladder had the highest automatic salary increases, followed by the clerical group. The increases for analysts were based on those in the clerical ladder. Since analysts had no union to negotiate their own rates, the personnel department applied the clerical standard to this group.

The second type of raises were merit based. These were monetary increases given in recognition for outstanding performance. Not regulated by contracts, they represented a 7 percent increase from the salary base. In theory, the policy for merit increases was formally regulated to allocate equal percentages throughout the agency. However, managers who had access to agency-wide personnel budget data claimed that there were significant differences among units. Working in a unit under an influential person increased an employee's prospects of (in PSA's lingo) "getting a merit." Linking merit increases to networking and luck, these managers argued (in a group interview) that "merit is a matter of being in the right place at the right time."

In theory, only supervisors and managers could receive "merits." In practice, selected premanagerial employees often received them. For example, during the reviewed month the action forms of several office associates, shop clerks, and staff analysts reported merit increases. In contrast, the policy was strictly enforced in the operator ladder, where premanagerial operators had no access to merit increases.

It could be argued that some flexibility in merit increases represented an advantage for premanagerial analysts and clerks over operators. However, a comparison of the average rates of salary increase among the three groups indicates that the operators did much better without any help from this policy. Moreover, the considerable discretion introduced in the staff group could be manipulated for personal or political purposes, as suggested in a union booklet's reference to the merit policy: "In agencies where merit increases are given, employees commonly complain that management rewards 'favorites' or 'friends' or 'political appointees' rather than those who might be more deserving." The potential advantage was thus accompanied by a high degree of uncertainty. This was complicated by the use of "merits" to replace promotions, since they required fewer bureaucratic manipulations and were less scrutinized by the city personnel department. D. Coleman's story, related earlier, illustrates this point. In her case, promotion was postponed twice. The inconveniences created by the original job match motivated both parties to settle for a merit increase. But this arrangement was less favorable than a promotion, in both money and status.

Promotion raises followed a similar pattern. Increases in salaries for operators were, as percentages, higher and more stable than for the two other groups. In addition, increases for provisional employees were higher than for permanent employees. Finally, increases for analysts were usually higher than for clerical employees. Two subgroups were thus clearly penalized under this distribution: the staff civil servants (compared to operators and to provisional employees of the same groups), and clerical employees (compared to analysts and to operators). For example, a permanent clerical employee who had received three promotions over the course of her work history at PSA suggested in an interview that her promotions had represented a trivial salary improvement. A review of civil service promotions among clerical and analytical employees confirms this report. Most had very small increases attached to them (usually in the hundreds of dollars).

Economic Value of the Jobs

The salary assigned to a job indicates its implicit social value in a hierarchical context. Figure 5 presents a snapshot of the relative value of the operator, clerical,

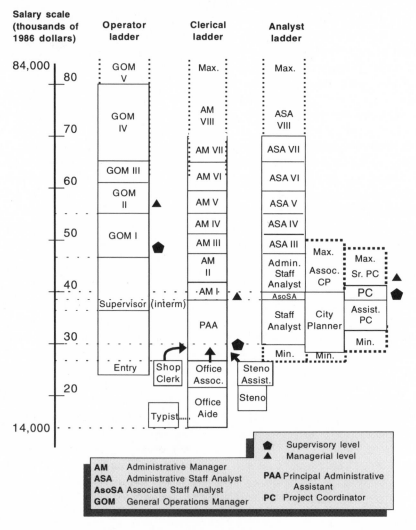

Figure 5. Relative value of career ladders at PSA against salary scale. Graphic by David Grossman.

and analytical ladders within PSA, using salary levels as standard of comparison. It confirms that operators had the highest economic value among the three ladders. Take for example the general operations manager job, level I. By design, this was the first level in the operator managerial job sequence. Even though its incumbents supervised supervisors, they were considered premanagerial employees in PSA's job structure. Indeed, this job had been classified, by a union agreement, as a supervisory position. Salary levels mirrored, however, its original location in the managerial sequence. Hence operator supervisors enjoyed considerable salary and status advantages compared to staff employees placed in equivalent premanagerial titles (e.g., principal administrative assistant in the clerical ladder; associate staff analyst and project coordinators in the analyst ladder).

The figure also shows peculiar compensation features for the analyst ladder. In theory salaries for analyst managers started at a significantly lower level than those for operator managers (and were sometimes even lower than for operators at the second supervisory level). Yet the supervisory salaries for some of the analyst job clusters (staff analysts, city planners, and project coordinators) were higher than the formal entry-level salaries for analyst managers. In practice very few analysts started their managerial career at the formally assigned entry-level salaries. Indeed, if they had been supervisors in one of the other analyst series (staff analyst, etc.) before entering management, their new salaries would automatically start at a higher level.

The clerical ladder had a relative lower status. Clerical supervisory and managerial levels were "deflated" compared to those of the other two ladders. By the time a clerical employee reached the first managerial position, he or she would be making a salary equivalent to that of the first supervisory level in the operator ladder. This is significant because jobs with different salary levels send social messages about the degree of control the incumbents have over organizational resources (including, for example, authority). People filling the slots may be labeled and treated in accord with their position in this implicit social scale (Tomaskovic-Devey 1993).

In terms of status, then, the clerical ladder had a lower rank. The analyst and operator ladders seemed at first glance to be relatively similar in value. However, although entry-level operators had a lower status than entry-level analysts, by the time both groups reached managerial positions their value had reversed. The status of managers in the operator ladder was higher.

Learning from Work

The literature in organizational behavior and human resource management attaches enormous importance to the developmental aspects of work (Hackman and Oldham 1980; Baird, Schneier, and Beatty 1988; Silvia and Meyer 1990). In contrast, there has been relatively little attention paid to this area of work in the organizational stratification literature. With few exceptions (Kalleberg and Griffin 1978; Berg, Freedman, and Freeman 1978; Rosenbaum 1984) the role that this opportunity dimension plays in creating inequality has not been considered sufficiently. There are no systematic studies of the opportunity for personal growth as a possible "resource" that may be differentially distributed in organizations in ways similar to earnings and promotions.

In his analysis of the market experience Lane (1991) proposes an excellent framework for developing this agenda. Reviewing a large set of empirical studies from numerous disciplines, he produces a powerful argument about the existence of stratification in what he calls "workplace learning." This he defines as the acquisition of a series of values and insights derived from work practices. These values and insights contribute to personal development by altering world views, improving cognitive complexity, imparting a sense of personal control, and enhancing self-esteem.

Lane further distinguishes between two characteristics that may be linked to workplace learning. One is "transcendence," or discovering purposes in work beyond survival and wealth (in other words, working for more than a paycheck). The other is "immanence," or aspects of work that bring intrinsic enjoyment (in other words, working for the pleasure of it). He argues that market economies must, for efficiency's sake, prioritize immanence over transcendence, and acknowledges, too, that jobs vary greatly in the degree to which immanence is actually present. But he argues that there are some lucky individuals who find both qualities in the workplace. Those who do he calls the "privileged class," thus acknowledging the existence of some sort of workplace learning inequality.

Empirical evidence of this type of inequality is not entirely absent from organizational inquiry. For example, studies report that women and people of color have been excluded in the past from task forces and special assignments, participation in which is often critical for developing skills and visibility for corporate success (Fernandez 1981).[17]

Because of the subjective nature of personal development, it is difficult to explore job challenge as an objective opportunity dimension in organizations without relying on employees' perceptions. Moreover, from a logical point of view, personal fulfillment cannot be viewed as a job reward because it derives *from* the performance of tasks rather than *for* such performance (Kalleberg and Griffin 1978 and 1980). Nevertheless, human resource specialists insist that organizational activities such as training and development can improve an organization's competitive advantage (Schuler 1992). These activities may represent a potentially important incentive, operating over and above direct compensation, to attract and retain competitive employees.

This discussion suggests that the study of job challenge as an opportunity dimension requires focusing less on the character of jobs and more on the organizational factors that affect employees' potential growth and fulfillment. By comparing both the availability of developmental programs and employee participation in them in the three ladders, one gains a relatively objective picture of this opportunity dimension in PSA.

Access to Training

In the survey, employees were asked several questions about their participation in formal training. Their responses indicate that operators took advantage of training programs more than any other group. Analysts reported having participated the least, but those analysts who participated did so on more occasions.[18] For example, most clerical employees who participated did so in only one program, whereas analysts did so in two or three programs, and most operators in four or more. This distribution is entirely consistent with the opportunity patterns described earlier for promotion and compensation.

PSA's formal efforts to provide training throw some light on the reasons behind these differences. The Division of Human Development was responsible for the training for different groups in the agency. At the time of the study this unit was relatively new. It had more projects planned for the future than it had actually offered. Its leaders were proud of their initial accomplishments, however. These included the design of the Basic Training Program for operators in entry and supervisory titles and the Executive and Management Development Program for incumbents of upper-level line and staff jobs.

The division's structure and the training it provided during its two years of existence mirrored the pattern found in the other dimensions of opportunity. PSA had put most of its effort in training operators. Premanagerial workers in this group were the only ones who had permanent and consistent training offerings. Training staff justified this decision by pointing to the importance of their work for PSA and by emphasizing the need to introduce operators to the complex equipment and work routines required for efficient job performance in the field.

There was, however, another reason for this emphasis, which was not entirely related to task complexity. The supply of courses was structured in such a way that lack of support from supervisors could become a critical obstacle. A formal policy of the Division of Human Development stated that the supply of inside courses depended on demand from unit managers. If staff managers did not request courses for their employees, the unit would not offer them. It seemed that there were important differences in the views of supervisors across career ladders. Although there was a concensus that operator training was necessary, staff supervisors often viewed the courses negatively, either as "remedial" solutions to perceived problems of performance or as "vacations" that took employees away from work. They were thus reluctant to request training for their own employees. Once in a while the division identified needs and offered staff courses. This was risky, however, because if the courses did not attract enough attention they had to be canceled, which meant wasted investments. After several fiascos, the division organizers developed a more conservative attitude, preferring to wait for specific requests from units.

Once courses were designed, the procedure for participation had several steps. The division announced the requested courses through posters. In coordination with the Employee Assistant Unit, supervisors approved the request of interested employees, who then registered. Since the participant's unit paid for in-house courses (the Division of Human Development paid for outside courses), supervisors were careful about their demands and approvals. Therefore, staff employees could encounter at least two obstacles in their access to training: a shortage in available offerings and a lack of support from superiors. By contrast, the training process for operators had become sufficiently institutionalized to take place independently of managerial attitudes.

These differences extended to other aspects of training. In-house courses for analysts and clerical employees were sporadic and less systematic than those offered to operators, and their topics varied from time to time. Analysts had been originally offered an orientation course, which introduced them to the agency and gave them a chance to observe the actual operations in the field. Later this course was opened to all new employees who wanted to participate. As it changed, its scope, depth, and duration were reduced. The original course for analysts disappeared as the program expanded, even though the division kept it as an available offering for the future. To replace it, selected analysts were sometimes invited to participate in the training programs organized for managers.

The Division of Human Development was also a source of information for employees, enabling them to take advantage of external training opportunities. In addition to in-house courses, it also coordinated educational efforts with other organizations and contracted training in skills such as computer proficiency. For example, the division had recently promoted and facilitated participation of PSA clerical employees in a Skills Enhancement Program. This offering, which represented one of the few systematic training programs available to clerical employees at PSA, was a union initiative. The lack of direct division interest in clerical training is illustrated by the fact that of the fifty employees in the unit, only three had the direct assignment to plan and implement clerical training.

Formal Employee Involvement Programs

Organized mechanisms of participation provided employees with the opportunity for systematic input into the decision-making process of PSA. However, the same pattern of advantage recurred: operators had priority, analysts were second, and clerical employees came third. An important story recounted in PSA's organizational culture linked the practice of involving operators in task forces to the initiative of an innovative commissioner. According to this account, the Commissioner wanted to work with line managers open to change. Having identified promising operators early in their careers, he trained them, rotated them into different borough offices, groomed them, and provided them with ample opportunities for exposure. He encouraged them to go back to school and to take the various management tests as early as possible. Eventually this strategy enlarged the pool of operators for managerial positions and gave many younger and more energetic line managers the opportunity to work at the center of power. The practice has since become institutionalized. At the time of the study, some managers in the executive team wanted to create a similar informal policy for young provisional analysts. Both D. Coleman's experience and that of Analyst Manager C (discussed earlier) indicate that highly visible assignments had a direct payoff beyond personal learning. They spilled over into promotions and increased compensation.

Quality circles were another participatory scheme that had been formally implemented among PSA employees since the early 1980s.[19] Although the circles had placed PSA in a pioneer role in the public sector, their use remained exclusive to the blue-collar trades in PSA, including operators. When I asked an operator manager if clerical or analyst employees ever participated in the circles, which he was describing with great enthusiasm, his puzzled expression and blunt "No" indicated that the idea of including these groups was foreign to him. This is hardly surprising, since in 1986 broad Total Quality Management efforts were still uncommon in the public sector. Quality circles were initially developed for factory work, and this perhaps explains why there were no attempts to provide office workers with similar opportunities. Their absence had a stronger negative effect on the clerical group than on analysts. The latter, after all, had the chance to be part of task forces, which also provided an opportunity to participate in PSA's decision-making process. The clerical group, in contrast, had no direct or indirect opportunities for participation. This is the same pattern as already observed in training and task force participation. Hence opportunities for job challenge replicated the same patterns observed for promotion and compensation.

Conclusion

PSA evolved mechanisms to distribute rewards unequally among employees located in different segments of its job structure. Incentives provided to some employees bypassed the civil service pace that regulated the city personnel dynamics. All this was accomplished with considerable subtlety, such that the organization appeared to comply totally with civil service law while at the same time providing managerial discretion when necessary.[20] PSA managers were not unique in practicing this type of manipulation, of course. The public administration literature reports similar practices among public managers at local, state, and even federal levels, although the extent of the practice has not been empirically measured (Rich 1982; Shafritz, Hyde, and Rosenbloom 1986; Moore 1988).

The gap between formal rules and actual staffing practices was in fact a function of the degree of enforcement of the civil service system for different employees in the same organization. The reward system, too, varied from one career ladder to another as a result of the varying formalization of the employment relationship. Although operators, analysts, and clerical employees shared their membership in an organization that claimed to have a unified reward system in place, in reality separate mechanisms of reward distribution predominated for members in each ladder.

This pattern of promotions, salary adjustments, and opportunities for personal growth in the three ladders is typical of contemporary work arrangements, and not just in the public sector. Permanent employees from the three ladders were subject to labor market rules defined by a formal merit system. This produced, in theory at least, a "closed" employment relationship characterized by institutional protections from external competition and job security. However, variations in the degree of enforcement created differences by career ladder. Operators had full protection, clerical employees had partial protection, and analysts had minimal protection. In contrast, provisional employees of the staff ladders participated in "open" employment relationships, which allowed economic rules of the market to affect individual attainment. This variation in the degree of openness has been documented for private organizations in the past (Doeringer and Piore 1971; Sorensen and Kalleberg 1981; Sorensen and Tuma 1981).

Yet, personal attention to networking seemed to be critical for all employees in PSA. This finding is consistent with Granovetter's (1985b) notion of organizational embeddedness as a determinant of organizational inequality. It also reinforces the proposition (in organization theory) that the most important skill needed to succeed in a bureaucratic structure is an awareness of the political nature of the competition and a willingness to act on it accordingly:

> The one who makes it to the top is the organizational politician, concerned above all with informal ties, maneuvering toward the crucial gatekeepers, avoiding the organizational contingencies that trap the less wary. (Collins 1979:31)

The need to be politically savvy was reinforced by the variation in employment practices. Uncertainty promoted attention to relationships in an environment characterized by a sharp contradiction between the dominant discourse of "equality of opportunity based on merit" and the reality of inconsistent applications of this principle. In this sense the main difference in the work experience of employees in the three groups may have been as much qualitative as it was quantitative. The political activity of the operators was facilitated by a context where information about the process was abundant, the direction of the path was obvious, and workers were protected from outside competitors. In contrast, analysts and clerical employees encountered an uncertainty that stemmed not only from the ubiquitous political nature of the workplace but also from a lack of structure in the ladder (in the case of analysts) or from a lack of enforcement of the structure (in the case of clerical employees).

Outcomes and Outputs: The Consequences of Patterned Opportunity

The direction of organizational careers is determined by a combination of personal and structural forces. Individual effort is a necessary but not a sufficient condition to explain why some people succeed while others fail in organizations. Additional ingredients in the formula for success include managerial selection preferences and processes of organizational growth and contraction (Stewman and Konda 1983); the timing of a person's past advancements (Grandjean 1981); the design characteristics of jobs and of the entire ladder in which they are located (Sorensen and Tuma 1981; Rosenbaum 1984); the strength of unions in the organization (Freeman and Medoff 1979); considerations of organizational demography such as cohort size (Pfeffer 1983), tenure distribution (Halaby 1978) and gender composition (Kanter 1977); and finally, existing patterns which, by inertia or by attribution, reinforce the way things are done. These are not considerations that individuals can entirely control.

This chapter further documents how factors external to individual performance shaped opportunity in PSA.[1] The focus is on the outputs and outcomes of opportunity dynamics in PSA. The chapter explores how job design contributed to distribute advantages and disadvantages unevenly among PSA employees. It also explores the aggregate impact of this distribution on the prospects of employees. In addition, the chapter explores some of the direct consequences that a range of opportunity outputs (attributes of jobs, career ladders, and managerial groups, including their demographic compositions) had for the real people who passed through the system.

The last chapter highlighted the degree of civil service enforcement as an important opportunity factor. This chapter stresses the relevance of the design of jobs (job requirements, descriptions, and evaluations), the social composition of jobs and ladders, and the opportunities and social statuses that employees derived from their positions in the career ladders.

The description of outputs and outcomes corroborates the existence of important differences between operators, analysts, and clerical employees. The differences refer to real opportunities and to the degree of uncertainty experienced in the employment relationship. They confirm that operators did have a better opportunity package than other groups studied.

Operators represented the occupational group with the skills required for PSA's critical tasks. It may be argued, therefore, that PSA had to provide higher incentives to ensure the quality of their work, and that this alone justified their advantages. This reasoning is partially correct but incomplete. As will become apparent in this chapter, participation in a career ladder conferred important structural and social attributes that were independent of the actual jobs that employees performed. These attributes had direct consequences for the emergence of opportunity structures in PSA.

Opportunity by Design

Criteria specified in job descriptions usually guide staffing decisions, from hiring and placement to promotion. Hence, career ladders can be ranked according to the formal opportunity their positions offer, using information from job descriptions alone.[2] The following pages report an analysis based on a systematic procedure developed by Peterson-Hardt and Pearlman (1979) in their study of employees in New York State public agencies. From answers to a range of questions—about the relative worth of the job ladders in PSA, about the requirements for climbing them, and about the difficulty and significance of movement —it became evident that job designs within each career ladder shaped the opportunities of PSA employees.

Relative Worth of the Career Ladders

The economic comparison of the ladders in Chapter 4 suggested that clerical jobs were at a disadvantage, that analytical and operator jobs were better off, and that operators had the most advantages of all. The comparison of the midpoints of the salary ranges in entry-level and ceiling jobs across ladders replicated these patterns.[3] Most of the analyst job clusters had a high entry-level status (see Table 1, A). In contrast, most of the ports of entry in the clerical ladder had low status. The single port of entry for the operator ladder ranked medium in status. The ranking changed slightly when focusing on the status of the career ceilings (Table 1, B). There was a difference of $17,000 in the potential yearly salary between the

Table 1. Opportunity for entry-level and ceiling titles ranked by salary ranges

A. Entry-level titles

Rank	Salary ranges	Job titles[a]	Career ladder
High	$30,000–$35,000	Staff analyst	Analyst
		Assistant project coordinator	Analyst
		City planner	Analyst
Medium	$25,000–$30,000	—	—
	$20,000–$25,000	Operator	Operator
		Assistant statistician	Analyst
		Shop clerk	Clerical
Low	$15,000–$20,000	Office aide	Clerical
		Steno/secretary	Clerical

B. Ceiling titles

Rank	Salary ranges	Job titles	Career ladder
High	$55,000–$80,000	General operations manager II	Operator
Low	$38,000–$69,000	Administrative manager	Clerical
Low	$38,000–$69,000	Administrative staff analyst	Analyst

[a] Ranked in descending order according to salary midpoint for each title.

lowest salary in the operator ceiling and the equivalent salaries in the clerical and analyst ceilings.

But analysts had some advantages over clerical employees. For example, several nonmanagerial titles for analysts (e.g., associate city planner, senior project coordinator, and some computer specialist titles) had salary ranges in the forty thousands. This salary was even higher than the average managerial entry-level salary. This would suggest that the status of the analyst progression was higher than that of the clerical job clusters.[4]

Job Requirements for Hiring and Promotion

Exploring how hard or easy it was to climb each ladder also suggested that promotion differences were built into the jobs themselves. Following Peterson-Hardt and Pearlman's methodology, the analysis included comparisons of mobility requirements, ease of mobility, and amount of possible mobility within each ladder.

Mobility Requirements. An assessment of the education, skill, and experience required for titles at each level in the hierarchy indicated that the operator ladder had the easiest entry requirements at the three levels.[5] The analyst ladder had the hardest job requirements at the supervisory and entry levels in terms of educational credentials or number of years of experience. The requirements for the managerial level were equally hard for the two staff groups and a bit looser for the operators. The clerical entry level had two routes, one of which was harder than the operator ladder but easier than the analyst ladder while the other was the easiest of the three.

Ease of Mobility. Did the requirements get tougher as the employee moved up or did they stay similar? An answer to this question would indicate the relative ease for an employee to move into a managerial status.[6] The clerical ladder was the hardest to climb once the employee was inside. The next in order was the operator ladder, and the easiest to climb was the analyst ladder.[7]

Amount of Possible Mobility. The distance between the lowest and the highest title in the progression represents the real impact of upward movement. For example, a ladder with a low entry level and low ease of mobility has low possible mobility because little status can be gained by moving up. In contrast, in a ladder with a low entry level and high mobility the progression is long and the possible status changes are substantial.[8] The impact of the changes produced by upward mobility had more substance in the operator ladder than they did in the clerical and analyst ladders.

Table 2 summarizes the results of the structural analysis for the three ladders. The operator career ladder had higher degrees of opportunity than the clerical ladder in all five dimensions, and higher than the analyst ladder in three. In contrast, the clerical ladder ranked lowest in most criteria. From the point of view of formal job design, then, the operator ladder was the most advantageous, whereas the clerical ladder provided its incumbents with the fewest structural advantages. The analyst ladder fell somewhere in the middle.

Table 2. Summary of analysis: degree of opportunity by career ladder

Criteria assessed	Operator ladder	Analyst ladder	Clerical ladder
Relative worth of jobs			
Entry-level titles	Medium	High	Low
Career ceiling	High	Medium	Low
Job requirements for hiring and promotion			
Mobility requirements	High	Low	Medium
Ease of mobility	Medium	High	Low
Amount of mobility	High	Low	Low
Degree of opportunity	High	Medium	Low

Note: High, Medium, and Low measures based on Peterson-Hardt and Pearlman's (1979) methodology. See text for explanations.

In practice, it was harder for an analyst to enter each job from outside, but once inside, it was easier to move up. As the analyst approached the managerial level, he or she already had most of the needed requirements for promotion. In contrast, a clerical employee could enter the ladder easily, but additional requirements appeared upon approaching the managerial level. Finally, an operator had a slightly harder time entering the ladder compared to the clerical employee, but once inside, movement was easy and the switch to management was relatively simple.

Moreover, although operators took longer to move up the ladder, their gains in status as they reached higher levels were more significant. On the other hand, an analyst reached the top more quickly but reaped fewer benefits. Clerical employees took the longest and yet reaped the least. The consequences of these dynamics were real in terms of financial opportunity and social status. After all, the size of potential increases in salary is normally a function of the position within the hierarchy.

Observing Opportunity from Above: The Managerial Group

Two indicators of the opportunity structure in PSA are the routes of entry into management and the characteristics of managers who move up from different segments of the organizational structure. This is so because managerial status is in itself a sign of career mobility and economic attainment.[9]

An examination of PSA's managerial group provided confirmation of the general promotion and compensation patterns described above.[10] Replicating Kanter's findings (1984), this analysis indicates that managerial opportunities in PSA were highly linked to structural design issues. Indeed, the main characteristic differentiating managers in PSA was their organizational function, that is, whether they were line or staff. Line managerial positions drew individuals exclusively from the operator career ladder. Potential candidates for staff managerial positions came from several job progressions, two of them being the analyst and the clerical ladders. The boundaries between these two groups had become institutionalized to the point that movement of individuals from one type of slot to the other was virtually impossible.[11] The implication of this boundary for PSA employees was that 58 percent of the most desired positions in PSA were open to any candidate whereas the remaining 42 percent could be accessed only by a selected group, the operators.[12]

A focus on managers who had been recruited to their present positions from within PSA suggests that there was a separate hiring policy for staff managers. The typical staff civil servant would take at least sixteen years to develop a successful career from entry to a managerial position.[13] In contrast, the tenure distribution of the managers who had held at least two positions in PSA indicated that only about 34 percent of the staff managers had in fact followed this type of movement up the ranks in PSA. At the other end, another 37 percent of them had ten or fewer years of tenure, which suggests that their careers did not follow the typical bureaucratic model.[14] These differences were also linked to historical variations in managerial recruitment patterns.

Changes in Managerial Career Patterns over Time

The changes in managerial careers over time were consistent with PSA's staffing patterns. The strong operator group was consolidated during the 1970s. Operators were represented by strong unions that fought to protect their working conditions and retain their privileges as new staff employees entered the agency in ever greater numbers. The staff managerial group slowly grew during the 1980s. Eventually PSA developed a highly professional group of staff managers consisting of a small number of staff "veterans," who had come up the ranks, and a larger number of provisional employees with educational credentials. This group developed its own niche in PSA.

While the newest group of operator managers moved up the ranks more swiftly than the veteran group, the promotion patterns did not change much in this career ladder. In contrast, non-operator managers who started their careers in the late 1970s and early 1980s seemed to be a totally different breed compared to older staff managers. Many of them had spent most of their careers in other city agencies before transferring to PSA. Others had no experience in managerial positions and substituted this with educational degrees. Upward movement for this group often took the form of reclassifications to higher managerial levels within the agency. For example:

M. Davis came to PSA with a master's degree in public administration. She started with an entry managerial analyst title, working in the executive office. Two years later she became the head of an important unit in PSA and her title was upgraded to level II. The yearly increase of salary in this fast track was of $5,333, the highest among all managers in the same cohort. (Source: personnel files)

The careers of the newer managers who crossed from premanagerial to managerial positions within PSA were fast and erratic. Unlike the older staff managers, who steadily followed civil service paths, they often skipped supervisory levels. And whereas most of the older staff managers held clerical titles and usually followed the traditional road, most of the younger staff managers held analyst titles.

There was in fact a recent agency emphasis on hiring analyst managers from the outside rather than promoting them from within. Internal competition for the desired staff positions intensified with the flow of outside rivals. These managers from the outside resembled the small group of provisional managers who held degrees in traditional professions such as engineering. Given the closed nature of the operator ladder, this competition did not affect line managers.

Differences in Managerial Returns on Earnings

A comparison of salary levels of managerial operators and those of managers from the two staff groups highlights, once again, the disparity in compensation across the ladders.[15] Table 3 summarizes the results of the regression model used for this comparison.[16] The numbers indicate that belonging to the operator ladder had a direct and significant impact on the salary of a manager, independent of other organizational and individual attributes. Operator managers, in fact, earned an average of $9,817 more than staff managers.[17]

The relative amount of time a manager waited before attaining the last promotion also had a significant effect on his or her present salary. For every one-percent increase in the waiting time there was a $4,000 decrease in salary. A significant loss of earnings was therefore associated with a long premanagerial

Table 3. Ordinary least squares (OLS) annual salary regression: managerial earnings in PSA

Dependent variable: annual salary (in thousands) Independent variables	Parameter estimates[a]	
Intercept[b]	36.96	(-21.75)***
Males	6.37	(-0.48)**
Time prior to most recent promotion[c]	−4.36	(-2.12)***
Managerial intermediate level	8.22	(-7.73)***
Managerial highest level	17.29	(-14.36)***
Line managers	9.82	(-6.50)***
R^2	0.74	
Sample size	175.00	

Source: Managerial Employment Roster, 1986 salaries.

[a] Numbers in parentheses represent T-statistics. Table reports only statistically significant variables. For a complete listing see the Appendix.

[b] Intercept represents female staff managers at lowest managerial level.

[c] $(T_1 - T_2/\text{seniority})$, where T_1 = year of most recent promotion; T_2 = year of previous promotion; and seniority = number of years in the job.

  * Statistically significant at the 10% level.

  ** Statistically significant at the 5% level.

  *** Statistically significant at the 1% level.

wait. As clerical and analyst civil servants had longer waits than operators, these numbers indicate that non-operator permanent managers were penalized twice for their participation in PSA staff ladders.

Additional analysis suggested that a manager in the operator career ladder earned an average of $10,635 more than a clerical manager, $9,541 more than an analytical counterpart, and $9,278 more than a manager from other miscellaneous titles.[18] These figures further confirm that within the staff group, clerical managers were most disadvantaged in relation to the operators, despite their civil service similarity. The analysis shows that analysts were also disadvantaged, although less so.[19]

Opportunity and Numbers: Demographic Composition of the Ladders

Organizational demography has been defined as "the composition, in terms of basic attributes such as age, sex, educational level, length of service or residence, race and so forth of the social entity under study" (Pfeffer 1983:303). The demographic distribution of the work force is directly connected to the patterns of opportunity that affect employees' prospects. It influences opportunity by affecting the promotion and the compensation structure of the organization. For example, in pyramidal organizations cohort size has an impact on the competition for career advancement. Not only is the competition more intense in large cohorts, there are also fewer opportunities for subsequent entrants.

The impact of demography on opportunity has been demonstrated empirically. Studies have found that persons in fairly small cohorts tend to benefit from having earlier career moves and rapid advancement (Stewman and Konda 1983), that the average length of service of personnel in public organizations affects the criteria for promotion and evaluation (Halaby 1978), that the percentage of college graduates in each job strongly affects the promotion chances of the incumbents of those jobs (Rosenbaum 1984), and that the racial and gender composition of jobs can strongly affect financial rewards (Rosenbaum 1984; Pfeffer 1983). The differential mix of ethnicity, gender, and civil service status in the three career ladders illustrates the existence of similar patterns in PSA.

The degree of diversity across PSA ladders was evident in their civil service composition. Differences in civil service enforcement made staff ladders more sensitive to the dynamics of the broader, nonbureaucratic labor markets and produced a degree of openness in the employment relationship that did not exist in the fully enforced operator ladder. Variations in civil service status illustrate these different opportunity structures. At the time of the study, 100 percent of the operators were permanent civil service employees. In contrast, in the clerical ladder 61 percent of the incumbents were permanent employees, 38 percent were

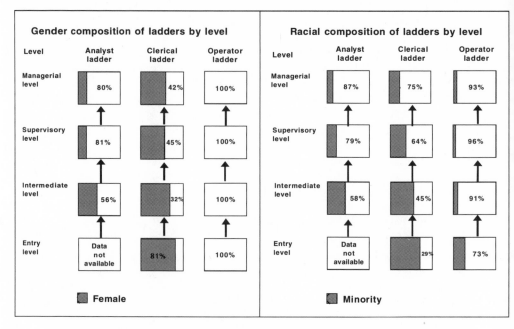

Figure 6. Gender and racial composition of career ladders by organizational level. Graphic by David Grossman.

provisional, and 1 percent occupied noncompetitive titles. In the analyst ladder the proportions shifted. Only 33 percent of the incumbents were permanent civil servants. Of those who were not, 30 percent were provisional employees and 37 percent were placed in noncompetitive titles originally designed for other purposes.

Ample evidence points to gender and racial typing of jobs in PSA. Figure 6 offers a visual comparison of the gender and ethnic composition of the three career ladders by hierarchical level.

Men and nonminority employees were at an advantage. More of them were located in the ladder with the most opportunities (i.e., the operator ladder), and they occupied the most desired jobs. All jobs of the operator ladder were filled by men, and in all levels they were predominantly whites. Using the formal definition of job segregation, this ladder was segregated by both sex and race (Bottini, Chertos, and Haignere n.d.). The two higher levels of the analyst ladder were also segregated by sex, with men dominating; the two lowest levels of the clerical ladder were likewise skewed, with females dominating. Furthermore, while the clerical ladder had the largest number of people of color, it was racially segregated at the top.

Linking Demography and Opportunity

The distribution of opportunity was highly correlated with the way sex, race, and civil service defined the career ladders in PSA. The high-opportunity ladder—that of the operators—was predominantly male and nonminority; the low-opportunity clerical ladder was largely filled by females and had the largest percentage of people of color. The medium-opportunity analyst ladder was more balanced, but it was still dominantly male and nonminority. In the two staff ladders, finally, the lower the level, the higher the proportion of women and minority employees.

The demographic composition of the managerial group showed much the same pattern (see Figure 7). Operator managers were predominantly white and entirely male; staff managers were more mixed, although the proportion of women and persons of color was small. There were no female line managers.[20] Only 23 percent of the staff managers were female. The proportion of minority managers in the staff group was twice that of minority operator managers (18 percent and 9 percent), although both figures suggest a rather low minority participation in management.

Moreover, as described earlier, operator managers represented a homogeneous work group. Recruited to their present positions from the inside, they held a generic civil service title and thus were all permanent employees. The staff group, on the other hand, was heterogeneous. It included many provisional managers who held a variety of generic or specific titles and who had entered management through various sources of recruitment. Furthermore, the managerial titles more often filled by minority and female managers were also those with the largest proportion of provisionals.[21] Indeed, 100 percent of the operator managers were permanent, whereas only 6 percent of the staff managers were.[22]

This discussion suggests that the closed nature of the operator ladder contributed to reproduce at higher levels the practice of exclusion of women and people of color that occurred at the entry level. In fact, the only way the agency could increase its managerial diversity was by hiring more people of color and women into the staff group. Efforts to diversify the operator managerial level had to be directed instead toward promoting employees from entry to supervisory and managerial titles at a faster rate and recruiting more candidates of the underrepresented groups to entry-level jobs.

Gender and Racial Inequality at Work

These descriptions coincide with previously documented efforts of women and people of color to achieve success in contemporary organizations, both public and private (Morrison and Von Glinow 1990). Powerful metaphors now

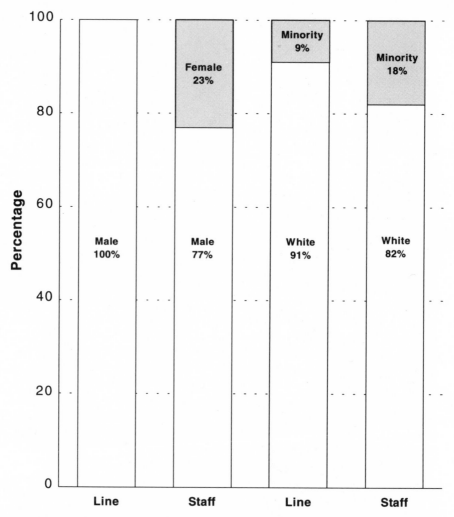

Figure 7. Gender and race of line and staff managers in PSA. Source: Managerial Roster. Graphic by David Grossman.

used in daily life illustrate the extent of the barriers for those who are "outside the loop" because of their color or their gender. There are "glass ceilings" in the movement toward the top (Kilborn 1995; Department of Labor 1991); there are also "glass walls" preventing movement from bad to good job progressions and "bottlenecks" between pre-supervisory and supervisory jobs (Department of Labor 1992; Lopez Amparano 1992). Finally, there are "sticky floors" which prevent upward movement from the lowest levels (Presley-Noble 1992; Center for Women in Government 1992).

Some comparative examples will help place the pervasiveness of gender and racial inequality at PSA in perspective. At the municipal level, studies have identified patterns of occupational and job segregation within and across career ladders in New York City mayoral agencies (Urban Research Center 1987; Stafford 1989). At the state level, several studies have found that the stereotyping of jobs by sex and gender represents a critical structural characteristic accounting for differences in promotional opportunities in the New York State civil service system (Peterson-Hardt and Pearlman 1979; Ratner 1981; Berheide, Chertos, Heignere, and Steinberg 1986; LaSalle and Bakst 1987). At the federal level of employment numerous studies have documented similar differences for women (Lewis 1994) and for selected ethnic groups (Kim and Lewis 1994; Page 1994). The most systematic study of organizational inequalities in the federal civil service concluded that both women and people of color disproportionately started their careers in the lower tier of the bureaucratic labor market. This itself made the achievement of parity with their white male counterparts very hard at the managerial levels (DiPrete 1989). Moreover, the structure of job ladders further contributed to inequality by creating group differences in advancement rates. If at the top the disadvantages seemed to disappear, very few women and minorities were there to benefit. The author of this study concluded that even though the federal civil service system has been a "merit" system since the 1880s, "merit has not translated into equality for women and minorities during its first 100 years" (DiPrete 1989:152).

These findings are linked to a generalized pattern of gender and racial inequality in U.S. society. Theorists of labor allocation in various schools of economics and sociology have long established an empirical connection between the social composition of jobs and other structural conditions. Such employment patterns contribute to accentuate social and economic inequalities (Doeringer and Piore 1974; Gordon, Edwards, and Reich 1982; Hodson and Kaufman 1982; Tomaskovic-Devey 1993). In this view, occupational and job segregation can be considered outcomes of the unequal opportunity workers encounter at several points of the employment relationship (including placement and promotion). This type of "ascriptive differentiation" of labor took place in PSA. Personal characteristics unrelated to job performance seemed to be linked to the location of people in different career ladders and at different levels of each progression.

The skewed demographic distribution in jobs and ladders suggests that one should seriously consider the possibility that "organizations and jobs may be every bit as much the product of racial and patriarchal practices in the workplace as they are of power and efficiency considerations" (Tomaskovic-Devey 1993:6). This author argues that job segregation not only is the reflection of processes of labor market segmentation but, in addition, has itself become an organizational process contributing to inequalities in the workplace. The implications of such a provocative statement will be helpful when, in later chapters, we explore the impact of demographics on the reactions of PSA employees toward their jobs.

Outcomes of Opportunity

Opportunity structures within PSA became most apparent when information about outputs, documented earlier, was used to interpret the results of a set of mathematical models designed to predict the impact of opportunity structures on personal success. The findings suggest that after taking into account human capital attributes often linked to attainment, individual prospects for promotion, compensation, and job challenge varied among PSA employees according to their position in different career ladders. Other things being equal, one's structural position had a direct impact on one's chances of accruing more promotions, receiving larger salary increments over time, and participating in training programs. In general, the impact on the individual prospects of analysts and clerical employees was negative when compared with operators. There were, however, important variations among staff employees. These were based on differences in civil service enforcement.

Three regression models assessed the impact of career ladder participation and other "human capital" variables on each dimension of opportunity (see Table 4). Assuming that levels of performance were normally distributed among employees from the three groups studied, the differences in reward distribution associated with the career ladder variable must be related to some attribute of the ladder rather than exclusively to individual performance.[23]

Prospects for Promotional Attainment

According to human capital theory, the number of promotions is a function of factors such as seniority, education, and organizational level, in addition to individual effort. The model tested the hypothesis that promotions were also a function of participation in each career ladder, combined with employee civil service status. The results accounted for 57 percent of the explained variation in the number of promotions for the sampled employees.[24]

According to these results (see Table 4, "Number of promotions"), when seniority, education, and organizational level were held constant, the impact of the career ladder on the number of promotions was significantly different for each staff subgroup compared to the operators. The differences were not significant, in the case of permanent clerical employees, however. The negative effect for all staff groups suggests that operators had accrued more promotions

Table 4. Ordinary least squares regressions: determinants of opportunity dimensions

Dependent variables: promotion, salary increase, and training programs taken[a]
Parameter estimates[b]

Independent variables	Model 1 Number of promotions		Model 2 Salary increase		Model 3 Training programs	
Intercept	−1.11		2.78		2.22	
Restrict[c]	3.25	(4.37)***	0.67	(2.44)**	3.59	(2.50)*
Seniority[d]	—	—	0.01	(10.76)***	—	—
(Seniority)²	0.00	(8.31)***	—	—	—	—
Log (seniority)	—	—	—	—	.25	(7.06)***
Education	0.07	(13.38)***	0.01	(3.14)***	0.07	(6.40)***
Promotions	—	—	0.15	(14.89)***	—	—
Permanent analysts	−0.35	(−3.80)***	−0.13	(−3.45)	−0.82	(−4.47)***
Provisional analysts	−0.44	(−5.13)***	−0.10	(−2.88)	−0.96	(−5.46)***
Permanent clerical employees	−0.01	(−0.19)	−0.15	(−6.05)	−0.44	(−3.77)***
Provisional clerical employees	−0.26	(−3.60)***	−0.10	(−3.17)	−0.07	(−4.55)***
Managerial level	0.21	(1.64)	−0.08	(−1.55)	0.25	(1.02)
Supervisory level	0.51	(−8.97)***	0.03	(0.03)	0.06	(0.55)
Entry level	−0.82	(−13.19)***	0.01	(0.03)	−0.25	(−1.97)**
R² =	0.57		0.78		0.30	
Sample size	363		363		371	

Sources: survey, personnel file. See the Appendix for the specification of each model.

[a] The models are based on the natural logarithm of the variable +1. See the Appendix for justification.

[b] Numbers in parentheses indicate T-Statistics.

[c] Restriction imposed to force regression through origin and to suppress constant term. See the Appendix for justification.

[d] Seniority refers to the number of years at work. Models 1 and 3 use the square of seniority and the natural log of seniority, respectively. See the Appendix for justification.

* Statistically significant at the 10% level.

** Statistically significant at the 5% level.

*** Statistically significant at the 1% level.

throughout their careers. But it is important to keep in mind that the number of promotions does not necessarily reflect the nature or the distance of upward movement, especially in a civil service context. Hence these differences are most relevant not because they indicate a direct advantage for operators but because they document the impact of structural location on promotion.

The group differences in mobility rates were moderate. The most striking difference was the degree of predictability of the employment relationship (how open or closed it was) on the promotion opportunity of employees located in each ladder. The similarity between operators and permanent clerks illustrates this point. These two groups had the highest civil service enforcement, and their promotion prospects were regulated in a similar manner. A comparison of

Table 5. Career ladder promotion rates by level

	Operator	Analyst	Clerical
Managerial	0.03	0.03	0.03
Supervisory	0.02	0.10[a]	0.02
Intermediate	0.01	0.27	0.65

Source: Title entry data breakdown for 1985 and 1986.
[a] Aggregate figure for the following titles: associate staff ananlyst, associate city planner, project coordinator.

promotion rates for these two groups yields no important differences at the supervisory and the managerial levels.

Promotion rates reported in Table 5 were calculated by comparing the number of promotions recorded for each job title with the number of employees in that title for a ten-month period. According to observations and interviews with PSA managers, the high rate for the intermediate clerical group did not accurately reflect their promotion chances, while the other rates seemed to be fairly accurate.[25] Ignoring the clerical anomaly, the table suggests a slight promotion advantage for analysts in the intermediate and supervisory levels, and similarly low rates for the three groups at the managerial level. This is consistent with the fact that operators and clerks tended to follow the pace of civil service, while analysts operated under looser employment conditions.

Hence, a proportionally higher number of employees in analyst titles moved up during the ten-month period studied. But at the same time, individual civil servants in the operator and clerical ladders experienced a larger number of promotions throughout their careers. These differences point to the complexity generated by heterogenous employment arrangements in PSA.

Prospects for Salary Increase

Another regression model assessed the impact of career ladder participation on employees' salary prospects (see Table 4, "Salary increase"). The ratio of current to starting salary represents a measure of salary increases for an employee throughout his or her career in PSA. To control for inflation, initial and present salaries were adjusted to constant dollars with a 1967 base.[26]

The model explained 78 percent of the variation in salary increases among the sampled employees. The table shows that employees in the clerical and analyst ladders had lower ratios of current to starting salaries compared to operators, after considering seniority, education, organizational level, and number of promotions. Operators had higher compensation prospects, as measured by the net amount of money they had accrued throughout their careers.

Furthermore, there was a greater salary difference between operators and civil servants in the two staff groups than between operators and provisional employees in those groups. This suggests that although civil service represented a financial advantage for line employees, it translated into a financial disadvantage for analysts and clerical employees. Such a paradox further illustrates the existence of patterns of opportunity, even among members of that public sector bureaucratic labor market commonly called the civil service.

Prospects for Participation in Training Programs

A third regression model examined job challenge (see Table 4, "Training programs taken"). It tested the effect of seniority, organizational level, education, and civil service status (by ladder) on the number of training programs in which employees had reported participation. The goal was to assess whether career ladder membership had a direct effect on training participation.

Here the explanatory power of the model proved weaker than in the case of promotions and salary increases. Only 30 percent of the variance was explained. Participation in training programs is largely a function of individual choice, a contingency factor that was not included in the analysis.[27] The results are nevertheless suggestive of the trend observed in the other opportunity dimensions; the negative signs of the coefficients confirm the pattern previously described. Everything else being equal, either by preference or for other reasons, clerical and analyst participation in training programs was significantly lower than operator participation. This can be interpreted as a disadvantage in access to a reward that can increase an employee's opportunity for workplace learning.

Conclusion

Information presented in this chapter suggests that the experience of the clerical supervisor reported in the opening of Chapter 4 represented a typical example of the way the employment relationship was structured in PSA for many clerical employees. Rather than illustrating an isolated instance affecting a single person, it exemplifies the experience of an entire group of individuals who shared a similar location in PSA's job structure.

Indeed, the sets of evidence we have examined—the structural nature of the jobs in the three career ladders, the traits of the managerial group, the demographic composition of managerial and premanagerial jobs, and employees' prospects for promotion, compensation and training—all point to the existence of opportunity structures in PSA. Together with the descriptions provided in the previous chapter, this information further clarifies how individual choice and organizational design interact to produce processes, outputs, and outcomes of opportunity. Employees experienced the consequences of this structural design on a day-to-day basis, and their choices were bound accordingly.

At least two if not three different types of work arrangements coexisted within PSA. Careers unfolded differently for operators on the one hand and for clerical employees and analysts on the other. Each arrangement benefited its employees in a different way. In addition, two subtypes of employment relationships regulated work within the clerical and analyst groups: a more open model for provisionals and a more closed model for permanent employees.

The operator progression fitted perfectly the notion of an internal labor market, defined as a cluster of jobs with "three basic structural features: (a) a job ladder, (b) entry only at the bottom, and (c) movement up the ladder which is associated with a progressive development of knowledge or skill" (Althausser and Kalleberg 1981:130). In this ladder the direction of the movement was clearly defined, the jobs at the top were few, and there was high predictability. Furthermore, the operator group experienced the conditions typical of most ILMs: high wages, mobility potential, protection from outside competition, stability, job security, and better opportunity overall. As a single employer, PSA had defined the rules for this particular group of employees independently of external labor markets and public sector dynamics. In this sense, the operator ladder was a perfect example of a firm internal labor market (FILM). It also represented a particular employment type, the bureaucratic internal labor market (BILM). A stern enforcement of civil service regulations, guarded by the union, sanctioned this employment relationship.

The clerical ladder was based, in theory, on the same ideal BILM typical of public sector employment. Its imperfect implementation produced internal variations in the employment relationship, however. This resulted in employment arrangements characterized by segregation based on race and sex, and in lower salaries and fewer real mobility prospects.

The clerical progression had the least opportunities and at the same time the largest proportion of women and people of color. This replicates a broader pattern of inequality: women and people of color have easiest access to "bad" jobs characterized by low pay, low advancement opportunities, poor working conditions, and instability (Osterman 1980). The same dynamic operates in reverse. We see another career ladder filled mostly by white males, who enjoy the many opportunities typical of "good" jobs. Notwithstanding, clerical jobs differed from those in the typical secondary labor market because a good portion of its employees, two-thirds of them, had the job security and the steady mobility prospects afforded by their civil service status. Both types of clerical employees, provisional and permanent, experienced a similar reality of deflated opportunity in PSA, however.

The work arrangements typical of the analyst ladder varied along a continuum depending on the degree of civil service enforcement. Some employment agreements in this ladder were similar to those of the clerical group participating in the city's BILM. Others were based on the dynamics of a broader occupational labor market (OLM), where the terms of employment were a function of the larger market's supply and demand for technical knowledge.

Variations in the employment relationship in PSA illustrate the condition of heterogeneity of work arrangements. Employees who worked side by side in PSA, often occupying titles with identical names, participated in a variety of work arrangements with rules typical of FILMs, BILMs, and generic OLMs. Moreover, these terms of employment varied in ways that produced advantages for some and disadvantages for others. These variations highlight the degree of workplace inequality that PSA employees confronted, despite the generalized societal expectation that organizations provide equality of opportunity based on merit.

All in all, the design of the operator career ladder offered far more opportunity to its members than the analyst and the clerical career ladders did. The work conditions of operators testify to their ability to take advantage of and monopolize the best features of the reward system in PSA. This suggests the importance of further exploring how power affects resource allocation in hierarchical organizations such as PSA (Perrow 1986; Collins 1985). The next chapter places our knowledge of opportunity in each career ladder within the broader organizational context of PSA. It is in this arena, where power occupies center stage, that employees ultimately experience feelings about work.

Power and the
Distribution of Rewards

Organizations are political systems. Those in charge must create order among people with different interests and agendas. Politics represents one of the processes that help determine *who gets what, when, and how* in a legitimate manner. Power, in turn, is the ability of individuals or groups to exercise control over these processes (Morgan 1986; Pfeffer 1981; Kanter 1977). Perrow suggests that power is

> the ability of persons or groups to extract for themselves valued outputs from a system in which other persons or groups either seek the same outputs for themselves or would prefer to expend their effort toward other outputs. (1986: 259)

Moreover, he suggests that power serves several functions, since actors struggle either over the content of the output or over its distribution. The exercise of power may be used to "alter the initial distribution of outputs, to establish an unequal distribution, or to change the outputs" (p. 259).

That people need resources to accomplish individual and collective tasks only enhances the political nature of organizations. Organizational resources are, after all, limited and sometimes scarce. The uneven outcomes of resource allocation are, to some extent, a function of the fact that this effort takes place in a contested setting (Edwards 1979; Perrow 1986; Morgan 1986; Pfeffer 1981, 1992). Work life, always involves some bargaining among groups with uneven amounts of power. Hence, this social force plays a critical role in the distribution of resources in formal organizations.

Perrow's metaphor of the pie can illustrate this view of power as control over distribution. At issue is the type of the pie and the way it is divided, not only its size. The question is whether the division follows some set of prescribed principles that appear legitimate to the members of the system. This means that the problem of distributive justice is inherent in the power dynamics of organizations. Power affects actors' perceptions of fairness in the distribution of the pie, in terms of both processes and outcomes.

The aim of this chapter, then, is to explore the social forces behind the power arrangements that sustained and legitimated the distribution of rewards in PSA, and to identify how the distributions of power, resources, and opportunity were all interconnected.[1] It may not be possible to claim which distribution came first, but it is possible to assert that the interaction of these three types of "organizational commodities" generated patterns of advantage and disadvantage for specific groups of PSA employees.

Power can be diagnosed by observing its consequences. The concentration of salary is a good measure of the concentration of power. Our study of inequalities in compensation has established that operators have an advantage compared to the two other groups. The size of operator entry-level salaries and their incremental raises point to their power to draw organizational resources. In contrast, analysts and clerical employees had no similar collective advantages, even though mechanisms such as "equity payments" did exist for other professional groups in PSA.[2] Another indicator of the power difference was the lower economic status of analysts and clerical employees compared to equivalent employees in other agencies. Some employees complained (in personal interviews) that, seven years after the separation from the parent agency, PSA analysts had received fewer salary increases than their counterparts who had stayed in the original organization.

Two examples of nonfinancial indicators of power are the proportional representation of groups in management positions and the participation of employees in interdepartmental task forces, teams, and committees (Pfeffer 1992). An ambitious provisional staff analyst pointed out that large chunks of PSA—the most interesting parts, in her mind—were closed to people like her. In fact, the operators' monopoly over line managerial positions represents yet another indication of the concentration of power in their hands. The systematic participation of operators and provisional analysts in special duty assignments is a final example of PSA's power distribution. Employees knew that the "clique" used special assignments to groom their people for future managerial positions.

What were the social forces behind this power distribution? Three important sources of power helped operators and (to a lesser extent) provisional analysts consolidate their power base in PSA. These were resource dependencies stemming from PSA's mission, the process of unionization, and organizational change. Each helped or hindered a group's ability to influence the terms of its employment relationship in PSA.

Resource Dependence and the Employment Relationship

According to Pfeffer, those units or individuals that address directly the critical concerns of an organization's mission tend to have more power because of the dependencies generated around their work. Operators and provisional analysts played strategic technical roles in PSA. This bestowed some legitimacy over their claims to organizational resources. Operators did so from their position in the operating core. Analysts in turn made similar claims based on their work within the technostructure.

The nature of the operators' tasks contributed to increase their potential power base. Operators' willingness to work productively represented perhaps the most important human resource issue PSA leaders had to address. Operators' field experience was the most valuable asset PSA had to cultivate in order to survive as an organization. Pfeffer argues that consensus and technological certainty surrounding a task enhances the potential power of those performing it. The more predictable, certain, and tangible the results, the more seriously the leaders will take the claims of the workers. Operator work was blue-collar; it was harsh in terms of working conditions, and it had little prestige outside of PSA. But at the same time, given proper training, the job was straightforward and easy to perform. It was also easy to measure. Consensus and certainty also facilitated internal and external communication, thus providing a united front and consistent messages about the best ways to accomplish goals. This further increased the technical credibility of the workers vis-à-vis other groups in PSA.

These attributes also contributed to enhance the social cohesion of operators in PSA. A consulting anthropologist described the high degree of operator solidarity she observed in PSA as follows:

> [Operators] always make some gesture of recognition when they meet up with each other on the streets during work time. Whatever a new recruit's attitude upon entry into the department, once there, he is socialized into a culture with a strong work ethic. Comradery among workers is important in maintaining this morale. Out in the districts, the tasks . . . are taken seriously. There is a "we're in this together" feeling among the work force.[3]

A high degree of social interaction complemented the workers' solidarity. The union organized picnics and family events. Extramural activities reinforced the sense of community, and many workers were friends outside of work. Some even took their vacations together. In general, there was a "clan" atmosphere at work. According to the same anthropologist,

> on-the-job sharing among comrades . . . is expressed in taking breaks together, playing cards or shooting pool during breaks, even in sharing pornography, sexual

innuendoes, and an occasional slap on the rear. As one worker put it, "We play a lot." Beside the security and salary, the shared on-the-job socializing is a large part of worker gratification.

By the time operators became line managers they had shared important rites of passage together. The belief that only someone who had been in the field can understand what supervisors and managers must confront daily was responsible for the operator monopoly over line managerial positions. The acceptance of this claim itself is an indication of how much PSA depended on the work of operators. It helps explain why operator managers tended to take unified positions about issues at work.

Operator social interaction occurred in the union, at home, and at work. Staffing practices and a cohesive culture helped reinforce the group's unity, consensus, and cohesion. This produced the important source of organizational power that Pfeffer has called "unity of action." The claim of a group over resources is much stronger if it comes as a unified voice, because this increases credibility as well as legitimacy in the eyes of the leaders. It also produces more pressure by sheer numbers.

The relative power of analysts can also be linked to resource dependencies. The professionalization of government provides the broader context for understanding the increased dependence of PSA decision makers on analytical skills (Benveniste 1987; Mosher and Stillman 1977). Kearney and Sinha have characterized this trend in public agencies as one based on dual streams of professionalism: the "invasion of public administration by the professions, and the professionalization of the vocation of public administration" (1988:572).[4] Indeed, large bureaucracies such as PSA have experienced a rapid growth of their technostructure. With the advent of information technologies, trained analysts have become increasingly essential to their efficient operation (Mintzberg 1979, 1989).

The greater development of a technocratic mentality in public administration may help explain the increased relevance of analysts in PSA. Pfeffer has noted the link between information and power: "Our belief that there is a right answer to most situations and that this answer can be uncovered by analysis and illuminated with more information means that those in control of the facts and the analysis can exercise substantial influence" (Pfeffer 1992:247). Technical analysis does serve an important legitimating function for public organizations. It provides the rational discourse required to attract and retain organizational resources from regulatory and authorizing agencies in a highly political environment. Analytical skills were thus important managerial tools in PSA.

Provisional analysts represented a new promise of professionalism and expertise in the bureaucracy. They had the ability to cope with critical organizational uncertainties in PSA, and they monopolized the complex information needed to make decisions. While information was crucial to monitor and evaluate the success of PSA's mission, its collection and interpretation required highly specialized skills such as budget and productivity analysis. These were potentially important sources of power for the group. Over time, the need for sophisticated analytical techniques to standardize and evaluate work in PSA forced decision makers to focus their attention on ways to attract and retain credentialed analysts. Often they had to negotiate employment conditions under open terms, despite the weight of the civil service ideology.

The growing importance of analysts in PSA is evidenced by the creation in the late 1970s of a special unit with direct control over humanpower planning in the main operation. Its organizational location, however, shows the subordination of analytical work to line authority. Despite its large analytical component, analysts reported to the agency's senior *operator* manager rather than to the commissioner or to some other high-ranking non-operator. This unit was conceived as a "think tank" which would integrate the experience of line officers and credentialed managers and analysts. It represented the technical heart of operations at headquarters.

Finally, in contrast to the operators and provisional analysts, clerical and analyst civil servants performed work which did not enhance their power. PSA leaders felt no compelling dependence on the work of these two groups of employees. Clerical employees performed simple, generic, and thus easily replaceable work. It was only indirectly related to PSA's critical task, and was white-collar in nature. Despite its secondary importance compared to the operator's job, it was performed in the comfort of an office. Similarly, tasks performed by permanent analysts did not require specialized skills. Experience rather than education provided the critical skills required for permanent analysts' efficient performance. By way of implicit understanding, permanent analysts tended to engage in tasks that overlapped with the most complex clerical work or with the supervision of clerical pools. In contrast, the younger provisional group tended to be involved in the "hard core" policy issues that required technical analysis.

Hence, permanent employees from the analyst and the clerical ladders could not legitimate in technical terms their claim to a share of the resources. This may be associated with the lower opportunity offered in their career ladders within PSA. In the case of the clerical group, this correlation happened despite the existence of a well-defined and structured career ladder that enjoyed union protection. In the case of the permanent staff analysts, it had happened in the context of the career ladder's recent development and the analysts' partially successful effort to gain the right to unionize. In both cases, collective efforts had helped employees gain some important civil service benefits (such as job security). But these efforts had not been successful in creating the clout needed to exert a stronger claim over other organizational rewards.

Unionization and the Employment Relationship

Collective bargaining represents a powerful source of control over organizational resources because it gives unions the ability to participate in rule making and its enforcement (Spero and Capozzola 1973). As we saw in Chapter 3, unions have shaped the conditions of employment for those organizational groups they represent. The real effect of union involvement depends, however, on the actual clout they can exert over those who manage municipal affairs. Some unions will be able to exert strong pressure to guard the system, while others will have a harder time. This produces variations in civil service enforcement and influences the degree of formalization of job progressions across occupational groups and city agencies. In PSA the operators' high degree of formalization and civil service enforcement contrasted with the moderate or low degrees of the clerical and analyst groups. These variations can be associated with differences in union strength across ladders.

The Operators' Union: A Unified Front

The operators' union had gained its strength during the late sixties when it organized and successfully won an important nine-day walkout from PSA. This job action violated a prohibition on strikes by public sector employees, and it paralyzed the city. It also generated heated debates and exposed political contradictions between city and state leaders. The final outcomes of the job action included a fundamental transformation of working conditions for operators, an improvement of their salary structure, and an upgrading of machinery and work facilities for the group. The success of this action, according to union documents and leaders, consolidated the rank and file into a stronger and more unified group.

The large number of workers represented by the union embodied a degree of electoral power in PSA. Union leadership did indeed have political leverage at the city and state levels. Their political clout also extended to operations within PSA. A critical indicator of their influence was the emergence during the late 1970s and early 1980s of labor-management committees and quality circles. These gave managers, supervisors, and workers from the field a new problem-solving tool. They were forms of worker participation designed to ensure the input of operators in the decision-making process. These devices helped institutionalize the operators' voice in PSA's affairs. They also helped move labor-management relations to a more productive, cooperative mode, compared to the traditional confrontational setting.

Operators were not the only group enjoying these participatory schemes in PSA. Other blue-collar career ladders also used them, suggesting that they, too, had some union power within the agency.[5] The main difference between other craft workers and the operators was that the employment conditions of the former were determined by their trades, which were external. This diluted their strength within PSA. For example, one of the main obstacles for the promotion of these workers was precisely the narrow job descriptions imposed by external rules. Another obstacle was a union agreement which prohibited non-operator managers to supervise operators. This strict code of supervision of operators by other operators hindered other trade employees' potential movement to supervisory positions in the line function.

The operator union enhanced its power by functioning exclusively for its constituency in PSA. While it was housed under the broad, traditional labor structure at city, state, and national levels, the labor-management contract negotiations focused exclusively on PSA operators' grievances. This special focus affected critical human resource management decisions within PSA, as the following example illustrates.

In the early 1980s, PSA leaders designed a productivity improvement strategy that required fundamental changes in operations around the city. The proposed reforms required drastic changes in equipment and the reduction of the crews servicing the field. A gain-sharing scheme gave the reduced crews a share of the savings generated by the reform. Labor-management committees, which had already been started, would become critical in implementing the experiment.

In the initial proposal, PSA wanted to sponsor team membership by creating a productivity savings fund for all district employees. This proposal included gain sharing for the clerks in the district, as a means of recognizing their collective contribution. The operators' union opposed the plan on the basis that only those members of the crews who actually did the work should benefit. Once this was resolved to the union's satisfaction, the discussions turned to the percentage of savings that workers would receive. Unresolvable differences around this issue resulted in arbitration. The final decision favored operators. Under the new arrangement, each member of the crew would receive a non-pensionable payment for each shift worked, as long as the crew maintained its productivity targets. After two years, the payments would become pensionable.

Implemented in seven districts, the experiment originally produced net savings of 24 percent in personnel costs. A year later, six new districts had made the same shift, with equivalent increased savings. By the end of that year the city estimated that the reforms had saved $7.7 million per year. As the program expanded and bonus payments became widespread, operators in other districts began to urge their union representatives to extend the gain-sharing program to their units. The union ratified an agreement three years after the experiment had begun. At the end of the fifth year all districts were working under similar arrangements.

This story highlights another important consequence of the union's exclusive representation of PSA operators. Its leadership was drawn exclusively from the pool of operators in PSA. Hence there was a close link between workers in the field and union negotiators. Indeed, they were one and the same. This unity was reinforced by the formal chain of command which went down from line managers at headquarters to field operators. Hence, the communication network, the capacity for immediate organization, and the degree of solidarity among workers converged both at work and in union meetings, providing great political strength.

Clerical Unions: Fragmented Power

Unions representing clerical employees had—over the last fifteen years—gained political clout throughout the city, growing rapidly in numbers as well as in strength. They had, however, only a moderate degree of leverage in shaping the conditions of employment in PSA. Part of the reason for this was that several unions represented PSA clerical employees, depending on their titles, and no single union fought exclusively for clerical employees. The unions served a larger constituency of clerical and nonclerical employees, and they covered a wide range of job titles in a multitude of city agencies. Hence, the specific claims of the clerical occupation, and of the PSA clerical group in particular, were subsumed within broader issues addressed by the entire union membership around the city. This diluted the power of PSA clerical employees, when they tried to press managers into solving problems specific to their agency. An illustration is the way clerical employees had to fight to protect their right to move into managerial positions.

When the city charter first introduced the clerical title of administrative manager in the 1970s, the first clerical managers in many agencies were provisionals. This reduced the urgency to prepare and schedule tests for civil service candidates to fill the jobs. As time passed, permanent clerical supervisors became eligible for the promotional test to enter the managerial position. But with no test in sight, they had to wait.[6]

The city Personnel Department did not offer the test, perhaps because their initial delay in recruiting civil servants had created a new problem. The appearance of civil service lists would force city agencies to reassign the provisional managers who had occupied the positions since their creation. Should these ad hoc managers be displaced by those working their way up the ladder? More importantly, what would be done with the present provisional managers, who had excellent qualifications and educational credentials? Their exit from the system would represent a loss of institutional memory and know-how, which the agencies could not afford. Furthermore, the managers themselves would not give up their jobs that easily.

Several unions, acting in the name of their clerical membership, pressed the city to address this problem. Eventually they took the city to court for not scheduling the exam. Almost ten years after the original job title was created, an administrative manager exam was finally scheduled. The test had an elaborate format that guaranteed that many supervisors would be screened out.

A PSA employee who took the exam described it as follows. It had three parts, offered during a period of three years. First there was a long qualifying test, which eliminated more than just a few candidates. Those who made the preliminary list took a written test, scheduled two years later. Those who passed again were then given an oral examination. After another delay in making the results public, the civil service list finally appeared. The process had required a court suit and four years of union struggle.

S. Miller, the clerical supervisor who earlier compared her working conditions with those of operator supervisors (see Chapter 4), was one of many clerical supervisors involved in this process. At the time of our interview she was waiting for the results of the last test. She was in doubt about her actual chances for advancement in PSA. If she made the list, she argued, she would have to wait until PSA solved the internal staffing problem of provisional managers before she could be appointed to a new position. It was obvious that the change could only be managed incrementally, to the disadvantage of those waiting in the lists.

The history of this test shows the different bargaining power employees had vis-à-vis the city and agency managers. It also illustrates the relative power clerical unions had in PSA. While the union was able to exert some pressure through collective action, the fight was neither easy nor fast. Helping supervisors expedite the testing process to enter management jobs involved great effort and frustrations. The final outcome represented less than a clear victory for the supervisors themselves.

The nuances of the civil service testing process also illustrate how personnel policy in large municipalities is political as much as technical. Many struggles over classification, testing, and compensation represent battles among changing coalitions with dissimilar interests and uneven power in the city personnel arena. The deals and delays and the final accommodations and agreements described above can be seen as examples of strategies to control the outcomes of such struggles (Rich 1992; Gottfried 1988).

The Organization of Staff Analysts: In Search of a Voice

The Organization of Staff Analysts had about three thousand members around the city. It had elected officers and its members paid dues by mail (no job shop clause was allowed). Even though this organization wanted to represent analysts in contract negotiations, city officials had not recognized it formally. They claimed that although they would listen to the concerns of its members, they would not necessarily follow their proposed solutions.[7]

The organization had emerged from a grievance among permanent employees who, one year after having made the staff analyst promotion list, had not been called to occupy their new positions. Behind this delay was the same dilemma described for the clerical group in the previous section. Like the clerical workers, permanent analysts wanted to do something about this problem. Since they had no union, their grievance had less credibility. A group of civil servants therefore decided to form an organization, which they then decided to change into a formal union. They encountered two obstacles. First, many provisional analysts were not interested in participating. Second, most city officials and PSA managers were not anxious to add another formal union to the existing list.

The permanent/provisional dichotomy created the first obstacle. Provisional analysts with master's degrees in fields like public administration, policy analysis, economics, or urban planning viewed themselves as professionals. Some aspired to build a career within the agency or across the city. Others wanted to gain experience in the public sector and then move to a private firm. Most had the ambition of achieving managerial positions in their immediate future. This made the idea of belonging to a union unattractive to them.

In contrast, permanent analysts believed the civil service tradition could promote merit in public employment. Some had been clerical employees who had switched to analyst positions when the slots were first created in the 1970s, before higher educational requirements were formalized. A few clerical supervisors had also used the flexibility of the new titles to take the supervisory test in the analyst ladder, skipping the entry port and avoiding the educational standard that later became the formal requirement. Once in the titles, they often sought to improve their educational credentials. Job security provided by civil service enforcement was an important concern for this group. They saw civil service as a means to maintain a good job attained through the system and through effort. Permanent and provisional analysts therefore had dissimilar definitions of the potential role that a collective organization should play for them.

Managers and city officials represented another obstacle toward the staff analysts' effort to unionize. With the threat of unionization imminent, city representatives made the claim that analysts could not engage in collective bargaining because they belonged to a special category. They argued, for example, that analysts held confidential information or that they might handle it at some point in time, perhaps during collective bargaining. The staff analyst organization claimed in turn that few analysts handled that type of material and that, in fact, they seldom evaluated budget items related to union negotiations. A desk audit ordered to clarify the nature of the analysts' jobs yielded mixed results. While some analysts did handle sensitive information, others did not.

As the energy built up for the forthcoming elections, dirty tactics against the unionization effort threatened the actual chances to gain certification. In the end, staff analysts won the right to organize and today permanent employees in this title have a bargaining unit. Analysts placed in other titles and provisional analysts cannot be union members. This internal split diminishes the potential strength of the group.

Organizational Change

The third force influencing the power distribution in PSA consisted of cycles of expansion and contraction in the agency. The dynamics of change contributed to enhance the provisional analysts' bargaining power, while at the same time they threatened the status quo that had granted operators their power base. Alternate processes of contraction and growth intensified the competition over organizational resources previously monopolized by the operator group. This affected the power distribution in the agency.

Retrenchment and the Loss of Operator Slots

Under a policy of retrenchment during the late 1970s and early 1980s, many operator jobs were officially transformed into staff jobs. These changes affected clerks in headquarters, clerks in the field, mechanics and other technical workers, and enforcement personnel. Between the years of 1977 and 1986, the agency replaced 745 operators with lower-paid non-operators, yielding an annual savings of more than $7.5 million (Brecher and Horton 1986). The process entailed the loss of some advantages that these jobs derived from their link to the operator ladder. Operators lost control over some jobs, thus setting a precedent for future losses. They countered the city comptroller's recommendation to extend the program with the argument that the process had reached the point of diminishing returns. They also furnished quantitative evidence to justify canceling further scheduled shifts.

A description of the conversion of an office-based job cluster from operator to non-operator status illustrates the power dynamics and opportunity consequences behind this process. Originally these slots were monopolized by an elite core of senior operators who found the field too stressful but who did not want to retire. They were thus allowed to use their experience in office work. Then retrenchment policies forced the opening of these jobs to younger non-operators. As the ladder consolidated and productivity was enforced more directly, the older operators ended up competing with younger employees who did not have (and apparently did not need) operator skills to perform well. The operators transferred or retired, and the jobs eventually shifted completely to staff employees. With full conversion, the ladder lost status and pay. It became characterized by poor working conditions and a high attrition rate. Individuals aspiring to operator positions would take these jobs as a last resource or as a strategy to gain information about the operator ladder. Many would take the civil service exams for both jobs and then enter whichever list they made first. Sometimes operators started in the non-operator job and later moved to the line job. The reverse, however, never occurred.

According to an employee from PSA's Equal Employment Opportunity Office, many of the jobs that operators monopolized in PSA could be performed equally well by other employees. The definition of a job sometimes seemed more a function of the particular development of the position than of any objective job evaluations. The boundary between line and staff jobs was justified by promoting, within PSA's culture, the strong belief that field experience for operator positions in headquarters and other office settings was critical. There was a belief, for example, that the clerk to the district manager had to be an operator. This clerk was almost an "alter ego" of the manager, and he made important operational decisions. It was indeed, a powerful position. Operators argued that this job required a way of knowing and thinking that could only be acquired by moving up through the ranks. The same argument had been previously made for every operator position that had been converted to non-operator status. Interestingly enough, no productivity harm had been reported from these conversions during PSA's entire history.

Operators did succeed, however, in keeping line managerial positions closed to employees from other ladders, with the argument that "Unless you've worked in the field, you don't know how to manage field operations." Referring to the ideological component of power, Pfeffer argues that "because decisions and actions inevitably have multiple components, which can be viewed along multiple dimensions, the ability to set the terms of the discussion is an important mechanism for influencing organizational behavior" (1992:206). Slowly, growth in PSA's technostructure gave rise to the view that the terms could in fact be challenged and changed.

The Growth of the Technostructure

The consolidation of the technostructure and the consequent demand for analytical tasks started in PSA at the same time that city decision makers switched jobs to non-operator status for financial reasons. This growth had also forced PSA managers to find new slots for analysts, within the constraints of city-imposed personnel caps. Instead of revising the traditional position classification system to incorporate the new skill requirements, managers tried to work around it, using rules of exception to accommodate the incoming employees. The result was that most provisional analysts landed in one of the many jobs that formed an unstructured job cluster, one with relatively advantageous individualized compensation and promotion arrangements. Indeed, the absence of a formal ladder stimulated bargaining for personal deals. With no collective voice to buffer the negative effects of this uncertainty, the views many analysts held about unions contributed to further atomize their potential group power.

That analysts represented a historically new job category in the city bureaucracy also contributed to weaken their power as a group. They were a relative young force within PSA, only recently starting to articulate their claims to organizational resources. Building a power base takes time because it requires changing not only objective conditions but also subjective perceptions about distributive justice. Organizational theorists connect these perceptions of justice to the production, reproduction, or transformation of given power arrangements. The resources at the disposal of the powerful enable them to induce attitudes and behaviors in others (such as compliance) and thus legitimate inequitable distributions (Cook and Hegtvedt 1983).

In his now classic discussion of distributive justice and salary allocations, Homans argues that power is a critical factor affecting *who* is rewarded, as well as *how much* one gets as a reward: "If one person or group has greater power in either the good or the bad (coercive) sense than another person or group, it is usually able to command greater rewards than the other" (Homans 1976:233; see also Homans 1974; Pfeffer 1992; Perrow 1986). The dominant distributive justice arrangements—that is, the predominant principles of justice used to allocate resources—become reflections of that distribution of power. Changes can occur only when one begins to question either the legitimacy of the allocator or the logic of the allocation (Cook and Hegtvedt 1983). That is why the new analyst group represented a real threat to operators. The new group was moving toward a clear articulation of its claims. It could only be a matter of time before it would have an input in agency processes and outcomes that had always been the preserve of operators.

Conclusion

There was a strong and positive association between power and opportunity in PSA. Operators had a clear ability to influence the organization, and they also had the best opportunity package. The combination of these two elements created a status quo that ensured further acquisition of power and resources. In contrast, the degree of power of analyst and clerical employees was correlated with lower degrees of opportunity in their ladders. This reduced their potential to acquire new organizational resources and diminished their power in PSA. These findings replicate opportunity dynamics already studied by scholars in various traditions. The social psychology of justice literature suggests that power imbalances in exchange networks produce unequal distribution of benefits across participants (Cook and Hegtvedt 1983). In addition, stratification scholars have highlighted the role of power in creating diverse employment arrangements within the same organization (Sorensen and Kalleberg 1981; Althauser 1987). Empirical evidence from both streams of research indicate that actors with advantages in power accumulate more benefits than those without power. In this sense the story line of power dynamics in PSA is idiosyncratic only in its details.

This process of accommodation is analogous to the tendency in stratified societies for the rich to get richer and the poor to get poorer. If one substitutes power for wealth and organizations for societies, this analogy conveys an image of a circular generation of power and opportunity, seen so often in social structures of all kinds. Two propositions about social interactions in stratified systems apply here. The first is that "the person with the gold makes the rules." Pfeffer (1992) claims that this New Golden Rule links power to hierarchy and other types of formal domination. The person with the capability to make the rules will in turn use them to his or her advantage, thus ensuring the generation of more advantages. This advantageous position may in turn make those in power more capable in exerting power successfully (Morgan 1986).

The second proposition asserts that "power begets power" (Kanter 1977). Here power refers to ability to get things done, to enjoy a favorable portion of resources and opportunities to be effective in controlling others. Kanter says with respect to this ability: "people who are thought to have power already and to be well placed in the hierarchies of prestige and status may also be more influential and more effective in getting the people around them to do things" (p. 168). Perceptions of power do mirror the distribution of this commodity in stratified systems, and thus influence the distribution of other, more tangible resources.

While these cycles are easier to visualize in the larger social system, this chapter has illustrated how they also operate at the micro level of organizational life. A combination of external and internal factors—the nature of PSA's mission, unionization, and processes of growth and contraction in PSA—influenced the degree of power accumulated by each group of employees. This in turn influenced their ability to define in favorable terms the job conditions that would define future patterns of opportunity. Thus the powerful within PSA had the ability to generate definitions of social reality that legitimated the process as well as the outcomes of the existing distribution patterns. Indeed, a status quo that was advantageous to operators became itself the source of more power. It created the conditions to control not just the desired resources but more importantly, the terms of the resource distribution itself.

Yet power dynamics in PSA were not simple. The picture that emerged in this chapter shows the importance of the constant process of negotiation and renegotiation of power arrangements occurring over time in a contested environment. The role of operators and provisional analysts in the technical division of labor gave them a relative advantage over other groups. But operators and provisional analysts represented, respectively, the most and the least consolidated employee groups in the agency. This translated into a sharp contrast between the degree of structuring of their career ladders, despite the similar technical dependency both groups generated. This may help explain the differences in opportunity between the two groups.

In the case of operators, collective action ensured favorable employment conditions and their enforcement via civil service. In contrast, the strength of the voice of analyst and clerical employees was not proportional to their numerical expansion within PSA. The weaker collective voice of these groups stemmed either from their recent insertion in the job structure (for provisional staff analysts) or from their fragmented bargaining capacity (for civil servants in both groups). The fragmentation of the analyst group also derived from the fact that provisional employees used their market power to enhance their individual interests, regardless of the needs of the group.

Finally, the low technical relevance of the clerical group's cultural capital placed them in a weaker position to claim a share of the resources. At the same time, the power of their unions was fragmented compared to the unified front of the operators' union. Hence, despite their well-structured ladder and the support of their unions, clerical employees were at a disadvantage.

Why did PSA employees accept these opportunity differences, given the strong emphasis that the civil service ideology placed on the equality justice principle? The answer to this question will emerge as the "subjective" side of opportunity is explored in future chapters. For now, it can be said that the slack introduced by the uneven enforcement of civil service rules may have contributed to legitimate inequality in distributive processes and outcomes. Indeed, an inconsistent enforcement introduced enough ambiguity to help a manager justify ad hoc staffing decisions based on some version of merit. This turned attention away from the fact that a given decision might have been guided more by a job candidate's location within a power structure than by actual merit. The use of merit criteria to distribute organizational rewards thus acquired the rubbery texture that scholars of municipal employment have documented elsewhere at the macro level of urban politics. Individuals and groups within PSA brought with them differing images of opportunity and used them to make sense of the contradictions typical of the organization of work. As they did so, merit definitions would stretch or contract to cover the prevailing views of those with power. Part III of this book will explore these dynamics in detail.

PERCEPTIONS: EXPERIENCING WORKPLACE INEQUALITY

Perceptions of Opportunity (1):
Realities and Myths

Employees may have a "gut" understanding of their chances for success in the workplace. They may even have rational opinions about the processes that define opportunity and affect their prospects. In this sense, the perception and the reality of opportunity may be closely aligned (Kanter 1977). But they are not the same. Indeed, individuals—both managers and employees—may not perceive the full extent to which their career opportunities are constrained by structural factors (Rosenbaum 1984). Yet the lack of awareness does not reduce the real impact of the experience of inequality.[1] For example, an office aide in PSA may not realize the extent to which his or her career is limited by participation in the clerical career ladder. This, however, does not diminish the actual impact that the participation has on the probability of promotion to management or on possible salary increases.

The link between the objective and the subjective sides of an individual's experience of opportunity therefore deserves empirical exploration. The extent of the overlap is important because the actual patterns of resource distribution, the beliefs people share about what they are getting, and their beliefs about what they deserve represent three different aspects of social reality. They all affect the cognitive maps employees use to interpret work experience. The next three chapters explore these dynamics in detail, highlighting the links between opportunity and employee perceptions of work.[2]

Operators, analysts, and clerical employees were well aware of the limitations and possibilities imposed by the unequal outcomes in resource allocation. In general, these perceptions were closely aligned with the actual patterns of opportunity they experienced. In particular, they mirrored two coexisting models of employment in PSA. This chapter illustrates the patterns of association between these models and employees' perceptions of their opportunities. It documents differences in the perception of job opportunities in general and of promotion, compensation, and job challenge in particular.

Two Models of Employment

The bureaucratic model of work organization has been described in the human resources literature as a closed employment model (Beer et al. 1985). In this model, merit is a function of position requirements, much as it is in Weber's ideal type of bureaucracy. This model has dominated public sector employment in the United States since the passing of the Pendleton Act in the late eighteen hundreds. It achieved full development with the design of position classification systems during the first quarter of this century.

In its ideal form, this model represents a *closed* employment relationship because competition for jobs is denied to external candidates. The notion of career is defined in terms of a sequence of jobs associated with higher experience and higher pay. The model implies the use of standardized and objective instruments for assessing merit (i.e., tests). It is built on the assumption that a successful career will usually take place within a single organization, to which the employee remains highly loyal. The ideal employee is therefore one who has invested his or her work life in the organization, who knows his or her job well, and who complies with imposed work standards and regulations, thus ensuring regularity and continuity in the operation.

This contrasts with what the literature calls a market model of employment (Beer et al. 1985). In this model, the employment relationship is defined as an "inducement-contribution contract." It can either be maintained or ended by any side involved in the agreement. Merit is a function of job performance, and the ideal employee is one who can adapt to the situation and bring to it whatever type of human capital is most needed. This model is based on flexibility; employees enter and leave at any level of a ladder. It thus represents an *open* employment relationship. As mobility is not necessarily vertical, nor restricted to a single organization, the notion of a career is more individualized. Furthermore, careers can be constructed around professional lines, which are often independent of organizational loyalties. Attuned with the ideology of credentialism, this model identifies higher education as the best predictor of productivity.

In theory, PSA sanctioned the bureaucratic model as the legitimate employment mode for most of its premanagerial employees. The civil service system embodied this model. In practice, the differences in civil service enforcement produced employment conditions that resembled those typical of open, market-based relationships for some employees. The way employees interpreted their opportunities in PSA reflected their actual participation in one of the two employment modes, closed or open.

The amount of opportunity employees experienced also affected whether the perceptions were positive or negative. Indeed, employees linked—in one way or another—the unequal distribution of resources to variations in civil service enforcement. Most employees complained about the inefficiency of the system. However, the explanations they gave for it varied from one career ladder to the next. Two occupational groups as different as the analysts and the clerical employees shared important common perceptions about their opportunity. Both shared the uncertainty typical of open employment. They also shared low opportunities, a result of their exclusion from organizational resources monopolized by operators. These two groups tended to highlight the negative aspects of their opportunity package. Operators, in contrast, tended to feel positive about the various opportunity dimensions of their jobs.

Reactions to the Opportunity Dimensions of the Job

If someone feels that having a promotion is important and that the present job offers no chance of one, that person will be dissatisfied with the promotion dimension of the job.[3] The contrast between what PSA employees felt they wanted from a job and what they actually got from it offers a first approximation of their feelings about the job, or selected dimensions of it. A survey supplied information about three dimensions of opportunity. All employees who answered it were assigned a "discrepancy score," reached by comparing separate answers about the opportunity dimensions of their job. One question assessed whether a certain opportunity existed and the other how important it was.[4] The presence of a discrepancy between the two answers indicated that the person was dissatisfied with that aspect of the job; no discrepancy meant the person was satisfied.[5]

These scores provide a useful comparison of how employees in the three ladders evaluated the opportunity dimensions of their jobs.[6] Figure 8 confirms the pattern of association between perceptions and participation in the open and closed types of employment. Indeed, the largest differences tended to occur between operators on one hand and the two groups participating in open employment relationships on the other. The magnitude of the differences highlights the striking dissatisfaction of analysts and clerical employees, especially with promotion and pay. Operators experienced more satisfaction with nearly all opportunity dimensions of their job. The only dimension in which analysts were more satisfied than operators was workplace learning. But even here, only slightly more than one-third of the operators reported dissatisfaction, and the difference between the two groups was only eight points.

In addition, more clerical employees were much more dissatisfied than operators and somewhat more dissatisfied than analysts in all opportunity dimensions

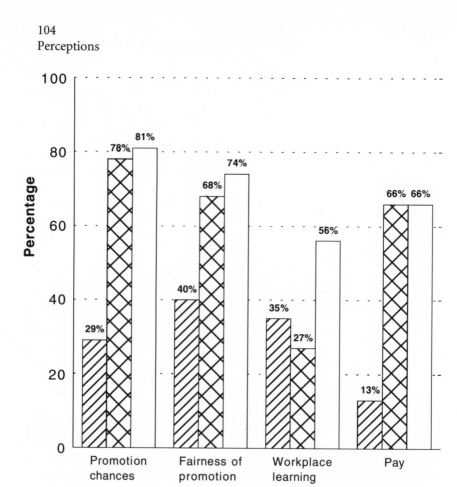

Figure 8. Percent of respondents dissatisfied with selected indicators of opportunity by career ladder. Graphic by David Grossman.

(except for pay, where equal numbers of clericals and analysts expressed dissatisfaction). Although both analysts and clerical employees reported ample dissatisfaction, the latter expressed the strongest feelings of dissatisfaction with all opportunity aspects of their jobs.

Perceptions of Opportunity for Promotion

H. Astor was a civil servant manager who had made her career as a step-up (provisionally promoted employee) through the clerical ranks. She compared civil service protection in her ladder to a double-edged sword because it was enforced in an organization where some did not have to comply. She argued that the rules could not work unless they were applied to all. Since they were not, following them could be detrimental. The union's advice to stay within the specifications of the job description, for example, prevented clerical employees from being noticed by their supervisors. In her view, emphasis on employee protection against out-of-title work could slow the employee's career. She believed that her supervisors would not have taken risks on her behalf—offering her opportunities as a step-up—had she not demonstrated a level of initiative by working over and above what the job formally required. She was also convinced that her decision to go back to college could only benefit her.

Astor's mind-set was consistent with an open employment model rather than with the closed model endorsed by the clerical union. But at the same time, paradoxically, she strongly advocated the importance of civil service enforcement. She claimed it was the only way to provide opportunities for employees who, like her, did not (yet) have a higher educational credential but who had a lot of experience and job commitment. The contradictions in her thinking stemmed from an environment characterized by uncertainty. This motivated her to pursue two separate strategies of career development. Her case provides a vivid example of the dualities produced by the coexistence of conflicting work arrangements within the same environment. Many permanent clerical employees and analysts had to make career decisions in this almost schizoid atmosphere.

Contrast this with the situation for operators. The certainty of their promotional criteria and practices and other relative advantages gave operators a sense that if they really wanted to, they could move up. The promise of equal opportunity based on a formalized, well-protected ladder was sufficient to offset the reality that only a few would actually move up. In the survey one operator manager expressed his satisfaction as follows: "I think that (PSA) is an excellent job with good promotional opportunities for anyone with a limited educational background. This job has enabled me to raise a family and give them all necessities and many extras."

The belief that operators have higher promotional opportunities was in part a "myth" of PSA's organizational culture. A consequent belief was that an operator's failure to move up was a function of the individual rather than of systemic limitations. In the words of a manager in the training division, those operators who succeeded at PSA did so because they "took charge" of their life. As one operator expressed it, "The opportunity is there to advance, but you find many workers do not apply themselves or inquire about certain things that might be beneficial to them." Regular movement, and the fact that two commissioners had been recruited from the ranks in the past, reinforced the belief that any operator who wanted to could make it to the top.

Contradicting this generalized belief, or perhaps as a way to protect themselves from its psychological impact, individual operators reported low expectations about their personal chances of moving up in the immediate future. The rating of their chances for promotion on a scale from 1 to 10 showed a shared realism about mobility prospects among employees (see Table 6).[7] Operators were the most pessimistic, followed by clerical employees and then analysts. Operators' pessimism can be linked to the higher enforcement of rules in their ladder. They believed that there were good opportunities, but they did not believe they would move up in the short run. Considering the reduced availability of positions in the pyramid, this was a realistic assessment. It also allowed operators to maintain the myth without compromising their personal integrity.

Analysts' higher expectations corresponded to the openness of their employment relationship. The general assessment of the promotion system was negative for this group. But individuals believed they could make it and were expecting to do so. They knew they had few opportunities, but precisely because the rules were not that structured, they felt they had better chances as individuals to move up in the system or, in the worst scenario, to find a better position elsewhere. Generic mobility rates and the work histories of analyst managers presented in previous chapters suggest that this was realistic. As for clerical employees, they were aware of the constraints of civil service, but they, too, knew that some employees found it possible to avoid them. The group's mixed expectations for mobility stemmed from an awareness that the ladder offered few opportunities and that the system moved at a slow pace. This realism was tempered with the knowledge that lax enforcement of civil service rules allowed some individuals to move up.

Employees also had differing opinions about how well or badly promotions were handled in their unit. While a large number of operators were pleased with the promotion system and did not want to see anything changed, fewer clerical employees and analysts felt that way. Many more clerical employees (76%) and analysts (81%) wanted changes compared to operators (57%). The same pattern was apparent when employees listed specific obstacles in getting a new job in PSA (Table 7). For more than one-third of the operators, no obstacles stood in their way; less than one-quarter of the clerical employees felt so, and only one-sixth of the analysts. Moreover, the operators who foresaw obstacles believed that they

Table 6. Expected chance of promotion by career ladder (%)

	Operator	Analyst	Clerical
Low chance of promotion	52	29	40
Moderate chance of promotion	28	39	43
High chance of promotion	20	32	16
Number of respondents	141	82	122

Note: Columns may not add up to 100 percent due to rounding.

Table 7. Anticipated obstacles to promotion by career ladder (%)

	Operator	Analyst	Clerical
No obstacles	37	16	24
Personal obstacles	24	13	20
Organizational obstacles	37	67	53
Other	2	4	3
Number of respondents	133	70	110

could overcome them eventually. Very few felt burdened by the organizational obstacles that the clerical and analyst employees typically mentioned. The latter also expressed pessimism about overcoming these obstacles.

Employees' descriptions of promotion barriers can be clustered into two broad categories. The first includes factors employees could overcome with personal effort. Examples are the lack of sufficient experience, qualifications, seniority, or credentials; lack of interest in new positions; and family constraints. The second category includes factors that were beyond an employee's direct control. Examples are managerial barriers (e.g., the persistent use of favoritism) or environmental factors (e.g., the absence of promotional tests). Most operators mentioned factors of the first category, whereas most analysts and clerks mentioned the second.

The obstacles most analysts and clerical employees experienced were, in fact, linked to the open nature of their employment relationship. Many believed that promotions in their units were blocked by the excessive use of *particularistic* criteria.[8] They mentioned political restrictions, lack of connections, patronage, nepotism, and favoritism as important obstacles in their effort to move up. Other barriers mentioned in this category included discrimination policies, a hiring preference for outsiders, a lack of visibility due to job type or location, performing a non-operator job, being caught in intra-agency conflicts, and direct interference by supervisors. A few mentioned lack of adequate information about opportunities, equal employment opportunity regulations, union or city restrictions, and civil service constraints. These last four factors were chiefly obstacles for provisional employees; the preceding ones were the worry of civil servants.

As for the sources of uncertainty that employees identified (Table 8), these mirrored the difference between the open and closed employment modes. For example, participants in the open mode (i.e., analysts and clericals) reported higher levels of uncertainty than those in the closed mode (operators). The nature of the fears employees reported likewise depended on the employment mode. Operators' apprehensions stemmed from city decisions to lay off personnel or terminate contracts due to political circumstances, fiscal crisis, or budget cuts. This fear was a reflection of the collective memory of the devastation

Table 8. Reasons for concern regarding job security by career ladder (%)

	Operator	Analyst	Clerical
Provisional status	0	14	54
City decisions	44	24	15
Conflicts at work	22	28	13
Miscellaneous/other	33	34	48
Number of respondents	18	29	39

produced by the fiscal crisis of the late seventies. It had little to do with internal employment practices in PSA. In contrast, employees who participated in the open employment mode feared forces inside PSA. Subtle distinctions among the analyst and clerical groups clearly mirrored the opportunity dynamics that characterized their ladders. Most of the clerical employees who felt insecure about their jobs mentioned their provisional status or their fear of failing civil service exams. More analysts were concerned with threats posed by conflicts at work.[9]

Perceptions of Financial Opportunity

In one of the early meetings of the Women's Advisory Committee in PSA,[10] the staff analyst Rose Lopez claimed that she knew a few female manager analysts who were making considerably less money than their male counterparts, although working under the same conditions. A female clerical employee also acknowledged knowing of similar instances in her unit. In the discussion that followed, the group agreed that pay inequities were an important problem in PSA. Yet they also agreed that it would be politically counterproductive to tackle this sensitive topic so early in the committee's life. They decided instead to promote career development activities for women.

The committee's decision was pragmatic. Indeed, given the demographic composition of the ladders, addressing differences in compensation would have required confronting the issue of equal pay for equal work at a systemic level (Gold 1983). Yet the disadvantages that clerical and analytical employees experienced with respect to their compensation packages transcended gender lines. With the exception of small pockets such as the women's committee, employees were less aware of the systemic nature of these contradictions; but their effects were real and thus they were part of an employee's cognition.

Employee perceptions of their opportunities for compensation mirrored the open/closed distinction. Many operators felt their pay was right in comparison to others doing a similar type of work in PSA (see Table 9). In contrast, fewer clerical employees and analysts felt this way. Participants in open work arrange-

Table 9. Perceived fairness of pay by career ladder (%)

	Operator	Analyst	Clerical
Pay is less than deserved	13	24	39
Pay is only somewhat less	37	46	29
Pay is right	50	30	32
Number of respondents	134	80	126

ments shared a more negative evaluation of the fairness of their pay. Employee perceptions were consistent with the actual patterns of compensation described in earlier chapters. Operators mainly felt their pay was right (50 percent); analysts generally felt they were paid somewhat less than they deserved (46 percent); and clerical employees felt they were paid much less than they deserved (39 percent). The same pattern was evident in the employees' perceptions of fairness in PSA's pay increase policy. Only 15 percent of the operators believed these policies were unfair, compared to 35 percent of the analysts and 47 percent of the clerical employees. Considering the actual differences in patterns of salary increases for each group, this assessment seems realistic. After all, pay increases for operators were automatic and not based on "merit." In contrast, the clerical and analyst groups had fewer automatic increases, and the most important raise, based on merit, was available only after a certain rank. Moreover, in the open context of these ladders, managers used merit pay as an expedient mechanism to reward staff employees, stretching its use even to cases that did not follow the legitimate criteria outlined by the rules. This often resulted in perceptions of unfairness.

This was the case, for example, of Tom Dale. He was one of the members of a team of analysts participating in a special budget project. He earned considerably less than his co-workers despite their equivalent assignments, which required working overtime without pay. Efforts from his superior to remedy the situation had encountered bureaucratic constraints set by the conditions defined during his original placement in the agency. At that time he was provisionally assigned to a statistician job title, which offered the salary range demanded in his initial negotiations. Since then, his experience and know-how had increased. After several merit adjustments Tom had hit the maximum salary allowed for the title. He would have to change titles in order to receive a higher compensation. But all possible titles that could be matched were unavailable. Thus, he was stuck, at least for a while. The initial match, intended only as a formality, made his work less "valuable" compared to that of the other analysts assigned to the same project. Working under such conditions, particularly under the stress generated in the context of a task force, his motivation and enthusiasm had waned. In general, perceptions of fairness and unfairness in compensation were clearly linked to the degree of managerial discretion that existed in the staff ladders. Ad hoc decisions often backfired, creating financial disadvantages to provisionals, as Dale's story illustrates.

Perceptions about job security also mirrored the variations in the degree of uncertainty across ladders (Table 10). Pessimistic views in this area were clearly influenced by the open nature of the analyst and the clerical ladders. More than two-thirds of the operators felt it was "not at all likely" they would lose their jobs, compared to one-third of the clerical employees and analysts. The pattern was even clearer at the other end of the spectrum: 28 percent of clerical employees and 11 percent of analysts, were uncertain about their job security prospects, compared to 6 percent of the operators. The assurance of stability was part of the operator package of benefits received automatically in their ladder. This assurance may have had a negative effect on those who did not receive it. Employees who participated in open ladders viewed it as one more potential "perk" denied to them.

The same pattern was obvious in the views about fringe benefits. A clerical supervisor responded to my question about the type of fringe benefits she received by looking at me cynically and asking, "What do you mean by *fringe*?" She proceeded to indicate that if I really wanted to see fringe benefits I should study carefully the operators' formal and informal benefits package. Since this supervisor worked in the field and experienced such differences daily, she was especially sensitive to the operators' advantages.

Because benefits were a function of the contract negotiations between unions and the city, most employees reported that they were adequate. Still, more operators were pleased with them. Most operators wanted a better retirement plan as the one fringe benefit they were not receiving. The concern of clerical employees and analysts centered instead on educational benefits. For the sake of consistency I will postpone discussion of this to the section on personal growth. The operators' concern with retirement deserves some attention, however. It, in fact, represented one of the few areas where members of this group expressed overtly negative views. They were linked to the recent introduction of a small degree of uncertainty in the operator ladder.

The retirement plan had been the subject of some controversy after important changes had occurred in the operator benefit package. This was a sensitive issue

Table 10. Expected likelihood of losing present job by career ladder (%)

	Operator	Analyst	Clerical
Not at all likely	68	26	32
Not too likely	26	63	40
Somewhat likely or very likely	6	11	28
Number of respondents	148	82	136

because it represented one of the few opportunity aspects in which allocation criteria were not uniform for all members of the ladder. At the time of the study, operators participated in three different retirement tiers depending on their time of arrival to the agency. The first group had a qualitatively better retirement plan. They retired after twenty years of work in PSA, regardless of their age. The other two tiers had an age requirement, and the number of years to retirement increased significantly.

The new operators, who belonged to the third tier, received the worst deal. Many resented it, as did the operator who told me, "The thirty-year pension is lousy. It's impossible for anyone to do this job every day for thirty years. The pension should be equal for all workers—twenty years." Another operator added, "How can one last thirty or more years in this job? I am sure you will be reading my obituary in the paper as time goes on and the pension laws aren't changed." The old timers felt, in contrast, that their pension plan was precisely what made the job worthwhile. As one supervisor from the "good" tier commented in my survey, "I will retire within the next year, God willing, and enjoy the rest of my life with my wife and try to travel if I can afford it." Another one remarked, "I can retire after twenty years of service at half pay. I now have twenty-one and a half years of service and may retire soon."

Even in the most "equalized" ladder, the introduction of differentiated allocation produced noise. It raised the level of uncertainty. This motivated operators to make comparisons, which in turn affected employee perceptions of their opportunities. As a first-rank operator said, "[PSA] is very unfair to the new worker—less pay, less benefits, no pension to speak of compared to our counterparts doing the same job—if anything comes of this it will show dissension among the rank and file, for we are the workers that get the job done and the managers and supervisors get all the credit."

This change in retirement rules had direct implications for other opportunity dimensions of the operator ladder. For example, incentives for early retirement disappeared with the implementation of the second tier. Thus, as employees reached managerial levels, they stayed longer in the system. This decreased the vacancies for lower-rank workers to fill. Even though operators did not express concern about the loss of mobility prospects, some supervisors realized the new policy would eventually create a bottleneck. For now, differences across retirement tiers in the operator ladder were the source of some strong negative perceptions concerning opportunity.

Perceptions of the Opportunity for Personal Growth

Perceptions of job challenge also mirrored the open/closed mode distinction. There were, however, important subtleties that added complexity to the analysis, because the actual amount of opportunity in each ladder also shaped people's perceptions. Comparing employees' views about opportunities for personal growth, one finds a pessimistic clerical group, an ambivalent analyst group, and a relatively optimistic operator group. Analysts agreed with the clerical group's negative assessment of training. But they also agreed with the operators' positive assessment of the actual opportunity to learn from their jobs.

Seventy-eight percent of the analysts and 77 percent of the operators felt they had opportunities to learn, compared to 54 percent of the clerical employees. Resource dependency theory may shed some light on this alignment of perceptions. PSA's reliance on operators and analysts prompted its decision makers to put effort into enhancing the job skills of these employees. It also created greater leverage for the incumbents of those career ladders to shape job conditions to their advantage. There was no equivalent incentive or group leverage for clerical workers. Training opportunities in PSA mirrored these motivations, and employees in turn responded accordingly. Operators not only had the largest participation in training programs, they also had a positive perception of the training they received. Analysts participated in fewer programs, but at least they felt that they were of high quality. In contrast, clerical employees participated in the fewest programs, and they disliked them.

The clerical ladder's negative views about opportunities to learn could be linked to the nature of clerical work, often characterized by boredom, task repetition, and little autonomy. Furthermore, clerical employees often had to work in field offices where they experienced an uncomfortable physical environment. One PSA clerical employee described his situation: "My present official assigned unit is the worst—work-wise and in the physical working environment—especially due to poor ventilation. At times—it is my purgatory. Eighty degrees and above is ridiculous for an office. Talk is cheap—we have been at this place for five years—and it's the same crap." But even clerical employees in headquarters, who did not suffer from hard working conditions, had fewer working incentives to counteract the poor quality of their jobs. On top of this, other intrinsic incentives offered to operators and analysts did not exist for clerical employees.

The previous chapters documented the unequal distribution of workplace learning through strategies of employee involvement. Operators took an active part in quality circles and task forces, and analysts participated in the latter. In contrast, clerical employees were excluded from both. One of the few instances of clerical participation was the Women's Advisory Committee, but this group had no decision-making capability.

The similarity between the operators' and the analysts' positive responses to workplace learning breaks down, however, when one turns to other areas of resource distribution. In the area of training the open/closed dichotomy appears again as an important factor. Analysts felt that their jobs offered good opportunities to learn, but they also felt, as clerical employees did, that the organization did not provide enough opportunities for systematic learning. In contrast to clerical employees, analysts felt that the few programs offered to them were good. In contrast to operators, they reported participation in fewer training programs. Analysts wanted more such programs and other forms of systematic opportunity for growth. Some analysts were fortunate to participate in task forces, but this was not a formal job attribute.

Both analysts and clerical employees expressed a desire for more educational benefits as part of their compensation package. They had in mind tuition reimbursement, on-the-job training, and general training programs.[11] Members of both groups also asked for training in broader issues. Some wanted to know about the structure of city government and public administration; others wanted a general orientation to PSA and its bureaus; still others wanted information about other jobs related to their own (to integrate the job into the larger picture or to open new job prospects); and, finally, some wanted to have a better understanding of civil service rules and regulations. These suggestions reflected a desire to understand the broader picture of work, both as an instrumental and a personal need.

Analysts were also aware that the job learning potential of analytical tasks diminished as time passed. Members of this ladder eventually hit a point where the learning curve became flat. Often, after about a year and a half, the job would start to feel repetitive. "Questions might have been answered differently one year ago," said one analyst in my survey, "Since many of my job duties have not changed over the last two years they have become tedious and the opportunity to learn has by now been exhausted." A different analyst, who had transferred to PSA from another public organization where he was skilled, described his job as follows: "My job is boring with little diversity. I have very limited ability to learn new things. My skills are going to waste."

It was at this point that analysts would start to look for promotional opportunities. As internal or external opportunities appeared, they would move on. Mobility thus served another important function in this ladder. It prevented burnout or boredom. One may conclude that analysts who felt their jobs provided opportunities to learn were those who had not yet hit the learning plateau at their present job.

The Social Construction of a "Good" Job

The large percentage of analysts reporting positive opinions about job challenge is not surprising, given the white-collar nature of the analyst job. The complexity of analytical tasks, as well as their insertion within broader organizational problems, may help explain the sense of opportunity for personal growth the group felt. Their work provided some degree of intellectual challenge.

That a significant portion of operators felt good about the prospects for personal growth is consistent with the general pattern of opportunity documented in this chapter. But it still seems puzzling, considering the nature of their jobs. Academic and popular accounts characterize blue-collar working conditions as lacking in desirable traits such as autonomy, skill variety, and meaning (Halle 1984; Rubin 1976; Terkel 1974). Blue-collar workers tend to accept "bad" jobs under compelling circumstances of economic need and only when confronted with a narrow set of alternatives. Although such work usually provides the means to a minimally decent life for workers and their families, it is done at the expense of personal growth. There is indeed, a trade-off between money and quality of work life. This is illustrated in the accounts of factory life presented by Hamper (1991). Describing his reluctance to follow his father's steps into the factory, he writes, "The idea that we were being paid handsome wages to mimic a bunch of overachieving simians suited us just dandy. . . . as long as the numbers of your pay stub justified your daily bread, there was nothing more to accomplish" (1991:2). And, further on, referring to his job, "every minute, every hour . . . and every movement was a plodding replica of the one that had gone before" (p. 41).

Like many other blue-collar workers, operators in PSA knew their jobs were not nice, but their wages compensated for this. Yet money cannot explain why operators reported a potential for learning in their jobs. Several unique features of the operator ladder help explain it.

The operator job was heavy, dirty, and often disgusting, but it was performed outside and it required moving around the city. This itself must have provided a sense of autonomy and task variety uncommon to equivalent blue-collar and pink-collar occupations. Operators also had some choice (of schedules, of sites, of partners) which in the traditional office or factory settings were denied to blue-collar workers. Hence, both in absolute and relative terms, a large number of operators felt fortunate about the nature of their jobs.

But what most influenced the operators' positive perception of opportunities for personal growth was the existence of quality circles.[12] The literature on Total Quality Management and on worker participation has demonstrated that these mechanisms represent, in and of themselves, opportunities for employees to feel empowered and to develop (Parker 1986; Cotton 1993). The potential for workplace learning multiplies as employees participate in the search for solutions to organizational problems. Moreover, quality circles reduce the gap between physical and intellectual work, a gap typical of most blue-collar settings. In PSA they also reduced the social distance created by the operator hierarchy, between an elite of thinkers and an indiscriminate mass of doers. They made work feel more democratic in a highly stratified context. This element of the operator opportunity package is critical to an understanding of the operators' perceptions of job challenge.

Perhaps here lies the root of the difference between the grim picture Hamper painted of his blue-collar job and the optimistic view that PSA operators conveyed of their own. Operators were offered much more than a good salary; they were offered a social situation that defined them as important members of the organization. PSA did not give members of this occupational group the message that they were a "bunch of overachieving simians" selling their souls for money. Instead, the organizational culture portrayed them as sacrificing individuals who were appreciated for doing the dirty jobs that somebody had to do, and for contributing their ideas about doing them well. Operators were, in the culture of PSA, the heroes, who sacrificed themselves for the sake of public service. Intense training and problem-solving mechanisms typical of private-sector ILMs and corporatist arrangements were used in PSA, thus sending the signal that the operator job was indeed critical. This provided a very different view of their work and their worth as human beings. The operator career ladder supplied the right incentives to turn potentially bad jobs into desirable ones. The opportunity structure motivated operators to plunge willingly into the type of work they did and even to feel challenged by it.

The image of the operator as a valuable resource was thus sustained both by the ideological discourse and by the design of work itself. The former provided a sense of personal worth; the latter confirmed it with the appropriate rewards. Ensuring protection from outside competition, the reward system offered an excellent compensation package and the possibility of moving up into managerial positions. It also offered the opportunity to participate in intensive organizational training efforts that would enhance the human capital required to move up the ladder. Finally, the system offered participation in the decision-making process through quality circles. All of these elements together sent the right message about the worth of the operator.

Conclusion

Scholars of work attitudes and behavior tend to attribute more weight to the perceptions of individuals than to actual realities. Some have argued, for example, that perceiving future opportunity can be more motivating than actually getting a raise, being promoted, or having broader responsibilities (Schneider, Gunnarson, and Wheeler 1992). Likewise, others claim that it is not enough for managers to be fair in the workplace; it is more important for them to *appear* fair in the eyes of employees (Greenberg and Cohen 1990). Both arguments reflect a conceptualization of opportunity that highlights its subjective nature. But opportunity is not just a subjective phenomenon. In stratified systems it also represents a social resource unequally distributed among individuals located in particular positions. Appearances of fairness and beliefs about future opportunities may well influence the perception of those employees who benefit from a given distribution, but that is because there is no cognitive contradiction to address. In addition, the discrepancy among appearances, beliefs, and actual reality will affect those who are at a disadvantage in the same work context. Appearances aside, the experience of being excluded from a share of the pie is real.

Using cultural and structural mechanisms, PSA constantly reminded operators how unique they were compared to other employees in the agency. The strength of the message had the desired impact on the operators' sense of worth. At the same time it sent different cues to other employees, thus affecting their cognition and their feelings. Clerical employees, who considered themselves equals to operators in many ways, felt excluded from their legitimate claims to equal opportunity as promised by the civil service. In the case of the analysts, the relative importance of their task gave them a moderate sense of job challenge and helped them negotiate good salaries. But the analysts' sense of deserving crashed against certain PSA realities. One was the absence of formal and systematic opportunities to move up the ladder. Another was the sense of betrayal when promises were broken, which sometimes happened after analysts were assigned certain job titles for administrative convenience.

Two conclusions emerge from the exploration of perceptions of opportunity in this chapter. First, PSA employees had fairly realistic perceptions of their opportunity, and these coincided with their participation in either an open or a closed type of employment mode. Second, employees' positive or negative evaluations correlated with the greater or lesser amounts of actual opportunity they experienced in their career ladders.

Even though the organizational culture tended to inflate the extent to which all operators had a real prospect of moving up the ladder, this group was realistic in their assessment of advantages and disadvantages. The perceptions of analysts and clerical employees were also realistic, and therefore they were more pessimistic about their overall opportunity in PSA. Both staff groups felt, for different reasons, that they had fewer advantages compared to operators. This heightened their perceptions of the disadvantages the system imposed on them.

Differences in perceptions thus reflected contradictions inherent in the dynamics of organizational inequality. Social interaction took place within a context where a strong merit ideology and civil service rules legitimated outcome allocation. Yet at the same time, actual practices often contradicted these rules and resulted in unequal opportunities to compete for resources. Violations of distributive justice became evident to employees experiencing the uncertainty typical of open employment relationships. The resulting dissonance became an important characteristic of many PSA employees' cognitive maps. It affected their perceptions of opportunity.

This chapter focused on the impact of structure and of actual advantages or disadvantages on employees' experiences of opportunity. The next chapter will explore the institutional dimensions of those experiences.

Perceptions of Opportunity (2): Conflicting Definitions of Merit and the Meaning of Work

As in many other public agencies, the espoused philosophy underlying the civil service in PSA was "equality of opportunity based on merit." This ideology supplied the dominant standards of deserving used to legitimate the distribution of organizational rewards. However, not all employees believed in the legitimacy of civil service as a merit system. Endorsement or rejection of this ideology represented a critical component of the cognitive maps through which employees interpreted their experience. Moreover, the relevance of education and experience as status marks of professionalism varied from one context to the next. These variations stemmed from the conflicting definitions of merit that employees used to make sense of their work experience.

All operators, most clerical employees, and some analysts tended to espouse a bureaucratic model of employment. Most analysts favored a market model. Employees were often positioned in structural contexts that reinforced these preferences. However, the uncertainty produced by differential enforcement intensified beliefs about the legitimacy of the endorsed model. Hence, employees often felt "trapped" by some of the attributes of the model they did not endorse. The description in Chapter 6 of the two analyst groups and their conflicting views about unions illustrates this powerfully. For permanent analysts, the union represented the hope of employment protection and civil service enforcement. It helped promote the formalization of the analyst career ladder. This encouraged selection from within, thus allowing employees at the bottom to move up as they gained experience on the job, rather than through educational credentials. In contrast, provisional analysts disliked the civil service staffing criteria of minimum job requirements and written examinations, just as many managers did. As for managers, the limited discretion granted them made the traditional civil service system an obstacle to their ambitions. Because they expected and

117

demanded employment conditions consistent with their definition of professionalism, the least of their concerns was a push toward the formalization of rules. They wanted more and faster opportunities rather than a formalized guarantee of upward mobility.

These conflicting views help us understand important differences in the perceptions of opportunity between analysts and clerical employees, even though both participated in open employment relationships. They also help explain similarities between the two groups with the largest number of civil servants—clerical employees and operators—despite the important differences in the amount of opportunity these two ladders offered, and despite the variations in the degree of civil service enforcement in them. Finally, these views also help us understand the significant differences between provisional and permanent employees, despite their belonging to the same occupational group.

The provisional/permanent dichotomy was a direct manifestation of the open mode of employment that characterized analysts and clerical employees. Both provisional and permanent employees had their own feelings about the civil service. Positions ranged from a strong endorsement to a weak acceptance to a total rejection of the civil service model. Most clerical employees and some analysts identified with the operators' belief that the civil service system, if well implemented, represented an important instrument to improve the quality of their lives. They endorsed it as the legitimate model for the public sector. In contrast, most analysts interpreted their experience using the more flexible market model of employment, which emphasized economic worth. These sets of merit beliefs, which employees made part of their image of opportunity, might be called—borrowing the terminology of cognitive science—"civil service schemata." Their importance lies in the fact that employee responses to opportunity were not just a mechanical reflection of their structural locations. Employees were also sensitive to the meanings provided by these schemata.

Differences in Civil Service Schemata

In the survey, PSA employees in the three groups stressed two distinct indicators of merit as factors associated with promotions in their units. For some, promotions were a function of what the person had demonstrated on the job or had brought to it. Examples included good knowledge of the job, the right qualifications and/or credentials, the necessary experience and skills, high job performance, and good performance evaluations. Others associated promotions with specific individual attitudes and behaviors displayed at work, which implied making a special effort to apply oneself to the job. These attitudes and behaviors included being bright, having initiative, demonstrating leadership, manifesting team spirit and positive attitudes, being responsive to departmental needs, having good communication with supervisors, having a good working relationship with others, demonstrating commitment, and possessing the determination and desire to be promoted. Of the two types of merit indicators—resources brought to the job and attitudes or behaviors displayed there—most employees mentioned the former. Thus they tended to accept the general belief that the civil service environment offers job security once one enters the system by some merit criteria. In this view, meeting a formal requirement (educational level or years of experience) was the main criterion for promotion, not good performance on the job. While most employees accepted this belief, it had a different impact on each occupational group. For most operators and clerical employees it represented the hope for actual protection from open market forces. For many analysts, it was a source of frustration. These reactions stemmed from differences in civil service schemata.

These differences affected how employees perceived their opportunities. For example, operators and clerical employees most often linked their promotion prospects to civil service, while analysts linked them more often to discretionary factors related to the organization. When they were asked if there was anything they could personally do to improve their opportunities, almost half of the respondents in each occupational group indicated that not much could be done. Fifty-three percent of the operators, 52 percent of the clerical employees, and 45 percent of the analysts said they had no control over their opportunities. This is consistent with the dominance of bureaucracy, so characteristic of the public sector. But a bit over half the analysts felt differently. They represented the largest group who believed that they had some control over their opportunities. This is typical of expectations stemming from the endorsement of a market model of employment.

Employees who felt they did indeed have some control over their career expressed a variety of opinions about what could be done. Operators and clerical employees gave similar answers (see Table 11, A). Almost half of the operators and one-quarter of the clerical employees mentioned civil service compliance as the main career strategy. Operators made an effort to comply to civil service requirements by taking tests when they were offered and studying hard to pass them. Some also felt they could improve their job performance, and a smaller number hoped to broaden their qualifications (through training, through learning about PSA and the jobs in it, and through formal schooling). The opinions of clerical employees were split almost equally among two groups. Some, like the operators, emphasized compliance to civil service regulations. Others assigned importance to job performance and broader qualifications. Although the operator and clerical groups differed slightly about the importance of the civil service, both pointed to factors intrinsic to the bureaucratic paradigm. The clerical group was somewhat more aware of human capital factors, however. In contrast, analysts dismissed civil service compliance (only 3 percent mentioned it as a strategy

Table 11. Perceived control over opportunities by career ladder (%)

	Operator	Analyst	Clerical
A. Initiatives that respondents feel they can take			
Civil service compliance	46	3	25
Job performance	25	37	31
Qualifications	17	26	27
Political activities	9	21	8
Number of respondents	65	38	64
B. Initiatives that their supervisors can take			
Direct sponsorship	7	43	26
Activities to support development	54	30	48
Provide a supportive environment	39	18	16
Change negative attitudes	0	9	10
Number of respondents	41	44	10

to control their careers). The broader variety of alternatives presented by this group suggests less consensus about possible career strategies, which is typical of a market model cognitive map. Some emphasized job performance, others the need to broaden their qualifications, and the rest the need for some form of political manipulation. "Political" here refers to the exercise of power, not to elective politics. Employees made reference to political and social games, ranging from cynical references to the need to "kiss ass" or smile to more neutral actions such as joining clubs or establishing networks.

Employee perceptions of whether their supervisors could do anything to improve their opportunities showed the same differences in schemata (Table 11, B). Very few operators and only some clerical employees felt that supervisors were important for their careers, while many analysts believed supervisors were critical. A provisional analyst working in the field enumerated the reasons why her supervisor played a crucial role in her career:

> One, a good supervisor can get people to work together, which also makes you look good; two, a good supervisor is important for promotions; three, a good supervisor is aware of what his people are doing and [therefore] can truly assess and compare their abilities, avoiding the problem of feeling unrecognized for your true value.

The minority of operators and clerical employees who saw room for supervisory intervention tended to associate their bosses' involvement with organizational and work actions acceptable within the bureaucratic paradigm. Examples mentioned in the survey included giving good recommendations and good performance evaluations, recommending employees for merit increases, and sending employees to training courses. These actions fitted the accepted role of supervision of employee development within a civil service framework. In contrast, many analysts (and a few clerical employees) wanted direct sponsorship, that is, a personal commitment from the supervisor to develop an aggressive promotional strategy for those subordinates who "deserved it." This attitude presumed some belief in the competitive market model of employment. Examples of what these employees expected from their supervisors included (here I paraphrase or quote from the survey) aggressively supporting their promotions ("push for it," "fight for me"), being aware of what opportunities exist and how they can be used by specific employees ("seek better jobs," "explore new titles"), publicizing or advertising employees' achievements and merits, nominating them for awards, writing letters, informing employees about specific opportunities, and broadening work assignments and diversifying tasks to increase employees' responsibilities and thus make them more visible.

Employees' opinions about the most important reasons for promotion also replicated the civil service schemata (Table 12). Most operators and many clerical employees offered as the main reason for promotion factors such as having passed a civil service examination and being on a waiting list. A permanent office associate complained about this situation as follows: "The job would be much more fulfilling if we had more opportunity to advance ourselves financially and if we had more promotional examinations instead of being trapped in a position for five years before being able to take a test leading to a promotion."

Operators and clerical employees were aware that the slow pace of the civil service system limited their promotional chances, and they accepted this as a feature of the system. In contrast, very few analysts listed the civil service as the main reason for promotion. For many of them, promotions were a function of individual effort, human capital investments linked to good job performance, politics, or particularistic criteria (that is, factors not formally relevant to the job). The same contradictions were apparent in this group's opinions about promotion obstacles, despite the fact that both analysts and clerical employees identified similar problems linked to the open nature of their employment relationship. For

Table 12. Main reasons for promotion by career ladder (%)

	Operator	Analyst	Clerical
Performance	31	38	33
Civil service rules	48	7	35
Particularistic criteria	11	33	16
Vacancies	7	9	6
Other	3	12	9
Number of respondents	141	75	124

many analysts the main obstacle to promotion was a lack of openings or too many people competing for too few positions, while for many clerical employees the obstacle was a lack of timely civil service exams.

As discussed in Chapter 7, few operators expressed a desire for change in the present promotion system, although many analysts and clerical employees did.[1] However, the latter groups had very different ideas about the changes they desired. The majority of clerical employees wanted more civil service enforcement. They asked for more promotional examinations, for the exclusive use of civil service criteria for promotions, and for more efficiency in assembling promotional lists. They did not want to change the system as much as they wanted it to work right. They believed it was the best way to handle promotions, but they considered it too inefficient and too unenforced.

Clerical employees emphasized the need to make the system more fair. In the survey they made direct references such as "more justice," "make it fair," "eliminate quotas," "remove the political aspect," "abolish prejudice," "give importance to *what* you know, not *who* you know." These comments reflected cynicism or resentment about the present situation. They also implied that although the system was not working, ideally it could. Thus clerical employees had a fairly realistic perception of their disadvantaged situation. Although they concurred with analysts about the need for change, the direction they proposed was toward achieving what operators had. When clericals were asked to name one single benefit they would like, their request—education—was consistent with this orientation. Training represents a structural prerequisite for the skills required in bureaucratic internal labor markets. In a perfect civil service system, training is, in fact, a prerequisite for upward movement. Operators received it automatically, while clerical employees did not. Hence they viewed operators' training programs as another perk denied them. Many clerical employees interpreted this as evidence of their "second-class citizen" status. For example, a clerical employee stated in the survey that operators received training in clerical jobs in field offices, whereas clerical employees entering similar jobs were not provided the same opportunity. He viewed this as an unfair practice. When this clerk requested better training in departmental forms and codes, he stated that it should be "like the one operators receive in this area." In contrast, the majority of analysts proposed moving away from the civil service system. They insisted on changes that would move the system toward a truly market model. They wanted *new opportunities*: more chances for promotion, more flexible promotion methods, the clarification of career paths, the opening of new connections between titles or the creation of more levels, the enforcement of a policy of promotion, and more promotions in their ladder as a means of encouragement.

Perceptions of available opportunity outside PSA provided an additional example of how civil service schemata influenced the sense of control employees had over their jobs. Employees from all three ladders felt they could use the skills

Table 13. Estimated difficulty of finding an equivalent job by career ladder (%)

	Operator	Analyst	Clerical
Very difficult or impossible	30	6	15
Somewhat difficult	50	33	39
Very easy or somewhat easy	20	61	46
Number of respondents	147	82	135

and knowledge acquired in the present job elsewhere. Yet more operators and clerks believed that their skills were not transferable, while most analysts felt that their skills were either fully transferable or at least somewhat transferable. Furthermore, when asked how easy it would be to find a job with another employer with conditions similar to those at present, almost all the operators and at least half of the clerical employees felt it would be either somewhat difficult, very difficult, or impossible, compared to one-third of the analysts (Table 13).

Operators most of all and clerical employees as well, felt they had low external opportunities. In contrast, a large proportion of analysts felt they had high external opportunities. In keeping with this expectation, analysts showed a more "cosmopolitan" orientation toward their jobs. For example, many members of the analyst group were not planning to stay for a long period of time in PSA. Of the entire group of analysts interviewed, less than a third estimated that they would still be working for the agency after two years, compared to about four-fifths of the operators and two-thirds of the clerical employees (Table 14).

Some scholars argue that the orientation that characterized analysts is typical of professionals working in large bureaucracies. These tend to be less loyal toward the organization than toward their profession. Other scholars suggest, however, that this orientation will emerge only when opportunities inside the organization are less than those outside (Blau and Scott 1963). Rather than a universal characteristic that professionals bring to agencies, loyalty and commitment would be the result of an assessment of what they bring, what they find inside, and what they see outside the bureaucracy. In PSA, many analysts were

Table 14. Estimated likelihood of staying in the job by career ladder (%)

	Operator	Analyst	Clerical
Very likely	82	28	59
Somewhat likely	7	25	24
Not likely at all	10	47	16
Number of respondents	135	80	128

caught in a dynamic that simultaneously "pushed" them out of the agency, where they perceived few opportunities, and "pulled" them toward other agencies, where they saw more.

The realistic perceptions described in the above examples not only reflected but also reinforced the alliance each group pledged to the open or closed models of employment. The lower educational background of operators and clerical employees made them less "marketable" outside of PSA. In this sense, the "on the job learning" criterion for success typical of civil service provided a haven for them. Aware of this, clerical employees and operators strongly defended the importance of "experience" as a job requirement, while analysts tended to give more importance to technical knowledge.

There was, however, an important difference between the opportunity perceptions of operators and clerical employees. While many employees from both groups felt "stuck" in PSA, one group had a positive internal reality to turn to while the other did not. Although both groups had a pessimistic view of their external opportunities, operators felt empowered by their work conditions, created by a perfect enforcement of civil service rules. For clerical employees the opportunity offered in the civil service system was an ideal rather than a reality. This points back to the structural differences between the operator and clerical ladders: the strong or lax enforcement of the system, participation in a closed versus an open mode of employment, and actual differences in the amount of opportunity independent of preference. These were all critical. So although both of these groups endorsed the merit system, there was an important difference between them. For the clerical group, endorsing the system did not necessarily translate into being viewed as a legitimate member of it.

The Permanent/Provisional Dichotomy

In the context of mixed career ladders, civil service labels assigned employees who carried them to specific social statuses. The meaning of these statuses varied, however, from one structural context to the next. "Permanent" status was not a strong social category for operators because they took it for granted. Likewise, the provisional status was literally nonexistent for members of this group. In contrast, the difference between these two statuses was a very real condition for many incumbents of the other two ladders. The meaning of permanent status was different for clerical and analyst employees than it was for operators. As for provisional status, this meant something different for clerical employees compared to analysts.

Members of these groups had dissimilar positions about the legitimacy of the civil service. Paradoxically, the absence of civil service enforcement in both groups produced a similar cognitive dissonance between expectations and realities. Those who believed in the bureaucratic model experienced a discrepancy because they originally expected to find protection and equal treatment. Those employees who espoused a market model found themselves unnerved by the system's rigidities.

Due to union protection, permanent clerical employees had a well-structured career ladder. Its formalization granted a sense of professionalism to this group, which lacked credentials in a system characterized by low opportunity. Stability was helpful to organize career plans. Total enforcement of the system, which clerical employees saw implemented in the operator ladder, was their main hope. The system could work in their favor, they believed, if the right definitions of equality and merit were fully enforced, as they should be. For these reasons, clerical employees sought permanent status. Provisional employees aspired to it, as expressed by this provisional shop clerk: "I love my job very much. People are the nicest and I get along with everyone. I only wish I could be called for my permanent position instead of being provisional."

Provisionals in this ladder knew they were at a disadvantage. The flexibility associated with their status was a source of constant insecurity. The group also lacked union protection. Provisional employees were located at the bottom of the clerical social ladder both in terms of vulnerability and uncertainty. They could be terminated at any time and for any reason, no matter how long they had served in the title. They could also be bumped to lower titles in the ladder.

Clerical "step-ups" felt they were the most vulnerable group. Most cases of simultaneous bumps and salary reductions took place in this ladder. If, at a personal level, moving up provisionally was positive, in the long run it represented an important source of ambivalence. Uncertainty became an attribute of the job. As we saw in Chapter 4, many work histories within the clerical ladder were accompanied by bumps and painful losses of salary. Consider for example the case of a clerical employee earning a formal yearly salary of $18,030 as a permanent shop clerk. His provisional title of administrative community relations specialist (a managerial title) had a salary of $44,642. If for some reason his real status was enforced, he would lose not only his managerial status but also $25,000 in salary! This would represent a very dramatic change in his career. It was only natural for negative feelings to emerge when such experiences occurred. This was particularly true when the difference in status between the permanent and the provisional job was large.

Going back to a lower status was painful both at a personal and at an organizational level. We see this in the letter a city employee wrote to her union, asking for advice:

I'm a provisional computer associate (technical support). I have served twenty-four months. A list just came out. I have been bumped from my job and I will be demoted to a technical support aide. Is this fair? Can I appeal this?

The answer from the union was not comforting:

> You have no appeal rights. Management can ask you to leave, and in fact is obligated by civil service law to do so, when an eligible list for permanent employees is released. That is why it is important to take tests leading up to the title you may be working at provisionally, so that you can qualify for permanent status.[2]

With no bargaining power, clerical employees could not put pressure on their superiors by expressing an intention to leave. Thus a bump was accepted as a better alternative than loss of the job. This only added insult to injury.

In the case of clerical civil servants, the system granted them legitimacy as deserving employees; hence permanent employees were better off than the provisional counterparts. In the case of analyst employees, however, the social status of the two subgroups was inverted. In an interview, a permanent analyst described the theoretical benefits the system offered as follows: "Civil service works for the benefit of permanent employees to the extent that it is enforced. Whoever takes the test and passes it is ensured that there is a one out of three chance of getting the job and keeping it." Yet low enforcement reduced those benefits. The numerical dominance of employees who espoused the market model in this ladder was itself a disadvantage for permanent analysts. They faced the same uncertainty as provisionals, but they did not enjoy the advantages provided by the latter's flexible contracts. Unlike their clerical counterparts, permanent analysts encountered fierce and unbalanced competition. On top, the rules of the competition changed constantly, making career moves unpredictable. Finally, permanent analysts were aware that for every civil servant promoted to a position previously occupied by a provisional analyst, the department had to find a slot equivalent in status and pay for that provisional. So civil servants in this ladder saw the jump from associate staff analyst to administrative staff analyst as a bottleneck. It represented a direct obstacle to development of their careers in PSA.

Provisional analysts had a higher social status because of the bargaining capacity their educational credentials afforded them. Two facts reinforced the credentialist ideology in this career ladder, even within the broader context of a civil service environment stressing experience. These were, first, the increasing importance of higher education in contemporary society (Collins 1979) and, second, the PSA rule allowing education to replace experience as a criterion for entry to most analytical titles.

Armed with the moral authority of credentialism, provisional analysts—as well as many managers—espoused a notion of professionalism that defined their contributions as superior to those of other civil servants. They used this as a lever to distinguish themselves from other PSA employees, thus legitimating their efforts to negotiate individual terms of employment. A provisional analyst I interviewed—she had been placed in a high-level clerical slot to meet her initial salary expectations—made this comment: "It does not feel right that, after spending two years of my life in a graduate program, I am placed in a clerical line. Even if it is only a formality, it makes me feel unappreciated in what I am worth." This analyst had followed the typical life cycle for provisionals in PSA. She had worked in the most prestigious analytical unit for two years and then moved to another agency, where she became the executive assistant of a high-ranking officer. In a follow-up interview, this analyst said that the move had helped her to improve not only her salary and her status but also her self-perception as a professional.

Endorsing the meritocratic ideology, provisional analysts took advantage of personal deals. In justifying these deals, they often assigned lower social statuses to members of the clerical ladder and to permanent analysts. Some even asserted that "increasing civil service will only increase the mediocrity of the work force." The provisionals' contempt for civil servants in this ladder was certainly intensified by the competition for rewards, but it did not originate there. It instead reflected a broader debate about opportunity and deservingness in public employment.

Professionalism, Merit Systems, and the Meaning of Merit

Public management scholars and practitioners agree about the desirability of creating conditions that promote a sense of professionalism among public employees (Benveniste 1987; Kearney and Sinha 1988; Mosher and Stillman 1977). However, this consensus disappears when the discussion focuses on the role that civil service systems can play. In a time of bureaucracy bashing and antigovernment feelings, many have argued that there is an incompatibility between professionalism and formal merit systems like the civil service.[3]

At the extremes of the spectrum in this debate lie two contrasting connotations of professionalism. On the one hand, a broad definition links professionalism to the proficiency involved in doing a certain job. It highlights a sense of pride in one's work and a desire to do a good job. A professional is defined as someone who emphasizes competence and strives for quality. At the other extreme lies a narrow view of professionalism defined as advanced and specific training (Fox 1993). This connotation defines professionalism as expertise based on credentials.

The conflict between the two views is present in most instances where there is a formalized personnel function. The broad view of merit predicts that a well-implemented merit system will foster professionalism. The narrow view predicts that a formal system will stifle it. This discussion represents perhaps one of the strongest points of contention among scholars and practitioners in public organizations. Yet it is not merely an academic debate. Its resolution has important implications for the management of human resources. The promotions-from-within versus recruitment-from-outside staffing dilemma, typical of decision makers in both the public and private sectors, illustrates the practical side of the discussion. Another example is the debate over the value of different types of human capital for evaluating people's worth and legitimating the distribution of organizational rewards. The pay-for-performance versus position-based-pay controversy is rooted precisely in these different interpretations of merit. In turn, each position proposes different reward structures.

The strongest manifestation of this debate can be found wherever formal civil service systems exist, at the local, state, and federal levels of public employment. For example, DiPrete (1989) found in his study of bureaucratic labor markets that the structure of job ladders for civil service careers in federal organizations was a function, among other factors, of a compromise between actors holding the two competing types of professionalism.[4] Tracing the institutional and technical forces separating "professional" from "administrative" jobs in federal government, this author documented the emergence of a two-tiered employment system with barriers between the tiers.[5] The terms of the debate changed over time as these tiers emerged and developed. In the early period of civil service reform, the dangers of patronage dominated the discourse and guided the search to improve the administrative capacity of government. With an institutionalized system, the debate shifted to other themes concerned with the nature and worth of public employment. These included topics such as the value of on-the-job training versus college education and the costs and benefits of providing government training to increase the promotability of civil servants.

These intellectual discussions cannot be isolated from other pressing social issues of the times. In the 1930s and 1950s efforts to promote a stronger state highlighted the relationship of politics to administration. In the 1960s and 1970s concerns about equal employment opportunity gave a new twist to the debate. They brought into focus the disparities in the demographic distribution of administrative positions. The 1980s were characterized by a technocratic discourse that highlighted the relevance of expertise and technique over politics and representation. The focus of the 1990s includes a change in emphasis from process to results and from the management of programs and operations to the management of visions and missions. Managers question the bureaucratic paradigm and flirt with ideas that move public management closer to private management. This new orientation has redefined the terms of the debate over which skills and qualifications are required for an effective public employee, or for a deserving manager.

Historically, the discussions have been framed as disagreements about the very nature of the tasks of administration. In the case of the creation of the two-tiered federal system, some argued that administrative work was largely a function of skill in dealing with people (i.e., personality) and organizational knowledge learned on the job; as such it was not highly related to education. Others argued that it was largely a function of intelligence. A third view was that administration was a secondary function of high-level technical jobs. Training for such jobs must therefore be primarily technical. A fourth view was that administrative skill came from a broad outlook on life learned through the right upbringing and through a liberal education. Technical skills were not necessarily unimportant, but they were a secondary priority. Finally, a fifth view was that administrative science was a profession of the same order as medicine and law and was properly learned through study at a university. (DiPrete 1989:26)

Be that as it may, civil service reform has been characterized by this recurrent debate. Those supporting the broad definition of professionalism stress the value of practical experience as a merit criterion. They argue that skill requirements between high and low jobs progress uniformly. They stress the importance of policies of promotion from within to enhance work morale. Employee unions, veterans, and, later, civil rights and women's groups have supported this view. These groups have emphasized the justice rule of equality to justify their claims. They conceive of the civil service system as the great equalizer.

In contrast, proponents of the narrow perspective have made the case for the existence of qualitative differences between skill requirements for positions at different levels of the hierarchy. According to this position, the competence of low-level employees hits a limit when they reach certain levels of the ladder. Above these, competence requires qualitatively different skills. Sponsors of this view have argued that formal knowledge of these skills is relevant enough to justify recruitment from universities. Supporters include academics of the progressive era and New Deal reformers, as well as personnel management professionals (DiPrete 1989). In contrast to equality, they espouse equity as the justice rule of preference.

Similar dynamics can be traced in the reform movements of local civil service systems. The emphasis on one set of values or another reflects the struggle for control over municipal employment (Fox 1993; Rich 1982). It is possible that one of the outcomes of these struggles is the existence or the absence of a formal merit system itself, at the local level of employment. Furthermore, the extent to which civil service law is enforced within jurisdictions, organizations, and career ladders (once a formal merit system exists) might also be the outcome of similar struggles.

The material base of the debate on merit becomes apparent when one realizes that social groups seeking maximum gains tend to restrict access to resources and opportunities to a limited circle of eligibles. Indeed, the exclusionary and status-enhancing view of professionalism described earlier brings to mind the notion of social closure developed by stratification theorists (Murphy 1988; Tomaskovic-Devey 1993). Tomaskovic-Devey defines social closure processes as

> the means by which superordinate groups preserve their advantage by tying access
> to jobs or other scarce goods to group characteristics. Educational credentials,
> capital ownership, ethnicity, race, religion, and gender are all group characteristics
> that are commonly the basis of formal and informal exclusionary rules. (p. 10)

For example, those who benefit from having educational credentials will insist that these are necessary for effective job performance. Those who do not have them will tend to minimize their value and insist on the importance of attributes they can use to justify their claims for a piece of the organizational pie.

Moreover, social closure results less from the passive acceptance of traditional privileges than from the deliberate efforts of the advantaged (to preserve privilege) and of the disadvantaged (to question the basis of that privilege) within a social world that is contested and where resources are scarce (Tomaskovic-Devey 1993). Social closure is thus a product of the existence of social inequality, while at the same time it promotes further inequalities.

Ultimately, espoused definitions of merit reflect a given correlation of forces among internal and external coalitions. Members fight for pieces of the pie within stratified organizations (Cook and Hegtvedt 1986; Cohen 1986). In the context of public employment, these definitions provide the institutional basis legitimating the distribution of resources in each public organization and jurisdiction. Similar tensions can be identified in the private sector, for example, between permanent employees, who enjoy benefits and protection by workers' rights, and "contingent" workers. Each of these espouse their own definition of merit.

The debate over the definition of merit remains unresolved. As new groups enter the arena of competition for jobs and resources, the arguments may take different forms. But they will always embody the struggle between those with clout, who seek to legitimate a system of resource and reward distribution that favors them, and those without, who contest this system.

The contradictions between the two civil service schemata in PSA, and the underlying values attributed to education and merit, are instances of the struggle over scarce resources in an uncertainty-ridden stratified system. Civil servants defended the closed view of employment and the importance of experience as the main criterion of merit. As we have seen, this criterion favored operators and, to a lesser extent, permanent clerical employees. Non–civil servants and managers, who wanted more discretion, defended the open view and the importance of education. Thus a crucial difference among the cognitive maps of operators, analysts, and clerical employees lay in the role assigned to "education" and "experience" as defining traits of success within ladders. Experience represented for operators a means to maintain their privileges, and for clerical employees a means to secure some for themselves. Education represented for analysts a means to change the dominant view and thus gain a position of advantage. Despite the internal struggle, claims resting on experience and on education are both valid, given their legitimacy in contemporary justice frameworks.

The Combined Effect of Positions and Beliefs

Two kinds of cognitive realities influenced work perceptions of PSA employees. Each can be thought of as a continuum and imagined visually as a horizontal line, yielding two parallel lines of influence. Each of the three occupational groups in PSA is located at a certain point on each line. Each group's perceptions—of work, of resources, of opportunties, etc.—depends on its place in this configuration. A visual image representing the impact of the two forces would look like this:

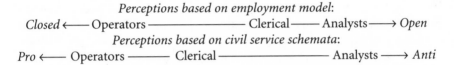

The first line represents the information conveyed in Chapter 7. This line depicts variations in employment models, from the closed to the open type. These variations resulted from the degree of enforcement of rules, from the consequent staffing practices, and from the actual amount of opportunity offered to employees. They represent one structural characteristic of employment in PSA. Actual participation in one or the other employment mode gave employees experiential information to evaluate and understand their present and future prospects. When one classifies the groups' perceptions of opportunity along this line, operators tended to cluster toward one side of the line (toward a closed model and relatively positive perceptions of opportunities); and both clerical employees and analysts tended to cluster together toward the other side (toward an open model and relatively negative perceptions). According to this pattern of association, employees had a fairly realistic and accurate perception of their opportunities. (Not all members followed the group pattern, of course.)

The second line—explored in this chapter—represents variations in perception that stem from institutional (value-related) forces. This line depicts beliefs about the legitimacy of the dominant merit system and justice perceptions associated with these beliefs. In this line, operators and most clerical employees (along with some analysts) clustered together toward one side (the pro–civil service side) and most analysts clustered toward the other (anti–civil service).

Employee efforts to bridge the discrepancy between expectations and realities was largely influenced by the way experiences were interpreted within the configuration described above. Analysts took sides with clerical employees in identifying themselves as members with lower social status in an operator-dominated agency. Since the advantages of the dominant group stemmed from the protection offered by closed employment, those participating in the open mode shared the perception that they had constrained opportunities compared to operators. But at the same time, many members of the analyst group clearly differentiated themselves from the clerical employees. The latter, in turn, considered themselves closer to the operators in terms of aspirations and expectations. Both analysts and clerical employees were aware of the social meaning of these differences.

Locating employee perceptions along these imaginary parallel lines shows the complexity of the social context, in which contradictions in work arrangements affected employees' experiences at the organizational level. One could argue that the perceptions of opportunity and rewards took one form for both clerical employees and analysts, on the one hand, and another form for operators, on the other. But the definitions of merit and professionalism took the same form for operators and clerical employees on the one hand and a different form for analysts on the other. The forces represented by these imaginary lines were, in reality, interconnected. It was, indeed, the complex combination of employee participation in a given type of employment and their civil service schemata that ultimately shaped their views of opportunity and their interpretations of work. Since responses stemming from each line did not necessarily coincide, the interconnections contributed to reinforce the contradictions within of the system.

As an illustration, consider the step-up clerical manager (mentioned in Chapter 7) who criticized the union for discouraging employees from working out of title. Evident in her case was some ambivalence about how to interpret her work life and organize her career strategies. Her ambivalence stemmed from her participation in an open employment mode and her formal endorsement of a closed one. Her strong verbal support of the civil service system, her ambivalent beliefs about the role of experience and education, and the importance she attributed to her supervisors in her own success are evidence of contradictions in the cognitive map she had of her work.

Conclusion

The adoption of an official merit system does not guarantee adherence either to professional values or to merit principles. After all, studies have documented differences between professional personnel norms and actual employment practices in city and county governments (Fox 1993). Fox's claim, however, is that jurisdictions with formal merit systems do seem to adhere closely to merit principles and tend to comply with legal and professional personnel standards, more so than governments lacking a formal merit system. If this is true, a large portion of the inefficiencies many critics attribute to formal civil service systems may be more a function of their partial implementation than of their design. There is also the possibility that the so-called inefficiencies have been identified as such by precisely those groups whose interests are not being well served by a particular definition of merit.

Rather than being an equalizer of status, an "imperfect" civil service legitimates differences in status among similar employees. In PSA the imperfections produced an elasticity in the definition of merit, which gave civil service status a different social meaning in each career ladder. These local meanings in turn helped employees interpret their personal experience and react to differential treatment based on the social statuses attributed to them. For operators, a strongly enforced civil service system coincided with the assignment of the same status for all individuals at each level of the career ladder. It also justified protection and perks that were not available to other employees. Therefore civil service did not create differences in reward distribution or in social statuses within the ladder. But it did set the operators apart from all others in the agency. This promoted and justified differences across ladders. It also assigned higher organizational status to this group.

Civil service status acquired a different meaning in the career ladders where a lower enforcement of the staffing process took place. Unequal enforcement resulted in differences in treatment *within* and *across* ladders for those outside the operator career ladder. In the clerical ladder, permanent employees considered the quality of their employment superior to that of provisionals. But comparing across ladders, both groups had lower organizational status than operators and analysts, even though in theory the "merit principle" should have protected them. In the case of the analyst ladder, permanent analysts felt they had lower organizational status, while provisionals felt they had higher status. Moreover, both groups felt they had higher status than the clerical group, but lower than the operators.

Opportunity perceptions of PSA employees were aligned with the type of employment relationship they could establish with PSA as an employer. But they were also strongly influenced by the legitimacy that employees attributed to the civil service system, regardless of the type of relationship they had. Indeed, the complex combination of these two forces ultimately shaped employee opportunity perceptions. Social meanings attributed to particular situations included definitions of opportunity, rewards, merit, and professionalism. These varied among advocates of each employment model, as well as among the actual participants of each type of relationship.

This was the social context in which PSA employees interpreted who they were and where they stood. It was a context that emerged from an organizational setting characterized by inequality, despite the fact that its ideology strongly endorsed fairness. Heterogeneous work arrangements within this organization created the possibility of the application of different principles of distributive justice, even while the same "blanket" philosophy appeared to be working for all. The emerging contradictions greatly affected people's perceptions of opportunity, and ultimately their reactions to work.

The Power of Comparisons: Perceptions of Justice and the Organizational Climate

N. Williams worked in the most prestigious analytical unit at headquarters. He had taken a leave of absence without pay from his permanent staff analyst position to accept the post of associate staff analyst on a provisional basis. As a "step-up," his salary increased considerably. During the three years following his "promotion," his personnel file reported simultaneous proportional salary adjustments in the permanent and provisional titles. Then a union filed a law suit against city management for abusing the use of provisional slots. PSA's personnel department held that Williams' situation was highly visible, and in consequence he was moved back to his original title, one level down the ladder. His boss told him that this was strictly a formality and that his employment conditions would not change. In an interview, however, Williams interpreted his experience as a psychological demotion.

Williams' reasoning was not totally out of line. To maintain his salary, personnel placed him in the highest level of his original permanent title (staff analyst). This was financially equivalent to the lowest level of the provisional title (associate staff analyst). But in the new position he was no longer formally eligible for the 7 percent merit increases because the permanent title was not a supervisory position. Hence Williams actually lost an important source of financial opportunity. Furthermore, he felt singled out by the system because not all step-ups had been reclassified. To make matters worse, when the legal problem disappeared after a few months, the vacancy for the position Williams had left was used to promote another provisional staff analyst in the same office. Williams kept his permanent title. While his job tasks remained the same, his work perceptions did change. He felt that his manager and PSA had treated him badly.

From the perspective of management, the episode represented an expedient staffing solution in a highly constrained environment. The maneuvers had saved

Williams' salary level while opening a new supervisory slot, which was used to reward another employee. From Williams' point of view, the situation had been handled arbitrarily. He felt deceived, and he experienced considerable bitterness. At the time of the interview, Williams was cynical about his work in PSA. He did only what was strictly required or what interested him.

Williams' experience illustrates how the forces described in the past chapters helped shape the references employees used to make workplace comparisons in PSA. His attitudes toward the agency were colored by the inconsistent staffing practices. They were also affected by the perceived inequitable outcomes in a career ladder characterized by uncertainty. The provisional/permanent dichotomy was implemented in decision-making procedures that were less than fair. These in turn produced opportunity outputs and outcomes that were clearly contradictory.

Ultimately, these situations increased the transparency of justice violations. Yet the institutional environment strongly endorsed the equality of opportunity. In this context, social comparisons emerged as a tool that helped employees make sense of their personal and collective experiences. Comparisons have a critical effect in producing a sense of justice or injustice in this society (Kulik and Ambrose 1992; Oppenheim 1980; Martin 1981). Indeed, distributive justice can be conceptualized as the coincidence of actual and expected allocations in a given social context. This is clearly linked to how and why individuals react to situations and interpret them.

Perceived differences in treatment, as well as perceived contradictions between explanations and realities, allowed feelings of distrust and resentment to flourish. Feelings of relative deprivation also arose when the expectation of equal treatment collided with the implementation of unequal procedures, which in turn produced unequal outcomes. The tendency was to direct these emotions against those who benefited. This promoted antagonisms among employees, despite an appearance of cordiality and respect.

Williams' response illustrates that PSA employees were not just passive receptacles of an ideological discourse. Nor were they mere puppets of a structure. External cues filtering through personal experience helped them process information and develop the cognitive maps they used to handle the dissonance. These mental operations promoted interactions charged with ambiguity. The result was an organizational climate reflecting distrust toward the agency and ambivalence toward other co-workers.

The Social Psychology of Comparisons

Comparison theories help explain individual reactions to a wide variety of opportunity outcomes such as pay and workplace status (Masters and Keil 1987).

Comparison evaluations can produce three possible types of consequences that directly affect organizational climate: cognitive consequences (the formation, strengthening, or alteration of opinions and judgements); affective consequences (the modification of emotional reactions, preferences, and attitudes) and behavioral consequences (actual attempts to affect the comparison, including leaving the field) (Masters and Keil 1987). Comparisons may therefore have important consequences for organizational life, affecting human resource variables such as satisfaction and turnover.

Comparisons presume the existence of a source and a target (or referent). Referents for comparisons can be of several kinds. For example, individuals do not only contrast their experiences with what they need, as the need-satisfaction model proposes. They also contrast themselves with other individuals and a *generalized* other. The latter provides an external reference to the self, based on a mixture of perceived generalized expectations and reactions rooted in the social world. Thus, in addition to self/self comparisons, individuals also engage in self/ other and group/group comparisons (Levine and Moreland 1987). To make matters more complex, individuals may see themselves in more than one comparative relationship to others, to themselves, or to a reference standard (Masters and Keil 1987). All these contrasts are based on normative expectations concerning the allocation of socially valued rewards (Greenberg and Cohen 1982).[1]

Referent cognitions theory assumes that a sense of one's treatment depends on the "story" (or explanation) one can tell about the situation. This story is constructed by comparing not only what outcomes might have been (referent outcomes), but also the process, that is, what other routes might have been taken to achieve those outcomes (referent instrumentalities) and, finally, what possible futures lie in store (the likelihood of amelioration) (Folger 1987). Understanding which are the appropriate referents and how they become the chosen ones represents a major research agenda on work perceptions and attitudes. It requires highlighting the social context in which the comparisons take place.

Situations or referent groups which "push buttons" and trigger comparisons may vary considerably from person to person and from group to group. But most importantly, they vary from social context to social context. These variations are a function of the salience of the object or instance of comparison. One important reason for the existence of salience is that the predominant type of information used for comparisons is acquired through direct experience. It is context specific. Salience can be linked to the intent of the individual who is making the comparison. It can also produce variations in the kinds of information the person will choose, when making comparison evaluations (Masters and Keil 1987).

The objects of comparison, their salience, the referent outcomes, and the referent instrumentalities that PSA employees used varied according to the structural and institutional forces that shaped their career ladders. The combination of these forces produced highly specific outcomes of resource distribution. They also produced specific ideas about merit and opportunity for each subgroup. But at the same time, each factor represented in and of itself a possible social category for comparative evaluations. As a reference for comparing the self to others, a person could use, depending on the motive, either location in a career ladder or status within the civil service system or a combination of both.

Given the degree of uncertainty surrounding the employment relationship in PSA, employees made judgements about their worth using different referent standards at one point or another. For example, a provisional clerical employee could ask, "How do I compare with permanent clerical employees?" (a self/other comparison within the same occupational category); or the person could ask, "How do I compare with provisional analysts?" (a self/other comparison within the same civil service category). An employee could also ask, "How do clerical employees in general compare to operators or to analysts?" (a group/group comparison); or finally, "Given my personal characteristics, what would I be if I did not have a public sector job?" (a self/self comparison). Which of these questions became most important for each group had a lot to do with the social context in which they were asked.

But civil service was only one of several important social categories of interaction. Information presented earlier suggests that race, gender, educational attainment, work experience, and occupational status represented not only personal attributes of employees but also compositional attributes of jobs. They thus affected the social nature of the ladder. As different "social types" of employees formed into clusters, and as those clusters varied from ladder to ladder, the "shared definitions" of organizational reality also shifted from one social context to the next. For example, N. Williams' identity as an African-American permanent civil servant played a critical role in shaping his negative evaluation of both the process and the outcomes in the story that opened this chapter. It is very likely that his interpretations of the situation would have been different had he been located in a career ladder where civil servants felt protected from external competition and where the most desired positions were equally distributed among employees of different ethnicities. In this sense, Williams' story is also an example of the importance of the demographic composition of jobs and career ladders in creating a social context for the emergence of particular meanings and reference groups.

Staffing patterns based on an uneven implementation of the closed model of employment produced the existing demographic composition for each ladder. They helped define who would be placed where. Recall from the analysis of Chapter 5 how the demographic composition of PSA ladders was patterned by sex, race, and educational attainment. Moreover, enforcement of civil service status seemed to vary with the clustering of individuals sharing the same types of demographic attributes. Thus the two groups with the highest enforcement were similar in terms of educational attainment, and they also reflected high levels of segregation by gender and race. Operators were all male and largely white. Clerical employees were largely female and had the largest proportion of people of color. While all operators were civil servants, only about two-thirds of the clerical group had this status. At the other end, the civil service composition of the analyst career ladder was also mixed, but the proportions shifted. About two-thirds of the group had provisional civil service status and higher educational levels. Demographics in this ladder were more balanced, with relatively equal proportions of men and women and of whites and people of color. However, fewer women and people of color were located at the upper levels.

The numbers and proportions of each ladder had an impact on how employees experienced work life. They helped define the salient attributes for comparison. Similarly, the structural and institutional variations across employment mode shaped the very meaning that each demographic attribute—gender, race, educational level, or civil service status—took for each particular occupational group. As the meaning of civil service status varied from one career to the next, the meaning of other social traits also became sensitive to context. For example, being a woman in the clerical ladder had a different connotation from being a woman in the analyst ladder. For obvious reasons, gender and race/ethnicity had even stronger connotations in the operator ladder. Once status attributes such as gender, race, education, and civil service helped define each ladder, they started to play a role in filling the slots. As new employees entered the system, these social categories also helped define the social nature of the job clusters where employees worked.

Tomaskovic-Devey (1993) explains this phenomenon by making a distinction between two interrelated but separate social processes affecting stratified work systems: status closure and status composition. Status closure refers to the use of ascribed attributes such as sex and race to determine who has access to valuable jobs. This is a direct process of discrimination in the workplace. In contrast, status composition refers to the process by which jobs become socially categorized, based on their composition by sex or race. Because of this categorization, as well as the pervasive racism and sexism of this society, employers and even employees tend to devalue jobs with many women or people of color. These jobs thus become the least desirable ones in the social system. Thus the sex or race that typically characterizes a group of jobs becomes a crucial attribute of the jobs, affecting their very nature, as well as the social evaluation of their worth within the organization.

Tomaskovic-Devey makes the interesting point that while status closure is a *cause* of job segregation, status composition represents one of its *consequences*. The denial of access to managerial positions for women (through the glass ceiling phenomenon) is an instance of the status closure process. The devaluing of women's work (in low-prestige clerical work or low-paying nursing positions) is an instance of status composition. Both processes contribute to reproduce inequality in the workplace. At the micro level of work life in PSA, the referent groups emerging from these dynamics of stratification became part of the cognitive maps employees used to interpret their situation. Referent standards that originated from personal information eventually became autonomous and emerged as shared evaluations for many members of each group.[2]

The Seeds of Conflict: Uncertainty in the Distribution of Resources

As N. Williams' case illustrates, permanent analysts have a sense of uncertainty stemming from their structural location. Many analysts were convinced that no matter how well they performed, other criteria could be used in making staffing decisions. Furthermore, Williams' bitter and resentful response fits with what the social comparison literature suggests about organizational injustice and relative deprivation. Resentment arises when a situation is deemed unjustifiable compared to imagined alternatives. Whether a situation is justifiable or not depends on whether one attaches blame to the situation or accepts its legitimacy (Folger 1987).

The gap between discourse about merit and practices inconsistent with merit created much of uncertainty, ambiguity, and a sense of injustice. These sentiments prepared the ground for antagonisms among groups and individuals competing for increasingly scarce jobs and resources. Frustration, which targeted either specific "others" or the system, played an ideological function in the organizational culture. It helped employees define one another as either "us" or "them." This social typing had an important function. It transformed individuals' experiences of dissonance into legitimate resentment. Categorizing oneself and others thus was a way of managing and ameliorating otherwise uncomfortable feelings of dissonance. The consequences for employee morale and for the organizational climate were immense.

Based on his experience, Williams believed that he had three characteristics which greatly reduced his chances for success in PSA: first, he was a civil service employee located in a career ladder strongly biased against permanent employees. Second, despite having an educational credential, he did not come from an Ivy League school. And third, being African-American, he had the "wrong" ethnic background. These reasons were, in his mind, interdependent. Williams was convinced that provisional analysts had a better chance of moving up than permanent analysts. He argued that even though the former had no job security, they had an important advantage: they had the look of many provisional managers at the top. Williams insisted that in the absence of civil service lists, managers chose—for succession purposes—those who were similar to them. Given their discretionary hiring practices, managers tended to be favorably disposed toward provisionals and toward a certain "type" of employee who fitted a particular demographic profile. The next sections explore Williams' arguments and their consequences for PSA's organizational climate.

The Reproduction of Patterns of Inequality

There was no way to verify Williams' reasoning about why his story ended as it did. Yet, information about patterns of opportunity in PSA do suggest that his assessment was at least plausible. I have already documented the social homogeneity of PSA's managerial group. Moreover other empirical studies of women and minorities in the workplace do suggest a similar pattern of exclusion (Fernandez 1981; Powell 1993; Kanter 1977, 1987). Williams' description of how managerial preferences produce inconsistent staffing decisions is not unique to PSA. Although he did not have a label for the phenomenon he observed, the literature does. These are instances of "homosocial reproduction" (Kanter 1977; Tomaskovic-Devey 1993).[3]

Social similarity can be an important attribute affecting a person's capacity to form alliances and to define others. Having educational credentials, the right ethnicity, and the right gender can be critically important for opening doors to organizational positions (Collins 1975, 1979; Young 1958). The sharing of a common social background "facilitates the formation of alliances and social networks, access to channels of information, the acquisition of a similar definition of reality and of the vocabulary and style to impress others with allegedly superior knowledge, and consensus concerning the course of action to be followed" (Murphy 1988:163).[4]

Social similarity, whatever criteria it uses, acts as a mechanism of exclusion or inclusion in circles of power and privilege, both in society at large and in organizations. Empirical evidence documents the pervasiveness of the reproduction of these patterns in contemporary organizations (Roos and Reskin 1984; Stafford 1989). Rather than instances of overt discrimination, they represent instances of "institutionalized discrimination" or what others refer to, in a more elegant form, as the group-specific disadvantages of the contemporary organization of work (DiPrete 1989).

Kanter (1977) clarifies how this process works in managerial succession. She stresses the impact of conditions typical of managerial work such as the uncertainty of managerial tasks, the difficulty of evaluating managerial roles, and managers' high dependency on communication flows. These structural conditions make managers' performance highly dependent upon their ability to develop trust in their work relationships. With escalating pressures to perform, promoting people who are socially similar to oneself can become an expedient shortcut to building trust.

The most convenient answer to questions such as "Who can I trust?" "Who can I communicate with accurately and efficiently?" and "How can I make sure that those under my supervision are doing a good job?" might very well be: "Someone who looks like me, talks like me, and acts like me." As employees in the lower levels are socialized into the organizational culture, they recognize this and try to adapt their attitudes and behaviors to reflect the traits that managers value and reward. The result is conformity and uniformity among those who aspire to join the club and become managers. The new managers will replicate the same attitudes, thus generating new cycles of social reproduction.

Homosocial reproduction can also be linked to the process of status closure. This is the denial of access to certain positions for groups of individuals who do not share the same attributes as the privileged (Tomaskovic-Devey 1993). Managers in PSA tended to prefer outside candidates to fill new supervisory and managerial jobs. Buying into the ideology of the meritocracy, the managers considered these credentialed candidates better qualified than internal ones. But more importantly, the outside candidates resembled the managers more closely. A manager justified his bias in favor of externals as follows: "The city government needs to attract a more professional staff to produce a more effective work flow." Here the definition of "professionalism" is clearly biased toward an open model of employment and against those hard-working individuals who were trying to "make it" up the ladder.

Despite strong institutional efforts for affirmative action in PSA, demographic imbalance characterized both the managerial group and many desirable jobs in the staff ladders. The vast majority of managerial employees were white males; and in each of the three career ladders the higher the position, the higher the probability that the incumbent would be a white male—even in the clerical ladder, where women and minorities predominated. Replicating many similar organizational settings in the public and the private sector, the work force distribution tended to penalize women and people of color. While managers did not engage in this process on purpose, its outcomes nevertheless were real. In this sense, Williams' situation illustrates a broader social process linked to a zero-sum distribution of resources.

The internal logic of homosocial reproduction in managerial succession may also work at lower levels of the organization. Granovetter (1981, 1985b) has used the notion of "structural embeddedness" to highlight the impact of networks and work relationships on organizational hiring and promotion. He suggests that upward mobility depends on the contacts a person establishes with others. These contacts facilitate decision makers' awareness of the person's attributes. The sequence of jobs, as well as the characteristics they have at each different level, provide the basis for the contacts. This condition is independent of the incumbent's personal desire to connect with the right people. It also frames the incumbent's actual prospects and choices. The same logic extends to other aspects of opportunity such as compensation and job challenge. A recent study of 185 managers in a large nonprofit organization found, for example, that managers' decisions about pay raises for their subordinates were largely influenced by their organizational connections (Schoderbeck and Deshpande 1993). This suggests that staffing decisions depend not only on performance level but also on the quality of organizational ties.

This logic can be applied to PSA. It is understandable why an office associate from the clerical career ladder would have few chances to participate in task forces (which could make her more visible or help her grow in the job) compared to a staff analyst or an operator. Clerical employees' positions provided them with little bargaining leverage in which they could exercise personal initiative. Since more women and people of color were located in the ladder with the least opportunity (or in the lowest levels of ladders with better opportunity), it could be said that their gender and ethnic background affected their opportunities. This has been demonstrated empirically in other work contexts. A study of New York State civil service jobs describes how women's promotional opportunities were constrained by sex segregation in at least four different ways. First, most promotional examinations involved male-dominated titles; second, few women were found among the top three candidates on lists for male-dominated jobs; third, women had fewer chances of being selected for a male-dominated job; and fourth, when selected, they had to compete with a pool of largely male candidates (Ratner 1981).

The reason for these patterns is the direct effect that organizational demography has on the quality and success of network ties for women and people of color. Ibarra (1993) highlights the link between organizational networks and career outcomes. She argues that because structural constraints differ by race and gender in organizations, network characteristics associated with success and effectiveness may also differ substantially for white males and for women and people of color. More specifically, she identifies the opportunity context as an important organizational factor that affects directly and indirectly behavior in network dynamics. The *direct* effect relates, in her view, to the types of network choices individuals make in their search for support and sponsorship. As an example from PSA, a woman analyst may prefer to be sponsored by another woman but may have to settle for a man. The *indirect* effect relates to the structure of the network that shapes available alternatives, their costs, and the benefits an individual seeks. For example, there will be fewer women sponsors to choose from in a ladder with few female managers, as is the case of the analyst ladder. Hence the actual probabilities of a good match are reduced.

It is not a surprise then that despite the influx of women and people of color into organizations of all types, managerial groups still tend to be fairly homogeneous. Some may argue that things are not as bad as they were—a belief based on successes that have been highly celebrated in popular culture. Yet there is

plenty of evidence to show that not enough progress has been made. For example, one federal study claims that if the present rate of hiring women managers
continues, by the year 2017 women will still remain underrepresented in senior
levels (Merit Systems Protection Board 1992). Many instances of job and occupational segregation are also well documented in the literature.

The discussion of the logic behind the dynamics of homosocial reproduction
is by no means an attempt to endorse it. The point, instead, is to highlight the
urgency of increasing the diversity of the work force at all levels of the organization. Attention to issues of justice and equality is a practical requirement for
organizational performance. Chapa (1992) suggests that homosocial dynamics
have a negative impact on organizational effectiveness. He argues that instances
of segregation based on sex, race, and class create compositional obstacles in
the communication process. They provoke the emergence of organizational
subcultures possessing different degrees of power, speaking different "lan-
guages," and experiencing different working conditions. Using data about
paraprofessionals in government, he concludes that the demographic composition typical of sex-segregated jobs and occupations has a direct impact on
the quality of the upward flow of information in public organizations, to the
detriment of organizational innovation.

There is considerable documentation of the extent of segregation within jobs
and ladders. Yet the impact of the compositional characteristics of work groups
on employees' personal experiences, work perceptions, and behaviors has not
been explored with equal intensity. One exception is Kanter's study of opportunity, power, and organizational demography (Kanter 1977, 1987). Kanter suggests that organizational behavior typically characterized as "feminine" (low
aspirations, emphasis on social relations, disengagement) instead represents
adaptive responses of individuals to the limited rewards and blocked opportunities inherent in jobs typically assigned to women. In other words, she argues that
it is the nature of the positions, and not the nature of their incumbents, that
influences behavior.

More specifically, Kanter suggests that the numerical composition of groups
creates interaction contexts that are experienced differently by majorities and
minorities in a group. She conceptualizes these experiences as exchanges based
on the stereotypical images that "tokens" and "dominants" develop of each
other. Three factors affect and reproduce these images.[5] First, visibility: tokens
receive a larger share of attention in contrast to dominants; this produces higher
levels of performance pressure on the token. Second, contrast: the differences
between the token and the dominants tend to be exaggerated; this generates a
sense of isolation for the token. And third, assimilation: people tend to interpret
the behavior of the token using familiar generalizations about the person's social
type; this "encapsulates" the token in the role expected by others. These factors
create self-fulfilling prophecies of success and failure. Choosing to respond
stereotypically as expected or to withdraw to avoid the pressure, many tokens fail

in the competition over rewards. This reinforces, in the minds of many, the sense of deserving of those who make it and the sense of failure of those who do not. The ultimate outcome of these perceptions is a negative work environment, which produces friction or discomfort for both types of individuals. Anecdotal evidence suggests that individuals experience these dynamics in a very real way. I have shown *The Tale of O*, a short film based on this analysis, to more than a hundred students over the course of three years. Empathy is the usual reaction from those who in one way or another have experienced tokenism in the work place. Many students have shared similar experiences of their own, telling stories of being excluded as women or as persons of color from desired jobs, career ladders, and managerial positions. More empirical studies are required, however, to understand the underlying logic in such accounts. The rest of this chapter moves in that direction, by illustrating how these dynamics got played out in the stratified context of PSA.

The Diversity Debate

Williams made some references to his race as a possible reason for his situation, and his comments point to an unresolved issue of diversity in PSA. These tensions would emerge from the organization's collective consciousness from time to time, and then submerge once again. The tensions arose over scarce resources. One such controversy ensued when people took sides over the debate created around some empirical data an analyst had collected. Having suspected that the agency's rate of attrition was affected by practices of racial discrimination, this analyst conducted an informal study. He found that there were statistically significant differences in the firing of nonwhites and whites. Others who believed that the agency did not have enough people of color in responsible positions, including some members of the EEO Office, joined forces to support the analyst. Those who opposed the study argued that this was a typical case of spurious correlations. They claimed that issues of "socialization" made people of color engage more often than other individuals in practices such as tardiness or absenteeism. It was those behaviors that got people into trouble. In response, those who supported the study argued that supervisors, usually white, tended to report fewer tardiness incidents among white workers than among minority workers.[6]

The analyst who authored the study demanded that the agency take action. He even threatened to publish the findings if nothing was done. The conflict, however, was not resolved. It dragged on for a while and finally died out after the analyst resigned. His claim had been that PSA was closing its eyes to a very real problem of organizational inequality. The agency clearly was not yet ready for an open confrontation of such a sensitive issue. Later efforts toward affirmative action may very well have been partially motivated by this incident.

At a personal level, most employees were aware of these tensions. Among employees surveyed, 24 percent reported that they had been discriminated against personally.[7] About two-thirds of this group attributed this experience to their minority status, one-fourth attributed it to their mainstream status, and the rest mentioned favoritism or discrimination without specifying a reason. The specific types of minority discrimination mentioned by respondents were sexism, racism, ageism, or a combination of these. Racism was mentioned most often and ageism the least. More analysts and clerical employees suggested racism or sexism as the reason for discrimination. More operators attributed their experiences of discrimination to being male, white, or both. A few operators mentioned the so called "reverse discrimination" and "quotas" that protected or favored minorities or women.

As we have seen, uncertainty characterized the PSA workplace: civil service enforcement was inconsistent and the existing distribution of resources bore signs of imminent change. Some employees labeled the inconsistencies as instances of discrimination. They linked these either to the poor implementation of the system, (unions took this view) or to the idiosyncrasies or prejudices of particular supervisors. Others, at the opposite end of the ideological spectrum, identified PSA's efforts of affirmative action as discriminatory. Paradoxically, both points of view promoted feelings of injustice and paved the way for conflict.

In the survey, various groups of employees expressed antagonisms based on race. One white analyst in a managerial position wrote,

> City government is being staffed by people who do not have basic work skills. Many promotions are based on race. A quota system, unofficial, is in effect. If you do not hire a minority, you are seriously questioned why not. Standards have been lowered to accommodate the minorities. White supervisors are scared to discipline because of racist charges. It is a mess.

A lower-rank minority clerical employee took a different view: "For male blacks, forget it. Any position with any high profile and salary held by a black male is strictly because of politics. They have to have some window dressing so as not to look overtly racist."

The first comment is paternalistic and the second is cynical; both represent negative attitudes about race relations. They must be placed in the context of competition for organizational resources in relatively segregated career ladders.

These attitudes have in common a belief that preferential treatment was given to certain groups based on irrelevant physical characteristics. The opinions vary in the interpretation of the practices. The first comment represents the typical backlash against affirmative action, in which changes to the status quo elicit resistance from previously advantaged workers (Tomaskovic-Devey 1993). The second comment represents the frustrations of the disadvantaged, who face obstacles in their effort to move up.

Overtly negative attitudes toward diversity in the operator ladder must be linked to the increasing degree of uncertainty they were experiencing as a result of organizational changes: PSA's implementation of a formal policy of affirmative action, the increasing number of employees recruited to support PSA's technostructure, a fiscal environment emphasizing the need to do more with fewer resources, and most importantly, a gradual shift from the bureaucratic to the market mode of employment among the managerial ranks of all ladders. These forces threatened the operators. They challenged the status quo and jeopardized their advantageous opportunity package. As evidence, 17 percent of the sample of operators surveyed insisted on the need for more civil service enforcement, despite the almost perfect enforcement described for the operator ladder. Even though this is a small percentage, that a group of operators wanted more enforcement is significant.

In fact, the operator managerial ladder had been gradually moving away from civil service standards toward other evaluation criteria. This change in policy had opened more room for managerial discretion in the promotion of upper-level operators. The comments of an operator manager about this new policy are illustrative of the disadvantages operators saw in opening the system:

> After introducing the use of merit for promotions above [the second level management position], we have gone back to the old days of patronage. This has created a background of fear and self-preservation that has changed the whole attitude and atmosphere of the job. When a person can be raised to a position that can mean up to $20,000 a year more money, he fears having it taken away at the whim of a rolling gripe, and strikes out at anything that can threaten his position and earnings.

Despite the fact that it did not represent a generalized feeling, this comment is important in two respects. First, it shows a new development in the opportunity structure of operators. Movement up the managerial levels was starting to occur independently of civil service exams, and it was becoming contingent on the discretion of superiors. This represented the slow shift from a bureaucratic to a market-oriented mode, at least at the apex. Second, the comment illustrates the comfort that operators felt about the formal merit system. Many operators disliked this change and wanted civil service standards to be strongly enforced.

It is easy to understand then how staffing outcomes that did not meet operators' expectations could be blamed on the new developments. Efforts to create a more balanced work force were starting to have an effect on the staffing of this career ladder. Women were in the process of being hired, and men of color were being strongly supported in their efforts to move up. These changes coincided with the stabilization and even reduction of the city's fiscal resources during the late 1980s. These trends negatively affected some members of the operator ladder. In the mind of the average operator, the changes were lumped together with work force diversification.

In the case of operators, the provisional/permanent dichotomy was irrelevant. So when they expressed resentment, they did so in terms of other social distinctions, specifically racial or sexual ones. Sometimes their comments were aggressive and bitter, like the intermediate operator who wrote in the survey, "Every gay, alcoholic, junkie, female, minority have some group or program or government quota to protect, aid, or cover up, or use as an excuse for. The white American straight male has nothing but a social security card."

There is no evidence to suggest that this represented a generalized point of view among operators in PSA. It is, however, illustrative of their growing sense of discomfort. As the rules of resource distribution were being renegotiated, the prospect of sharing scarce resources with a broader community of employees set the stage first for uncertainty and later for resentment. Distorted beliefs were not uncommon: any career success by a person of color was a function of an artificial staffing decision induced by affirmative action; any individual from a "protected" group was taking a job away from a qualified unprotected employee.

In his discussion of affirmative action backlashes, Tomaskovic-Devey characterizes their context as one "of exaggeration, envy, and mistrust" (1993:162). Such sentiments are typical of competitions for scarce resources under the zero-sum type conditions generated by sharp pyramidal structures. My own general sense, based on comments in the survey and informal conversations with PSA employees, is that backlash attitudes were common in pockets of the agency at all levels, even the supervisory and managerial levels. Some individuals in the operator ladder were having a hard time indeed with the opening up of their ladder. That new employees differed physically from the average operator (as women or as persons of color) made it easy to direct negative feelings toward those traits. Many operators inevitably experienced the gains won first by minorities and later by women as their own losses.

Internal "Bureaucratic Bashing"

Williams' contempt for his fellow provisional co-workers stemmed from two factors. One was his belief in the legitimacy of the system. The other was his experience of the lax enforcement of the merit principles endorsed by the system. For groups participating in an open contract, the provisional/permanent dichotomy was critical. The "others" who would be blamed for problems at work were often members of the same occupational group but of a different civil service status. Comparisons among these subgroups, each typifying the other in some way, created conflicts among employees working side by side. In some situations employees would reproduce societal notions of contempt for public employees—an example of internal "bureaucracy bashing."

Not only did the provisional/permanent dichotomy promote conflict among employees within the same occupational group, it did so among same-status employees in different ladders. Provisional employees and step-ups in the clerical ladder, for example, felt disadvantaged compared to civil servants. When the system was enforced seriously, the legal protection granted to permanent clerical employees restricted the movement of provisionals. Many provisionals resented this. Here, to illustrate, is what one provisional office associate wrote in the survey:

> The civil service system is extremely messed up because no matter how bad an employee you may be, if you are civil service you won't get fired. People literally do no work and get an unsatisfactory rating on their performance evaluation year after year, and nothing happens to them. Even a felony conviction won't cause you to lose your job. On the other hand, *as a provisional, you mess up just once, and you're on the unemployment line.* Practices like these are unfair and cause low job morale and laziness. (emphasis added)

Thus, employees themselves perpetuated the stereotype of the lazy civil servant. Another provisional shop clerk expressed a similar dissatisfaction:

> There are many [employees] who have gotten away with hardly working for so long—that everyone else has to pick up the slack. Supervisors refuse to do anything about it for fear of being written up. It's easier to give these people good reviews than being sued according to the supervisors. So there are people getting paid for sitting around doing nothing while other people have to cover for them. Great situation—especially when these "old timers" tell me not to get involved, "don't do too much work" and "don't be so helpful."

The same feelings emerged in the analytical ladder. One provisional staff analyst complained, "It definitely is aggravating when you see a civil service manager make $35,000 and you're making $26,000 and you're doing his job!" The salary difference she had observed contradicted the social value she attributed to civil servants. "Among provisionals," the same analyst said, "the feeling is we're more qualified than the civil servants. Our perception of them is [that they are] unmotivated and not bound for as great career achievements as the provisional hopes for."

Permanent analysts, those who had come up the ranks, had a similarly negative attitude toward provisionals. As one permanent staff analyst said, "Because I come off a list I make less than anyone in my unit for the same job. People hired off the street after me are in higher titles with more money, with the same qualifications as me."

Note the derogatory reference to provisionals as people coming "off the street." Civil servants made the same negative comparisons when they observed differences across career ladders. For example, a permanent shop clerk (clerical group) stated, "Many positions are held by operators, foremen making $34,000 per year, supervisors $48,364 per annum and above, whereas clerical supervisors levels 1 to 3 and managers are barely making as much as $30,000, for doing the same job." Here the "others," the objects of comparison, were operator supervisors and managers. In this clerk's mind, they should have had the same social value as their clerical counterparts, given their equal status in the civil service system.

The feeling extended to promotion prospects. The generalized perception was that operators had easier access to higher positions in the hierarchy. A career development study conducted by one of the agency's units illustrates this:

> [There is a] feeling expressed by many [staff employees] of being pinned up against the [operator] work force, and of having their career advancement completely overshadowed by what they see as an almost automatic chain of promotion that exists for the operators. During the field interviews, for example, a number of [non-operators] pointed to the fact that they, as [non-operators], would never be appointed to the top managerial levels within the Bureau. (Source: a PSA memorandum, dated 1985)

PSA decision makers associated this situation with problems such as high attrition rates, low motivation, and lack of commitment within different occupational groups that composed the staff personnel in the agency.[8]

In all these cases, comparisons were with other individuals who belonged to well-defined referent groups based on participation in different opportunity structures. The permanent clerical employee felt bad when he compared himself with his operator counterparts. The provisional analyst saw herself at a monetary disadvantage when she compared herself to higher ranked civil servants to whom she was accountable. The permanent analyst felt deprived in contrast to a provisional doing the same job. And finally, analysts and clerical employees, who both shared an open employment mode, felt deprived compared to operators, who enjoyed ILM protection. These feelings were necessarily connected to differences in opportunity and the consequent discrepancies that these generated.

Elasticity in the definition of merit, described earlier, is critical for an understanding of these strong feelings among people who worked side by side. A sense of injustice in a given system may be based on how "merit" is defined in that system, even when there is an agreement about the dominant justice rule being used, such as equity (Deutch 1985). But the feelings can also stem from incongruence in the distributive rules, for example equity versus equality. Both factors worked in PSA when employees tried to make sense of the contradictions experienced by the organization of work and the consequent inconsistencies in staffing practices.

Revisiting the "Merit" Debate

Behind Williams' assertion that his educational credentials were not as valuable as they could be was a belief based on personal experience. In the analyst ladder, the competition between provisional and permanent employees was fierce, even when the contenders carried the "mark" of success, namely education. Conflicting definitions of merit and professionalism in PSA were directly linked to particular notions of deserving. Both the narrow and the broad perspectives of professionalism (and their respective merit connotations) reflected underlying justice values that were part of employees' images of opportunity. The underlying assumption was a generalized belief that "technical competence and fairness are the proper guidelines for personnel decisions" (DiPrete 1989:27). The main distinction between employees in different structural contexts had to do with the interpretation of the terms "competence" and "fairness." This varied depending on the rule of distributive justice that was emphasized.

The dominant notion of merit in the workplace reflects the distributive justice principle of equity (Deutsch 1985). According to this principle, the outcomes of a fair exchange of resources will be based on people's contributions. There is however, a large degree of ambiguity in defining the value of contributions (Törnblom and Jonsson 1985; McClintock and Keil 1982; Greenberg and Cohen 1982). It may be argued, for example, that how much one puts in should be the primary determinant of how much of the outcome one receives. Hence, someone who contributes a lot deserves a large share of the final distribution. An illustration of this position is the union's definition of seniority as a proxy for experience, institutional memory, and organizational loyalty. Others argue instead that an individual's contributions must be measured with reference to the costs and investments incurred to be able to contribute. This latter argument is the bases for assigning importance to formal education, and is illustrated by the managerial emphasis on educational credentials as a proxy for technical knowledge and competence.

The two views emphasize different types of human capital in the allocation of, say, money (salaries) or positions (promotions). The first would imply that those who work harder, longer, or under harsher conditions deserve a higher salary, regardless of who they are or what type of credentials they bring. The second view would suggest that other factors, such as technical competence, expertise, or actual productivity should be considered in determining who gets a better pay.

Both views represent possible ways of enforcing the equity principle, yet each uses a different notion of merit to evaluate the contribution.[9]

Furthermore, despite the dominance of the equity principle, equality has also permeated the notions of deserving in today's workplace (Lane 1986; Bell 1973). The maxim that graphically illustrates this principle says "to each according to his or her inherent human worth." Employees' and workers' belief in this principle has led to the organization of collective actions to fight, first for bread-and-butter issues and later to preserve the inherent dignity of human beings in the workplace. Alongside values such as instrumentalism, individualism, and competition, equality emphasizes the values of parity, collectivism, and cooperation. These two sets of values sometimes overlap in the organizational culture, since they have both been espoused by different groups at different times (Lane 1986; Sampson 1983).

The institutional context of the workplace is complex because of the simultaneous, and often contradictory, use of these justice principles and their sub-rules to implement policies and justify the distribution of resources. The contradictions stemming from the overlap may create cognitive dissonance. Taylor's insightful study (1991) of affirmative action in a public bureaucracy provides illustrations of this. He found that employees' ambivalences toward this policy were rooted in the contradictions between competing justice theories—or fragmented assumptions from them. Most employees espoused a commitment to the goal of equal opportunities based on individual merit. Yet some emphasized individual interests, while others subordinated these in the interest of group solidarity.[10]

In PSA, carriers of the two civil service schemata sanctioned the legitimacy of equity rules of distributive justice. But the nature of an individual's contributions—education versus experience—was disputed. On the other hand, unions and fraternal organizations constantly reinforced the principle of equality. Hence two competing perceptions of merit provided two interpretations of fairness in PSA. As described in Chapter 8, recently hired analysts and some clerical employees used individual performance and expertise to define merit. The dominant rule of justice here was equity, which presumes that one is judged and rewarded in proportion to contributions. In contrast, civil servants (operators, permanent clerical employees, and permanent analysts) stressed a conception of merit based on job experience and seniority. This was reinforced by the union ideology, which promoted the values of parity and social solidarity. Civil servants and the unions therefore stressed simultaneously the principles of equity and equality.

Indeed, the strength of the civil service ideology in PSA's organizational culture encouraged the blanket use of a definition of justice as "fairness," a definition that emphasizes the equality principle of distribution. The view was, however, narrow enough to allow internal distinctions within and across ladders.[11] The operator unions provided protection to people in the group at the expense of employees from other groups. Despite the theoretical uniformity among civil servants, permanent employees from the non-operator ladders felt excluded, and were excluded, from many of the advantages granted to operators. In this sense, the operator ILM served another important latent social function in PSA. It provided the psychological frame that helped operators define themselves as "different" from other organizational members, even in a context that stressed equality under the law. This served to maintain the legitimacy of different treatment for others outside the operators' own moral community.[12] Operators were thus able to enjoy the advantages of a better treatment in PSA and at the same time espouse a discourse of equality and working-class solidarity.

Yet operators and others experienced the contradictions directly in their work. Grappling with them, they developed strong opinions about the nature of deserving. Negative feelings had to be directed somewhere if one was to maintain a sense of integrity. The last three sections of this chapter have shown how these strategies for coping contributed to create an organizational climate characterized by latent conflicts between different "types" of employees who, in theory, shared the same organizational mission.

Conclusion

Important transformations within PSA inevitably affected the way employees interacted. Each occupational group had specific stakes in the changes. Indeed, the dynamics identified in the last three chapters—around definitions of gender and race, educational status and experience, provisional and permanent civil service status—can be linked to a common thread. Each of the three pairs of social categories reflect exclusionary codes in the struggle to monopolize organizational resources (Murphy 1988).

Theories of exclusion in both the Weberian and the Marxist traditions suggest that rules—formal and informal, overt and covert—create practices whereby desirable social goods come to be monopolized by a few. These practices by necessity require the exclusion of the majority from access to the goods. "World images" provide standards for defining which groups or individuals are excluded or included. These exclusionary codes legitimate the privileged groups and help expand their power. Among examples of exclusionary codes Murphy includes education, race, ethnicity, gender, class origin, religion, and national identity. These are all criteria of membership of status groups and, as well, the sources of cultural codes of behavior. In contemporary postindustrial society some exclusionary codes are more acceptable than others. Yet they all contribute to create and legitimate social classifications that then are used to justify ranking and position in a stratified system.

Exclusionary codes are not permanent, of course; they change over time and across space. This is illustrated by the historical transformation of traditional exclusionary codes. For example, today many individuals question exclusion rules based on distinctions between men and women. While discrimination by sex has not yet disappeared, advances in this direction are a reminder of the precarious stability of social meanings. This has important implications for the present discussion. As codes of exclusion, indicators of merit such as credentials and experience carry within themselves the likelihood of suffering the same fate as previous codes:

> Exclusion based on credentials and experience seems today very different from previous forms of exclusion. They seem necessary and inevitable because they appear to be closely connected with efficiency. It must be remembered, however, that previous exclusionary codes appeared just as inevitable to contemporaries during long periods of history. (Murphy 1988:3)

The application of this type of macro analysis to the case of PSA can be instructive. PSA was experiencing a progressive shift in the locus of power from an operator-dominated agency to one where other groups were gaining importance. The latter were shaping their own claims with respect to distributive justice, based on their own definitions of merit. This transformation necessarily gave rise to grievances among members of two groups: those who were starting to gain power but still had no real voice, and those who felt they deserved the same treatment as operators because of their civil service status, but who remained in a disadvantaged position. Both groups were far from gaining the advantages or the clout of operators. But at the same time, feelings of uncertainty and fear were spreading among those who had the most to lose because of these changes, that is, the operators.

The situation was therefore one of tension. Those who were holding power would not give it up easily. Yet they were forced to address the issues emerging from the change process. At this point, for different reasons, clerical employees and analysts had a stronger sense of their claim, and even though they did not have sufficient power to exercise it, events in the right direction were taking place. For clerical employees the legitimacy of their claim came from their adherence to civil service ideology. The union's demand to enforce the system and to promote equal employment opportunities for women and minorities represented hope for them. The claim of provisional analysts came from a growing sense of relevance of their task in PSA. They believed that the educational credentials they brought did indeed contribute to increased productivity in PSA.

Reference groups—sets of employees sharing the same social attributes—gave PSA employees a means of assessing their experience. Unfavorable comparisons, perceived in a context of differential treatment and unequal outcomes, created resentments that pitted employees against each other dividing them by civil service status, by race, by sex, or by degree of experience and educational attainment.

These processes and the resulting ambiguities ultimately acted as important catalysts that shaped not only the social and demographic profile of each ladder but PSA's climate as a whole. Issues of distributive justice became a focal concern of the many employees who felt their sense of deserving threatened, or who saw officially sanctioned notions of merit and equality violated.

PART IV

REACTIONS:
THE SOCIAL CONTEXT
OF WORK ATTITUDES

Job Satisfaction

Commonsense interpretations of work, managerial ideologies pertaining to human resource practices, social science explanations of work attitudes—all take for granted that organizations are hierarchically stratified systems. Yet hierarchy generates invidious distinctions among people who are told, by institutions in the larger system, that all humans have an inherent dignity as equal human beings. So a contradiction arises, one that can not be ignored when studying attitudes in the workplace: employees' images of human worth and opportunity conflict with a reality of work organized around competition for rewards, a competition in which all employees do not meet on equal terms. In this book I have studied this contradiction by exploring the impact of the distribution of organizational rewards on the experience of work. This has meant using a conceptual framework that simultaneously focuses on the overall organizational picture and on the individual reactions of employees to their jobs. I have presented the pieces of this puzzle incrementally. Part II documented the existence of opportunity structures; Part III showed the link between opportunity and perceptions of work. Now, in Part IV, I intend to explore the link between perceptions and affective reactions to work. Chapters 10 and 11 take the last step of our analytical strategy, investigating the important relationship between opportunity and work attitudes. Chapter 12 summarizes the argument and places it within the broader literatures of stratification and organization theory.

This chapter focuses on the strong link between job perceptions and job satisfaction in PSA. It examines which factors—personal, organizational, objective, and subjective—influenced the job satisfaction of employees, considered as participants of specific career ladders. Consistent with previous research, most PSA employees surveyed expressed a relative degree of general satisfaction with their jobs. However, the more specific the questions became, the more employees began to express some degree of dissatisfaction.[1] The emerging picture was one of ambivalent reactions to their jobs, their supervisors, their co-workers, and the organization as a whole. The reactions were clearly patterned by career ladder. There were interesting differences among the ladders both in levels of satisfaction and in the effects of different job attributes on satisfaction.

Opportunity Structures and Job Satisfaction

What follows is a systematic study of the determinants of job satisfaction for each occupational group. The goal is to explore how the structural and institutional factors shaped employees' affective reactions to their jobs.[2] The following factors were considered:[3]

1. Individual and organizational attributes: race, sex, civil service status, education, seniority, and organizational level
2. The "objective" degree of opportunity experienced by each person: number of promotions, increments in salary from entry to present position, and the amount of training received
3. "Subjective" perceptions of opportunity: perceptions of personal discrimination and perceptions of external opportunities
4. "Subjective" perceptions of the job: social relations (chance to make friends, helpful co-workers); adequate resources (equipment, authority, supervision); comfort (pleasant physical conditions); advancement (good and fair promotion chances); job learning (opportunity to learn); and financial security (salary, benefits, and security).

Three separate regression models were used to isolate the direct impact of these factors on global job satisfaction. Results of the exercise suggested that individual attributes were relatively unimportant in explaining satisfaction variations within ladders. Some of them acquired more relevance, however, when considered as social attributes which helped interpret the opportunity context of work.

The models included the same factors studied in traditional job satisfaction research. The added value of this exercise lies in viewing the experience of work as embedded within larger opportunity structures. Indeed, distinctions in the opportunity of incumbents from the three career ladders provided light to understand how perceptions about the job influenced job satisfaction.

A number of individual and job characteristics had a direct impact on job satisfaction in all three models.[4] Table 15 summarizes how these factors were associated with employee job satisfaction in the three ladders.

Table 15. Factors associated with job satisfaction in PSA

Factors	Operators	Clerical employees	Analysts
Being a woman $(-)$[a]	n.a.		X
Discrimination $(-)$[a]		X	
Training			X
Job learning	X	X	
Good social relations			X
Availability of resources	X		X
Good advancement prospects			X
Financial resources	X		
R^2	54%	50%	70%

[a] The negative sign indicates that the relationship between this variable and job satisfaction was negative. This means that women were less satisfied than men and that employees who felt discriminated against were less satisfied than those who did not feel this way. All other variables were positively associated with job satisfaction.

The high R squares indicate that the factors included in the analysis were indeed relevant. These factors accounted for half of the variation in job satisfaction for the clerical group, a bit more than half for operators, and 70 percent for the analyst group. This last figure and the number of variables that were significant for this group (five) indicate that the generic model works best in explaining job satisfaction in the analyst ladder. On the other hand, only two variables were significant for the clerical ladder, and three for the operators. In both cases the variables explained about half the variation. This suggests that although the models did tap relevant factors for these groups, they missed other variables that affected job satisfaction.

The table also provides a visual statement of the importance of opportunity for understanding job satisfaction. Of the eight factors that affected the satisfaction of any particular group, five were directly linked to opportunity: feelings of discrimination, opportunities to learn, chance of receiving training, advancement, and financial security. In addition, two factors were indirectly linked to the opportunity of analysts: being a woman and the opportunity to develop social relations. The implications of these findings are the subject of the rest of this chapter.

Operators: Working in a Supportive Environment

"Working for PSA is great. It's the best job I have ever had. This job has been good for me and my family." This opinion, expressed by an entry-level operator in the survey, was widely shared among operators, who were quite satisfied with their jobs. As a group, operators expressed a greater degree of satisfaction than

Table 16. Employee job satisfaction by career ladder (%)

	Operator	Analyst	Clerical
Very satisfied	53	18	23
Somewhat satisfied	36	65	56
Not too satisfied	7	11	15
Not at all satisfied	4	6	6
Number of respondents	150	84	135

analysts or clerical employees. Fifty-three percent of the operators said they were very satisfied, compared with only 18 percent of the analysts and 23 percent of the clerical employees (Table 16).

The same pattern was clear in the responses to indirect measures of satisfaction (Table 17). About three-fourths of the operators claimed they would strongly recommend their job to a friend, would take the same job again if they had to start over, and would be very reluctant to quit their present job. These positive responses contrasted with those of clerical employees and analysts, who were more ambivalent. For example, 46 percent of both the analysts and the clerical employees said they would recommend the job to a good friend. The flip side of this is that whereas only 4 percent of the operators said they would discourage a friend from taking a job like theirs, a higher percentage of analysts and clerical employees (12 percent and 10 percent) said they would do so.

Table 17. Indirect measures of job satisfaction by career ladder (%)

	Operator	Analyst	Clerical
A. Respondents who would recommend the job to a friend			
Would strongly recommend	75	46	46
Would have doubts	21	42	44
Would not recommend	4	12	10
Number of respondents	151	83	135
B. Respondents who would take the same job again			
Would take the same job again	78	50	46
Would have second thoughts	17	39	47
Would not take the job	5	11	7
Number of respondents	151	84	136
C. Respondents willing to quit the present job			
Reluctant to quit	73	53	51
Indifferent	13	19	27
Glad to quit	14	28	22
Number of respondents	146	83	135

The column headed "Operators" in Table 18 provides the results of the analytical model of factors affecting operators' job satisfaction.[5] Table 19 describes all the variables included in the analysis. In brief, operator satisfaction was related to three perceptions about their jobs. Most important was that the job offered opportunity to learn; the second was that the job offered financial security, and the third was that it offered enough resources to perform well.

In contrast, several factors did *not* affect the satisfaction of operators in a significant way: the level of education operators had, the amount of time they had worked for PSA, where they were located in the hierarchy, and their race and ethnic backgrounds. This might be connected to the fact that, in general, the operator ladder was relatively homogeneous from a demographic point of view. Indeed, the 8849 operators who were members of this ladder at the time of the study were distributed among a very steep pyramid: 94 percent were entry-level operators, 15 percent were supervisors, and only 1 percent were managers. The largest proportion of operators (76 percent) were white, while only 17 percent were black and 7 percent were of other ethnic backgrounds. All operators were permanent employees and all were men at the time of the study. All in all, the

Table 18. Ordinary least squares regressions: determinants of job satisfaction for operators, clerical employees, and analysts

Dependent variable: job satisfaction	Parameter estimates[a]		
Independent variables[b]	Model 1 Operators	Model 2 Clerical employees	Model 3 Analysts
Intercept	−5.39	4.99	−4.59
Females	—	—	−2.79 (−2.50)**
Has felt discriminated against at work	—	−3.77 (−3.65)***	—
Training received	—	—	1.202 (2.16)**
Job offers opportunities to learn	2.79 (3.30)***	4.33 (4.18)***	—
Job offers adequate resources to do the work	0.62 (3.08)*	—	0.968 (3.36)***
Job offers financial security	0.80 (2.95)*	—	
Job offers opportunity to develop social relations		—	0.973 (2.21)**
Job offers opportunity for advancement		—	0.040 (2.20)**
R^2	0.54	0.48	0.70
Sample size	130	120	69

[a] Numbers in parentheses indicate T-statistics.
[b] Only statistically significant results are included. For a list and description of all variables used in the models see Table 19. For a discussion see the Appendix.
* Statistically significant at the 10% level.
** Statistically significant at the 5% level.
*** Statistically significant at the 1% level.

Table 19. Description of variables included in ordinary least squares models of job satisfaction for operators, clerical employees, and analysts[a]

Dependent variable: job satisfaction score (from −12 to 12) Independent variables	Definition
Individual characteristics	
Race/ethnicity	Dummy = 1, if respondent is minority employee
Education	Number of years of schooling
Sex	Dummy = 1, if respondent is female[b]
Seniority	Number of years in a city job
Civil service status	Dummy = 1, if provisional status[b]
Organizational level	Omitted variable: entry level
	Other levels: managerial,[c] supervisory, intermediate
Opportunity	
Objective measures	
Chances for promotion compared to others in sample	Score from −0.89 to 2.99[d]
Chances for salary increase compared to others	Score from −0.85 to 6.20
Chances for receiving training compared to others	Score from 0.47 to 2.10
Subjective measures	
Has felt discriminated against at work	Dummy = 1, if response is yes
Estimates it is easy to find a job in another agency	Dummy = 1, if response is yes
Perceived job dimensions	
Job offers opportunities to learn	Dummy = 1, if response is yes
Job is pleasant	Dummy = 1, if response is yes
Job offers opportunity to develop social relations	Score from 0 to 6, where 0 = not true at all, 6 = very true
Job offers opportunity for advancement	Score from 0 to 6, where 0 = not true at all, 6 = very true
Job offers adequate resources to do the work	Score from 0 to 9, where 0 = not true at all, 9 = very true
Job offers financial security	Score from 0 to 9, where 0 = not true at all, 9 = very true

[a] For full discussion of the logic of each model, its variables and their measurement see the Appendix.

[b] For analyst and clerical employee ladders only.

[c] For operator ladder only.

[d] Scores obtained from computations based on ordinary least squares (OLS) regression models reported in Table 4, described in the Appendix.

group was formed by blue-collar workers who entered PSA with low job skills and a high-school diploma. Many had fathers, uncles, brothers, or nephews in PSA. Parents and friends coached and prepared interested young people to take the civil service test. A middle-level operator made this statement in the survey, emphasizing how glad he felt about being part of PSA: "I am very grateful that I left the computer field [as a computer operator] eighteen years ago, thanks to the urging of my father." (His father had worked in PSA for thirty-seven years.) Parents encouraged their children to follow their steps because of the advantages the job offered over other blue-collar alternatives. After all, the operator position provided job security, a good compensation package, and prospects of upward mobility for individuals with low educational profiles. This represented an excellent job prospect for someone with a working-class background, and many operators had made a conscious decision to choose this line of work as a life investment.

Job candidates were willing to wait a long time to be hired after having taken the civil service entry test. They would work in other manual jobs, or in low-level clerical and technical jobs such as computer operator or clerk, patiently anticipating the time when they would be called from the operator list.[6] Sometimes they would get provisional clerical jobs while they waited. Some clerical males decided to take the operator test after they had entered PSA, intending to switch from the clerical to the operator career ladder. Although these switches did not represent the most traditional entry routes, they illustrate the high demand for the job among young men of working-class background. Demographic homogeneity thus was a critical social attribute of the operator job. In a quantitative model that focuses on differences, the social significance of this homogeneity gets lost.

The strongest factor affecting job satisfaction for operators was their perception that the job offered opportunities to improve their knowledge or work skills. Despite the harsh nature of the work, the operator ladder provided several attributes that made the job challenging. Two of them, discussed in previous chapters, were the automatic provision of formal training and participation in quality circles.

However, when operators were asked to report what their jobs predominantly meant to them, only 9 percent of the group defined it primarily as providing an opportunity for personal growth. Alternative definitions were that it provided an opportunity to earn a living and to build a career (Table 20).

Table 20. Primary meaning attached to current job, by career ladder (%)

	Operator	Analyst	Clerical
It provides opportunities to build a career	37	42	20
It provides opportunity to earn a living	54	·45	70
It provides opportunity for personal growth	9	13	10
Number of respondents	147	82	131

Most operators saw the job as a tool to earn a living. As one operator in the sample said, "The job itself is not a rewarding one. . . . The major reason for continuing this job is the twenty-year pension which will give me an opportunity to seek out new and more fulfilling employment at an age that I can truly benefit." This definition of the job itself did not diminish the importance job learning had for operators, however. This points to the instrumental nature of the operators' interest in learning. Opportunities to learn had for them a very pragmatic function. In their closed employment setting, promotion took place exclusively from within. Civil service tests were designed to measure knowledge learned on the job. Whatever operators observed and absorbed on the job would make or break their chances to move up. An ability to learn on the job was in fact the most important mechanism, perhaps the only objective one, to show who truly "deserved" to move to higher positions in this ladder.

Financial security was the second strongest factor affecting the satisfaction of operators. They saw their job as offering good pay, adequate fringe benefits, and job security. The more operators saw their jobs as offering these features, the happier they were with them.[7] This was consistent with the distribution shown in Table 20. Fifty-four percent of the operators said that their job primarily provided an opportunity to earn a living.

The importance of financial rewards is consistent with empirical evidence in previous studies of blue-collar workers. Extrinsic rewards play an important role in employees' assessments of their jobs largely because they offer access to other social rewards (Kalleberg 1975). Moreover, the operator job also offered the possibility of earning additional money. "You have three different shifts you can choose," one operator explained. "Many night workers have daytime jobs to supplement their income." Hence for many operators, the job was part of their long-term financial planning.

Finally, perceptions of adequate resources in the job were significant in explaining differences in operators' job satisfaction. This variable included two factors: having a competent supervisor who successfully promoted teamwork, and having enough help, equipment, and authority to do the job. The more operators felt their jobs offered these resources, the happier they felt with them. This is not surprising. The nature of operators' jobs required substantive technological support (well-maintained vehicles, for example). Moreover, the hierarchical chain of command required a high degree of social cohesion. The importance of a supportive supervisor seems only natural in a context where authority was tightly structured and effective communication was critical.

In sum, the primary determinants of satisfaction for operators were challenges on the job and a supportive organization. These sources of satisfaction reflected the operators' advantaged location within PSA.

Clerical Employees: A Prevailing Sense of Injustice

Clerical employees represented the office equivalent to the blue-collar operator group in PSA. Like operators, the approximately nine hundred members of this ladder were distributed, at the time of the study, in a steep pyramid (86 percent were entry-level employees, 13 percent were supervisors, and less than 0.5 percent were managers). Like operators, clerical employees entered PSA with relatively low job skills and relatively low educational attainment. Finally, while clerical employees participated in a career ladder that included open employment relationships, there was a constant push from unions to move it toward the closed mode. This benefited the civil servants in the ladder, whose employment relationship was already highly formalized.

Yet, in contrast to the operator homogeneity, there was considerable demographic variability in this ladder. Sixty-one percent of the clerical employees were permanent, 38 percent were provisionals and 1 percent were in noncompetitive titles. In terms of gender, 67 percent of the clerical employees were female. In terms of race, 57 percent were people of color (46 percent black and 11 percent of other ethnic backgrounds).

Only 23 percent of the clerical respondents said they were very satisfied with their jobs, while 56 percent said they were somewhat satisfied and 21 percent expressed dissatisfaction (Table 16). Other feelings expressed by this group suggested even more ambivalence toward the job. Only about half of the clerical respondents said they would recommend their job to a friend or that they would take the same job again were they to start over. Most of the rest would hesitate to recommend the job or have second thoughts about taking it again. Moreover, about half the group said they would either be glad to quit their jobs (22 percent) or would feel indifferent doing so (27 percent). These numbers offer a sharp contrast with those for operators (Table 17).

The multivariate analysis for this group indicated that the global satisfaction of clerical employees was influenced by only two perceived job factors (Table 18). These two alone, however, explained almost half of the variation in job satisfaction within this ladder. The factors were the opportunity to learn on the job and the experience of personal discrimination. Interestingly enough, both related to opportunity.

As with the operator group, personal characteristics were not significant for this group. Whether clerical employees were male or female, minority or nonminority, or permanent or provisional had no direct effect on their satisfaction. Neither did education, years spent in PSA, or organizational level. Instead, those clerical employees who felt that the job provided opportunities to learn were happier than those who felt they would learn nothing. This is not surprising. As in the operator ladder, learning on the job was the way to move up. In this ladder, indeed, experience could replace educational attainment as the critical human capital component.

The instrumental nature of job learning is evidenced again in the clerical employees' responses to what their jobs represented (Table 20). Only 10 percent defined the job as primarily providing an opportunity for personal growth. Like operators, clerical employees had expectations about what their employment would offer them. Working for the municipal government would provide the desired job security in an environment characterized by high competition for both private and public employment. Moreover, it would provide an environment in which to learn and, hopefully, progress within the system. A provisional shop clerk noted,

> I took the job for mental stimulation and other reasons. PSA being a government agency have somewhat possibility of upward mobility and good benefits. . . . With the erratic trend in employment and the constant failure of private business, this job does provide some stability . . . but I definitely do not want to stagnate myself.

The last sentence reflects the degree of realism that clerical employees had about the opportunities they were offered in PSA. The job was relatively good, but it was not a job that would take them to high places, nor was it one that would provide them with great challenges.

Indeed, even those clerical employees who aspired to move up would always be at a disadvantage compared to other co-workers in the same agency. The comments made by the clerical supervisor in an earlier chapter about the differences between her career trajectory and that of a fellow operator supervisor seem relevant here. In a context where civil service should guarantee equal opportunity based on merit, the deck seemed to be highly stacked against the clerical group. When asked in the survey to offer suggestions about their work, a permanent shop clerk made this request: "Enable the clerical staff in this agency, especially field personnel, to work with more latitude for promotions and equity in pay."

Indeed, soon after entering the agency, clerical employees realized that their job security was not accompanied by good prospects. A provisional office associate expressed her concern:

> Before becoming an employee of the City of————I was under the impression that a city job was one of the best places for employment. Being here for the past year, I now know working for the city is no better than private industry. Chances for promotion and/or money increase for me would come more easily in private industry.

This disenchantment points to a second factor affecting job satisfaction in the clerical ladder. Clerical employees who felt discriminated against in PSA were significantly more dissatisfied than those who didn't. In fact, as reported in a previous chapter, one-third of the clerical group claimed they had been discriminated against in PSA (in contrast to only 14 percent of the operators and 28 percent of the analysts). Moreover, although analysts reported a similar percentage, discrimination did not affect their satisfaction. The distinction explored earlier, concerning how obstacles for promotion were personally experienced by members of the two groups may shed some light here. While more analysts reported seeing particularistic criteria as the main reason for promotion in their unit, fewer of them reported it as a personal obstacle to their individual mobility. On the other hand, more clerical employees viewed this as a factor that affected them personally. Analysts tended to portray obstacles in terms of favoritism toward others. They mentioned nepotism, political patronage, and good connections as important reasons for promotion in their units. Clerical employees, on the other hand, tended to describe these obstacles in terms of discrimination toward themselves, by race, sex, age, appearance, and function (e.g., whether one was an operator or not).

To explore how characteristic these feelings of discrimination were, I looked at the distribution by gender and race of employees across occupational groups. Clerical employees always represented the largest group who felt discriminated against, regardless of sex and race. For example, more nonminority employees in the clerical ladder than in the analyst or operator ladders expressed having been discriminated against. Comparing all minority employees, male and female, in all ladders, the results were the same: more clerical employees felt discriminated against. There was something specific to this ladder that created a strong sense of discrimination. This in turn affected employee satisfaction.

Descriptions of discriminatory actions mentioned by at least two or more respondents in the survey shed light on the effect of discrimination on the work experience of clerical employees. I have classified them in three general categories, based on answers to an open ended question. Many statements are given verbatim.

1. *Unfair treatment in human resources practices*: there are preferences in job assignments, in equipment assignments, in schedule assignments, and in hiring; there are differential standards of evaluation; there are no promotions, or there is a lack of opportunities for some employees; there are no pay raises; there are no merit increases.

2. *Generic mistreatment*: treatment of clerical employees conveys arrogance in power and position; opinions and suggestions of some persons are ignored or not even asked for; some employees are forced to transfer; employees receive little support to use opportunities when they exist.

3. *Direct sexism and racism*: opportunities for blacks and women are blocked; inferior salaries are given for similar jobs (women are paid less); secretaries are

expected to serve coffee; sexual harassment; sexual and ethnic jokes; derogatory or sexist name-calling (baby, girl, honey, nigger); women are assigned to non-core, "support" jobs.

This last set points directly to the feeling that low opportunity was partly a consequence of direct racist and sexist interactions. Gender and race, as *demographic* characteristics, did not themselves explain the sense of discrimination in the ladder, nor were they significant determinants of job satisfaction. But their social significance cannot be denied. As illustrated in earlier chapters, gender and race were relevant structural attributes of the clerical career ladder as much as they were individual attributes of employees. Filled predominantly by women and people of color, the ladder at the same time offered fewer opportunities for promotion, compensation, and job challenge than the other ladders. In fact, this ladder provided a perfect example of gender and racial segregation at work.

The notions of status closure and status composition are helpful here. They show the indirect but critical role gender and race played in shaping employee feelings. Clerical employees' sensitivity to discrimination and its impact on satisfaction may be linked to them. The demographic composition of this ladder suggests the latent use of gender and race to determine who would have access to many of these jobs. This is an example of status closure. A large number of job incumbents were women and people of color as a consequence of this process. At the same time, the jobs were characterized as low in quality and opportunity. The demographic composition that characterized this group of jobs thus became directly associated with the social evaluation of the jobs' worth in the organization. This is a consequence of status composition. Tomaskovic-Devey clarifies this pervasive effect as follows:

> Racial and gender segregation are intertwined with the very fabric of work, influencing not only the allocation of people to jobs but the character of jobs and workplaces themselves. *They are organizational processes independent of the race or sex of the individuals who populate work places.* (1993:4, emphasis added)

Individuals located in this ladder—men or women, African-American or white—experienced a work reality tainted by the devalued character of their jobs. This pervasive feature of the ladder clearly affected their work life, although the effect was hard to measure.

As elsewhere, what really mattered about race and gender in the clerical ladder was not so much the physical traits as the socially constructed categories. Both status closure and status composition contributed to promote the processes of classification, ranking, and staffing of the slots in the stratified system of PSA.[8] A basic weakness of the traditional literature on job satisfaction may be its blindness toward the existence of these processes and their indirect but fundamental effect on the work experience.

To the extent that these dynamics played a role in clerical attitudes, the experience of being wronged may have become even stronger because it occurred in a group that endorsed the civil service system. After all, civil service ideology supposes a certain degree of fairness in the treatment of individuals with similar backgrounds, for example clerical employees and operators. So when clerical employees saw that they were receiving less than a just reward for their efforts, they felt wronged.[9] Since clerical employees saw themselves at a comparative disadvantage in terms of most dimensions of the job, furthermore, they may have interpreted being wronged as a sign of discrimination both at a personal and at a collective level.

The sense of injustice that marked the work experience of clerical employees profoundly affected their job satisfaction and work morale. It also made them highly sensitive to issues of procedural, distributive, and interactive justice. These feelings directly mirrored the position clerical employees occupied in PSA and were in direct contrast to what operators experienced. What feels fair and just to those holding (and benefiting from) the dominant version of reality may seem unjust to those holding marginal versions of the same reality. Homans makes this point. "Injustice", he says, is the curse of the weak not the strong; for the strong, the more powerful, just because they are that, can successfully insist on getting what they think they deserve" (Homans 1976:232). So the sense of injustice that clerical employees felt was very much tied to socially constructed definitions of organizational reality.

Analysts: Carving Their Path amid Uncertainty

Analyst jobs were staffed by white-collar workers who entered PSA with relatively good job skills. Only about one-third of this group were permanent employees. The other two-thirds were provisional employees, half of whom were assigned to noncompetitive titles. Since provisionals had educational credentials, these jobs had generally favorable salaries and promotional opportunities. Moreover, the pyramidal distribution was slightly flatter than the other two ladders. Of the 176 members of the ladder, 77 percent were entry-level employees, 20 percent were supervisors, and 2 percent were managers.

A bit over two-thirds of the analysts (65 percent) said they were only "somewhat" satisfied with their jobs, compared with 18 percent who were very satisfied and 17 percent who were dissatisfied (Table 16). This distribution is consistent with the fact that more than half of them claimed they would either hesitate or refuse to recommend their job to a friend (Table 17). Also, exactly half of the analysts said they would either have second thoughts about taking the same job again or not take it again. Finally, half of them claimed they would feel either indifferent or glad about quitting their job. These numbers suggest that the analyst group felt at best ambivalent about their jobs.

This group had the greatest social diversity among the three ladders studied. For example, 34 percent of employees in this ladder were female and 66 percent were male. With respect to ethnic composition, 61 percent were white, 25 percent were black, and 14 percent were of other ethnic backgrounds. This may help explain why, of the three ladders, this was the only one where one individual characteristic—gender—made a difference in how satisfied employees were. The high degree of uncertainty in the ladder set the scene for comparisons among individuals and groups. Indeed, female analysts were significantly less satisfied than male analysts (see Table 18). I will return to this point after exploring the other four factors, which also strongly influenced the job satisfaction of this group. In order of importance, these were the availability of training programs, the perception of good social relations on the job, the perceived availability of resources to do their jobs, and perceived advancement opportunities.

Most of these job dimensions can be directly related to this group's need to "administer" their personal conditions for success. This ladder was characterized by the absence of formalized rules typical of closed labor markets. The analyst ladder was open to outsiders, and the uncertainty of career movement was great. Hence, analysts were aware of the need to engage in a certain amount of "networking" and "politicking." They had to rely heavily on personal contacts and individual negotiation to get what they wanted. This reality influenced the degree of importance they gave to certain job attributes.

In contrast to both clerical employees and operators, analysts did not feel any better or worse because of the opportunities to learn offered by the job. The instrumental function that job learning played in the civil service context was replaced in this ladder by the power of educational credentials. However, another important job challenge factor was significant and positively related to analysts' satisfaction: the higher the chances for participation in training programs at PSA, the more satisfied analysts felt with their job.

Like job learning for those in the closed employment settings, formal training provided a career function for members of the analyst ladder. Analysts were eligible to participate in management training programs. These represented as much an opportunity to network as an opportunity to learn. An analyst's participation in one of these programs could make him or her more visible to high-ranking individuals around the agency. In the same way, both managerial training and a general orientation program (designed initially for analysts only) may have represented a career investment for those who participated. Both provided a global overview of PSA, which employees would find hard to obtain on their own.

Positive social relations in the job were another important determinant of the analysts' satisfaction. This factor included perceptions about the chance to make friends on the job and about the friendliness and helpfulness of co-workers. The more positive the social relations were, the more satisfied analysts were. This finding contradicts previous claims in the literature about the lack of interest in social relations among professional/technical employees (Campbell, Converse, and Rodgers 1976). It does, however, seem consistent in the context of the analyst career ladder. Social relations were helpful to establish networks at work. As documented in a previous chapter, of all analysts who reported feeling they had some control over their opportunities, one-fifth indicated that they could improve their opportunities by being political.[10] Moreover, one-third of the entire analyst sample said that the main reason for promotion in their career ladder was some form of favoritism.[11] Forms of particularism mentioned in the survey were nepotism, political patronage, and having the right connections. Specific examples of right connections included "having pull," "departmental clout," "friendships," "knowing the right person," "who you know," "belonging to a clique," "belonging to an inner circle," "having social ties," "brownnosing," and "being liked by someone." It is not surprising that perceptions of social relations were a predictor of the analysts' job satisfaction.

The third perceived job factor that explained analysts' degree of satisfaction was advancement prospects. This job attribute included both the availability of good chances and the perception that promotions were handled fairly. The more promotion chances were perceived as available and fair, the more satisfied analysts were. As a group, analysts had strong career aspirations in PSA, in city government, or in some cases in the private sector. This was consistent with the fact that a bit more than two-fifths of this group saw their jobs as opportunities to build careers, rather than opportunities to earn a living or for personal growth (Table 20). Any obstacle to their career goals would clearly affect their satisfaction. The complaints about the absence of promotional opportunities in PSA conveys a work environment that was not as friendly as analysts would have wanted.

The analysts' level of satisfaction was also affected by their perceptions about the availability of resources provided in the job. This is consistent with empirical studies that have suggested the importance of job scope for employees in general and for professional/technical employees in particular (Hackman and Lawler 1971; Campbell, Converse, and Rodgers 1976). Moreover, given the level of interdependency required to do analytical work, it is not surprising that analysts would give importance to the quality of supervision, assistance, equipment, and authority.

Finally, despite the fact that this ladder was less sex-segregated than the clerical and operator ladders, female analysts were significantly less satisfied than male analysts. There were fewer females than males in the ladder, and they occupied lower positions. These facts do not suffice to explain the women's dissatisfaction, however. The clerical ladder had a similar if not an ever more skewed distribution, yet, gender differences there were not significant. Something more specific to this ladder triggered the difference.

Some female analysts expressed direct and open dissatisfaction about their prospects of promotion and compensation, especially when they compared them with those of their male counterparts. The nature of analytical work itself may have sensitized them to the real differences between employment contracts for men and for women in a male-dominated agency. Analysts manipulated confidential information that included salary and promotion data. It was therefore easier for them to see the consequences of the patterns of opportunity at work. An illustration of this is the analyst who reported pay inequities among female managerial analysts in the Women's Advisory Committee meeting described in Chapter 7.

Both their work and their participation in managerial training gave analysts an opportunity to interact more directly with managers. This made them more sensitive to the managerial conditions of employment. Several characteristics of PSA's managerial group were a constant reminder to women analysts of their disadvantages vis-à-vis their male counterparts. First, most PSA managers belonged to the male-dominated operator career ladder; second, women did not have access to some of the line managerial positions located in the operating core; third, women managers were at a financial disadvantage compared to male managers. The analysis of managerial salaries reported earlier confirms that the disadvantages were real. Women managers earned an average of $6,368 less per year than male managers.[12] This figure did not include the loss associated with being a non-operator manager—an additional sum of $9,817—which affected directly all women, since they were excluded from operator jobs. In assessing their future prospects, female analysts had only to see the scarcity of women managers to predict their own futures. Given the male-dominated environment in PSA, as well as the predominance of men in the upper echelons of the agency, women were well aware that their probabilities of success were low.

Female analysts experienced this constrained opportunity structure in two ways. First, like their male counterparts, they came with high career expectations. When they did not find opportunities available through the formal structure, they were forced to rely heavily on mentoring and networking. Second, for these women, finding mentors in a predominantly male-dominated agency was a difficult and risky undertaking. Mentoring itself had the potential of becoming an asymmetric and therefore negative relationship. Studies have shown that the probability of this happening is greater when the dynamics are complicated by the type of interactions which develop in the cross-gender ties of a male-dominated network (Hill and Kamprath 1991). In this sense women analysts' sensitivity may have been heightened by a workplace where they were usually in a numerical minority. Often at the upper levels of management or in the field, they were tokens, defined as "one of a kind among many of another kind" (Kanter 1977). Therefore, in addition to the uncertainty associated with the lack of formalization of opportunity, they also experienced decreased opportunities because of social dynamics stemming from proportions and numbers.

To recap, whether one is a woman (in a male-dominated agency), whether one can participate in training (usually managerial in nature), whether one perceives social relations as good (for networking), whether resources are available for the job, and whether one sees a chance for promotion (in a context where the chance seems slim)—all these factors had a direct impact on analysts' satisfaction. All pointed to the importance of social context in general and of opportunity in particular.

The Importance of Opportunity

The impact of opportunity on job satisfaction was not uniform across ladders, yet its presence was constant. Job challenge was a significant determinant of job satisfaction for the three groups. Advancement prospects were important for the analyst group, although financial security was not. Inversely, financial security was important for the operators, while advancement was not. Finally, neither advancement nor financial security was significant in explaining the satisfaction of clerical employees, but a sense of discrimination was.

One could argue that these findings highlight the role of the socio-economic status of employees, the expectations associated with that status, and the values pertinent to each occupation. One could also assume that employees acquire these expectations and values even before entering the organization. This is partially true. Expectations however, must be understood against the background of the structural context in which the images of opportunity were enacted. The operator ladder guaranteed a job that combined a good salary, good benefits (pension/retirement plans), and job security, the three indicators of compensation. Moreover, in this ladder financial factors were relatively independent of upward movement or accumulation of educational capital. Indeed, the clue to the lack of interest in advancement in the operator group may be their understanding that, even if they chose not to move up the ladder, their financial rewards would still increase over time. In other words, the operator ladder represented a unique arena where increases in salary were not exclusively associated with significant increases in status. In this context, promotion became less important. Furthermore, recall the operators' stance with respect to their promotion opportunities, described in Chapter 4. They were convinced that they had high mobility chances, but at a personal level they did not expect to move up soon. This way of protecting their personal integrity may also help explain why promotion did not affect operators' satisfaction.

In contrast, for analysts, good pay was associated with their credentials or specialized skills. However, after the original negotiation at placement, it could only be significantly enhanced by new changes in status. Analysts needed and wanted an opportunity to achieve their career ambitions. This was consistent with their professional orientation, as well as a way to improve their financial prospects. So in a situation of high uncertainty about future prospects, the chances for promotion took priority in their job assessment.

Finally, clerical employees expressed dissatisfaction with respect to their financial security and their advancement prospects. Yet neither of the two factors had an effect on their global job satisfaction. Like operators, clerical employees had some of their initial expectations of financial security and job mobility met in city employment. But the different treatment they received compared to operators contradicted their expectations of equal treatment. This was particularly evident in the discrepancies in the salary structures of the ladders. The sense of injustice was so strong that the power of discrimination overshadowed the impact of specific extrinsic rewards in the clerical employees' assessment.

The Opportunity Nature of Job Challenge

Job challenge affected the satisfaction of all three groups. *Job learning* (a subjectively perceived job attribute) was significant for the two occupational groups whose work was performed according to the bureaucratic mode. *Training received* (an objective attribute) was important for analysts. Those who reported having one or the other attribute were significantly more satisfied than those who reported not having either. The case of PSA confirms the importance of this job dimension, which has been previously reported in the traditional literature. But there is an interesting twist in the PSA findings. Although there was a strong link between job challenge and job satisfaction for all groups, none of the groups defined the job primarily as an opportunity for personal growth. The large majority of operators and clerical employees candidly indicated that the job represented for them an opportunity to earn a living. For most analysts, it represented an opportunity to build a career. This suggests that job challenge as an intrinsic reward may be linked to the role intrinsic rewards play in opening future opportunities for extrinsic rewards (advancement and better salaries).

Indeed, in hierarchical work systems extrinsic and intrinsic rewards are interdependent. The tendency to prefer jobs that are challenging or that offer training is surely related to the requirements placed on employees to attain organizational success in a stratified context. In most pyramidal organizations, upward movement, as a sign of success, is usually tied to better compensation. A job that offers opportunities to learn more also offers the opportunities for the employee to become more competitive and thus earn more money.

Stratification theorists argue that in contemporary organizations it is hard to find job challenge as a prize independent of other rewards associated with higher status. For example, Rosenbaum's findings support the notion that organizations often make status a prerequisite for the pursuit of other rewards:

> Organizational psychologists have noted that employees seek many kinds of personal fulfillment from their work . . . such as variety, autonomy, challenge, and interpersonal influence. . . . However, the organizational structure tends to make them all contingent upon status advancement. Job evaluation systems formalize this relationship by using these features of jobs as factors in the determination of job pay and job status. (Rosenbaum 1983:302)

Rosenbaum further argues that job analysts often consider job challenge only as a "compensable factor" that increases job status. As a consequence, if employees want job challenge they must seek job status, even if status does not interest them. The consistency in the patterns of distribution of promotions, salary increases, and training programs, presented in earlier chapters, suggests that this was indeed the case in PSA.

The instrumental function of job challenge may be intensified in public employment, and specifically when there are differences in civil service enforcement. An illustration is the direct link observed earlier between an analyst's training and the networking required to succeed. In the case of permanent employees, a fully enforced civil service system transforms skills acquired on the job and personal development into effective investments for moving up the ladder. The broad definition of merit endorsed by the civil service promises equal opportunities to compete for desired jobs. A job that offers opportunities to learn can replace the "schooling" required to be competitive, especially in the case of individuals who do not have adequate credentials to bargain for competitive job rewards. Opportunity to learn was thus, in PSA, a desirable characteristic of the job, because it was essential for success. As evidence, many operators and clerical employees who lacked educational credentials had been able to move up into managerial positions.

The job redesign literature has linked the high value employees place on job challenge to an inherent, universal need for human development. In this tradition, employees seek challenge as an intrinsic reward. The PSA context suggests, however, that job challenge must also be associated with the way workplace learning leads to promotions and increased compensation.

The Role of Individual Attributes

The list in Table 15 presents only those factors that were significant in explaining variations in job satisfaction. Other factors not included in that list may add important information. With the exception of the female analysts, individual attributes made no difference in the level of satisfaction of PSA employees. Race, civil service status, education, seniority, and organizational level did not affect the satisfaction of any employees who participated in the study. This finding contrasts with the recent emphasis placed by the literature on individual characteristics. Yet it is entirely consistent within the organizational context of PSA. The most significant social differences affecting employee conditions of employment occurred across ladders rather than within ladders.

Moreover, some social psychology scholars have suggested that the effect of individual and personality factors on work attitudes varies according to whether situations are strong or weak (Weiss and Adler 1984). Strong situations refer to instances where well-recognized and widely accepted rules of conduct direct behavior. In these cases, individual variability is low and will have little predictive value. In contrast, weak situations, or those instances which are not uniformly encoded, do not generate uniform expectancies. Where weak situations predominate, the impact of individual differences will be significant. Differences in civil service enforcement created both strong and weak situations in PSA. This is helpful to understand why the only significant individual variable appeared where it did: in the analyst model. The least structured career ladder was the one where women were significantly less satisfied than men. The open employment mode typical of the staffing practices in the analytical ladder represents undoubtedly a weak situation, in contrast to the clearly defined civil service contexts of the other two ladders.

The important point, however, is that the weak/strong characterization is clearly linked to differences in the application of the rules, which in turn resulted in unequal opportunity outcomes. The meaning of the weak/strong characterization derived, in the particular case of PSA, from the degree of formalization of civil service rules. This affected not only expectancies but also the objective aspects of the ladder, for example the variability of the ladder's demographic composition or the patterns of opportunity employees encountered there. This points to an observation that Kalleberg and Griffin made in their empirical study of job satisfaction (1978). The linkage between individual characteristics (such as race, sex, and age) and reactions to work is mediated by an employee's position in an organizational labor market with particular employment characteristics. But an emphasis on gender and racial inequality typical of these ladders has only recently become a research interest for work scholars.[13] For example, in the organizational behavior literature there has been a resurgence of interest in the indirect and more complex links between job satisfaction, individual factors, and opportunities (Cranny, Smith, and Stone 1992). In a provocative article on this topic, Schneider, Gunnarson, and Wheeler (1992) suggest that it is possible that sex, age, and race are not the key variables. Instead, a better predictor of job satisfaction may be "the availability of opportunities mediated differently in different situations because of an individual's sex, age, or race" (1992:60). This represents an encouraging insight which deserves further exploration. The authors go on to explain these differences as a function of individual instances of direct discrimination: "individuals of different sexes, age groups, or races may be offered varying opportunities *because of prejudiced notions about what a particular "type" of person is capable of*"(1992:60, emphasis added).

It is true that prejudice may affect the opportunity of specific individuals and, through this, their satisfaction. But the reality is even more complex. Prejudiced notions may have become institutionalized through the rules that shape organizational labor markets in a stratified work system. This may play an additional role in the formation of work attitudes.

Tomaskovic-Devey suggests, for example, that structural factors such as job segregation help explain why dissatisfaction with work tends to be high among blacks, particularly relative to white women. Some of the reasons he proposes are that African-American workers are more closely supervised because of their race, that the average black worker is formally better qualified for his or her job than the white worker next to him or her,[14] and that most blacks work in jobs in which the majority of the co-workers are white.

Individual traits such as gender, race, and age have not been conceptualized as social categories that have particular meanings in stratified workplaces. This may help explain why the results of traditional studies linking them to job satisfaction have been neither consistent nor decisive (Schneider, Gunnarson, and Wheeler 1992; Mustari 1992). I will return to this discussion in the next chapter. Here I want to give some further discussion to the findings about the impact of gender on job satisfaction.

There are several ways in which gender, race, and other ascribed traits can have a real effect on the experience of work. Empirical studies have documented that being a woman can affect the placement of an individual in specific career ladders. In turn, her position in certain ladders and not others will affect factors such as her compensation, her opportunity to develop a successful career, and the direction that such a career will take (Kanter 1977; Roos and Reskin 1984; Haberfeld 1992; DiPrete 1989). Examples of similar dynamics in PSA were the absence of women in the operator career ladder, the small number of women in the upper levels of the analytical ladder, and the overrepresentation of women in the clerical career ladder.

That gender had no significant effect on the job satisfaction of clerical employees but had a critical effect for employees in the analytical ladder is related precisely to these institutional components of opportunity. Given an organizational labor market that was predominantly female and was low in opportunity, gender and racial discrimination came to be institutionalized in the clerical jobs themselves. In this ladder everyone—both the few men and all the women incumbents—experienced the consequences of the patterned distribution of "bad" jobs to certain "types" of employees, regardless of their gender or their color. But the clerical employees' strong sense of discrimination had much to do with the demographic composition of the ladder and its association with inferior work conditions and levels of opportunity. This link to race and gender, however, did not emerge in the quantitative model.

Indeed, personal attributes were less important than the perceived job characteristics in explaining general employee job satisfaction. This, however, is insufficient reason to disregard the social significance of ascribed attributes such as sex or race and achieved attributes such as civil service and education in shaping employees' cognitive maps. We have seen in earlier chapters how being a woman or a member of a minority, or being a provisional or a permanent employee, or even being educated or not, influenced employees' views of their job. Yet these attributes did so less as individual traits and more as categories that helped defined the social nature of the ladder. In other words, far from being insignificant or irrelevant from a substantive point of view, these individual attributes were embedded within the employee's participation in the career ladder. Quantitative models fail to capture these subtleties of organizational life.

Conclusion

The most accepted models of job satisfaction are based on the notion of the "person-environment fit."[15] In this view,

> the perceived characteristics of the job are evaluated in relation to the person's frame of reference, which in turn is shaped by the available alternatives, by expectations, by experience, and by the person's general adaptation level. The interrelationships of person variables (individual capacities, experience, values) and environment variables (objective factors of the job, available alternatives) are seen as the major predictors of satisfaction and performance as well. (Dawis 1992:73)

This summarizes the state of the art in the field, but it also delineates the basic debate that characterizes the study of job satisfaction: which are ultimately more important, individual or environmental factors? Numerous studies using different assumptions, methodologies, and measurements have created more questions than answers in an effort to resolve this debate.[16]

In the absence of a comprehensive model, the pendulum keeps swinging between individual and environmental factors. The job redesign school's emphasis on the impact of the structural context gained considerable ground in the seventies and early eighties. In the late eighties the pendulum started to swing back toward the dispositional perspective (Staw, Bell, and Clausen 1986). The analysis presented here suggests that the solution to the debate lies, in an integration of insights provided by both sides.

In PSA's stratified system, social comparisons were largely based on an objectively unequal distribution of resources. This reality affected an individual's entire experience of work, including psychological tendencies, personal traits, and everyday acts. Employees entering the organization found a given job structure and its particular dynamics waiting for them, and to these they had to respond. They also brought with them their personal and social baggage, which helped them interpret, evaluate, and incorporate into their individual universe the organizational world they found. Personal and job attributes, however, were perceived from the specific structural position in a career ladder. It was the ladder that determined the quality of the employment relationship. It guided the social interactions of employees, and it influenced their reactions to organizational life.

As we have seen in this chapter, operators' satisfaction with their work was influenced by a supportive environment. In contrast, the unsupportive work conditions in the clerical ladder led to overpowering feelings of injustice. Finally, analysts' job attitudes were linked to their need to carve a path through the uncertainty of an open employment environment. We are ready now to explore, in Chapter 11, how the documented differences in job satisfaction helped members of the career ladders address the cognitive dissonance produced by the experience of inequality in the face of the strong ideology of equal opportunity.

Relative Deprivation, Self-Evaluation, and Work Attitudes

Thus far, PSA's story illustrates how affective reactions in the workplace are largely influenced by opportunity dynamics. Employees are sensitive to the organizational process through which some of them are included in "circles of advantage" while others are excluded. PSA employees tried to make sense of this uneven reward competition. They struggled to reconcile it with beliefs about equality, opportunity, and merit. Principles of distributive justice helped justify or put into question the way opportunity affected them directly. It will become increasingly clear in this chapter that these images also helped people rationalize the consequences of patterned opportunity. This allowed them to reassert their sense of integrity, or to return some rationality to their world in the midst of the contradiction.

The nature of workplace attitudes is *relational*. This chapter explores the interdependencies involved in shaping them. It compares the differences in job satisfaction *across* ladders and relates them to the different employment modes participants espoused. A multivariate model of job satisfaction for the entire employee sample—differentiated according to their participation in open or closed employment settings—provides evidence of the strength and significance of differences in satisfaction across subgroups.[1] This model evaluates the statistical significance of the variations in employee satisfaction associated *exclusively* with employee membership in a particular subgroup, independent of how employees perceived other relevant dimensions of their job.[2]

The goal of the exercise was to verify whether the differences in satisfaction among employees who participated in different opportunity structures were significant, independent of individual perceptions of job attributes.[3] The model also provided evidence of the direction of these differences, thus clarifying if all groups were indeed less satisfied than operators, once other factors were

182

Table 21. Ordinary least squares regression: determinants of job satisfaction for all employees

Dependent variable: job satisfaction score Independent variables	Parameter estimates[a]	
Intercept	-2.69	(-1.62)
Permanent analysts	-2.36	(-2.60)*
Provisional analysts	-1.85	(-2.26)**
Permanent clerical employees	-1.33	(-1.66)
Provisional clerical employees	-1.69	(-1.95)**
Job complexity[b]	0.20	(0.03)
Has felt discriminated against at work	-1.38	(-2.35)**
Job offers opportunities to learn	3.26	(5.77)***
Job offers adequate resources to perform the job	0.68	(3.30)***
Job offers opportunity to develop social relations	0.68	(4.90)***
Job offers opportunity for advancement	0.31	(1.94)**
R^2	0.51	
Sample size	330	

Source: Survey and personnel files.
[a] Numbers in parentheses indicate T-Statistics.
[b] Dummy = 1 if low complexity. For full explanation see the Appendix.
* Statistically significant at the 10% level.
** Statistically significant at the 5% level.
*** Statistically significant at the 1% level.

accounted for. To stress the qualitative importance of the degree of enforcement of civil service, the model differentiated employee participation in five types of career ladder membership: operators (all were permanent), permanent clerical employees, permanent analysts, provisional clerical employees, and provisional analysts.[4] Table 21 presents the results of this quantitative analysis.

The findings about differences in satisfaction are shown in the diagram below. There were no significant differences in global satisfaction between operators and permanent clerical employees.[5] The other three subgroups in the open ladders were, in contrast, significantly less satisfied than operators.[6] Ranking these differences, permanent analysts were the most dissatisfied group, followed by provisional analysts, and then by provisional clerical employees.[7]

The clue to these findings lies in the distinction theorists of relative deprivation make between two negative affective reactions: dissatisfaction and resent-

Operators ⟶	Most satisfied group
Other groups compared with operators:	
Permanent clerical employees ⟶	No difference in satisfaction
Provisional clerical employees ⟶	Slightly less satisfied
Provisional analysts ⟶	Even less satisfied
Permanent analysts ⟶	Least Satisfied

ment. Even though the two feelings tend to go together, they are not the same. A person can feel either dissatisfied, resentful, or both. Dissatisfaction relates to the factual dislike of a given situation. Resentment is a counterfactual emotion (similar to frustration, regret, indignation, grief, and envy). It arises when a person compares reality with a favored alternative, one that he or she had failed to reach but could easily imagine reaching. This emotion implies, therefore, an accusation of wrongdoing (Folger 1987). Perhaps permanent clerical employees were dissatisfied with specific aspects of the job and resentful about their opportunity package. But this may not have translated into a global sense of dissatisfaction with their job. Subtle differences characterizing the affective reactions of each group must be explored. The critical questions to be answered in this chapter are therefore:

- why, if clerical employees had the lowest opportunities and the strongest sense of injustice, was their global satisfaction relatively equivalent to that of operators, once other factors were controlled for?
- what was common to the three groups whose members were more dissatisfied than operator and clerical civil servants?
- why were permanent analysts the most dissatisfied group?

The stratified social context of PSA provides invaluable information to answer these questions.

The Possible Impact of Human Capital

Occupational status and education are two of the most frequently studied variables in the literature on work attitudes (Weaver 1980; Hopkins 1983). Following traditional interpretations, one could argue that operators were more satisfied as a function of their lower educational attainment and that analysts were less satisfied because of their higher attainment. Indeed, one could accept at face value the proposition that education and occupation explain some of the cross-ladder differences in job satisfaction. But this proposition is not entirely convincing because there was also a difference in satisfaction between operators and clerical *provisionals*. In addition, this reasoning would have predicted the most dissatisfied group to be provisional analysts, and this was not the case. To sort out this puzzle, it is helpful to view the career ladder as the critical contextual variable within which education and occupational status acquire meaning.

This immediately adds another critical piece of information about the distribution of opportunity in PSA. Educational credentials represented an important job requirement in particular occupational categories. Thus education played a critical role in placing individuals in careers reserved for certain "types" of employees. As this became institutionalized over time, incumbents of each ladder would tend to assign particular social meanings to their cultural capital.

In reality the meaning employees assigned to education was totally dependent upon the structural context of the ladder (including its occupational and civil service composition). After all, a person's level of education was used differently as a criterion for recruitment, placement, and mobility in each ladder. Take for example the case of provisional analysts. A high level of education would make a person attractive as an external candidate to fill an analyst position. So, by definition, provisional analysts were individuals with high levels of education.[8] This was not the case for groups whose decisive human capital contribution derived from "experience."

Two points become important here. First, the occupational status of an employee and his or her membership in a particular career ladder are two sides of the same coin. After all, occupational status is an important symbol that society uses to classify and rank individuals. Education influences placement in particular career ladders; it prevents access to others. It therefore affects location within different strata (as well as within different tracks) at the organizational level. As a consequence, the relationship between education and satisfaction cannot be explained outside of the context of career ladder participation.[9]

Indeed, in the ladders characterized by uncertainty, there were variations in the value of education as cultural capital. In the operator ladder, in contrast, education was inconsequential. This implies that education would have a variable effect on the satisfaction of subgroups of the open employment mode, but no effect on the satisfaction of the operators. A simple regression model can provide a preliminary test of this hypothesis.[10] The results of this exercise indicated that indeed the relationship between satisfaction and education was significant; the signs were negative for the three staff subgroups affected by the weak enforcement of the merit system. Thus, the higher the education, the lower the satisfaction of permanent analysts, provisional analysts, and provisional clerical employees.

Social context helps explain this. Variations in civil service enforcement provoked a high degree of career uncertainty for all analysts and for provisional clerks. Education, experience, or any other resource could be used according to specific circumstances and at the discretion of the superiors making the decisions. In such an unpredictable environment, those with more education felt cheated or confused by the mixed messages. This in turn must have had an effect on their satisfaction. In contrast, education did not have a negative impact on the satisfaction of permanent clerical employees. As in the operator case, civil service predictability and an emphasis on experience over education explain this result. It is clear, then, that the relationship between education and satisfaction was either slightly intensified or weakened according to the degree of enforcement of the system.[11] These results are not surprising in the light of opportunity structures in PSA. They point again to the contextual nature of job satisfaction and to the importance of the different degrees of enforcement among the various subgroups. They also point to the need for further exploration of the "referents" that employees use, both to define their personal positions in the structure and to understand how their peers or superiors define them.

Referent Comparisons among PSA Employees

Imagine a matrix of the possible salient comparative evaluations taking place within the work context at PSA. This matrix results from identifying how each of the five subgroups viewed itself and the four others (see Table 22). The signs in the cells represent a positive or negative outcome of the comparison between the source (the group making the comparison) and the target (the group being compared). When the comparison between a potential source and a potential target was not relevant, "n.r." appears in the cell. For example, operators and clerical employees saw no point in comparing themselves to provisional analysts, given these groups' self-definition in the context of a strong credentialist ideology. In contrast, the most valid comparisons that provisional analysts made were with themselves. They also compared themselves to their counterparts, the permanent analysts. Finally, they were also willing to make an indirect comparison with those who represented the true competitors for organizational resources, the operators. Provisional clerical employees and permanent analysts had no commonality, whether based on civil service status or on task/occupation. Thus they were not salient referents to each other, despite the clear commonalities in socioeconomic background.

The cells in the diagonal of the matrix represent the comparisons that individuals from each subgroup made with themselves or with similar individuals. They answer the question: Given who I am (or what I bring to the job), how do I fare in PSA? This diagonal represents the input/outcome comparison identified by equity theory as critical in determining feelings of justice (Martin 1981). It represents the concerns with the justice principle of equity or proportionality. More than psychological, these "self-self" comparisons are social in nature, because they represent individuals' perceptions of the social value that others

Table 22. Referent comparisons among PSA employees

Sources of comparison	Targets of comparison				
	Operators	Permanent clerical	Provisional clerical	Permanent analysts	Provisional analysts
Operators	+	+	+	+	n.r.
Permanent clerical	−	+	+	+	n.r.
Provisional clerical	−	−	±	n.r.	n.r.
Permanent analysts	−	−	n.r.	−	−
Provisional analysts	(−)	n.r.	n.r.	±	−

attribute to them (Della Fave 1980, 1986a; Ritzman and Tomaskovic-Devey 1992).

"Self-other" comparisons are of course also social. But they provide comparisons based on the distributive justice principle of equality. Civil service in PSA legitimated the validity of comparisons among individuals from different occupational groups. Here the question is: Given my inherent value as an employee, how do I fare against my equals by right? This table is helpful to illustrate the types of mental exercises that employees performed when evaluating themselves as organizational members.

Comparing the Self

It is fairly clear why operators, as a group, would have positive self-self and self-other evaluations. Both the structure and the culture of PSA reinforced an image of the operator as a valuable resource. The sense of personal worth was confirmed with an appropriate reward system. Operators believed they deserved the opportunity advantages they enjoyed. This organizational message kept them from internalizing the outsiders' view that their work was of low social value. References to low external opportunities only reinforced the positive evaluation of their situation in PSA. What about the other four subgroups?

Permanent clerical employees had a negative internalized sense of their occupational self. This was based both on societal attitudes toward clerical work and on the messages sent by PSA. They were, however, well aware of the advantages that civil service offered. With unions ensuring their job security and stability, civil service enforcement provided them with the dignity to counter external negative messages. Like operators, clerical employees felt privileged compared to others in the open occupational labor market. But unlike operators, they did not feel they enjoyed all the advantages they should. Hence, their evaluation was negative compared to operators but positive compared to their provisional counterparts. They also fared positively compared to permanent analysts. After all, union protection meant they would not have to face fierce competition from external candidates. Permanent analysts were not so lucky. Finally, clerical civil servants considered it irrelevant to compare themselves to provisional analysts. In their minds, they represented a very different "brand" of employee.

Provisional clerical employees appreciated the nature of their job, but they wanted permanent status. Hence their self-evaluation was ambivalent, although more positive than negative. The comparison with other relevant referents (other civil servants) was negative. They felt that they were deprived of the label they wanted so badly: civil service status.

Provisional analysts were more concerned with their status as individuals than as a group. They knew they were in an open labor market, and they expected to compete as individuals. Rejecting an image of themselves as civil servants, they did not perceive other occupational groups as relevant targets for comparison. Comparisons with the only group with which there was some affinity based on job title (permanent analysts) were positive, so long as they did not represent real competition. Comparisons could be negative if these other analysts were in positions of supervision. But it was primarily in self-evaluation (who they were, where else they could be, and how constrained they felt by the system) that the outcome was negative. Even though this group did not make direct comparisons with operators, they did feel they deserved more than what they were getting within an organization whose resources were largely monopolized by operators. Thus, in a zero-sum competition, operators became a salient self-other referent for this group.[12]

Permanent analysts had many salient referents. They were more likely to compare themselves as civil servants, first with operators (on the basis of socio-economic background, levels of education, and seniority) and second with their provisional counterparts in the analyst ladder. Permanent analysts were torn between two worlds. The group expected to claim the rewards that the job title conferred on them, as they were conferred on provisional analysts. As civil servants, they also wanted to claim the protection of civil service (they demonstrated this in their effort to form a union). Paradoxically, although their jobs were of a professional nature (in the narrow sense), they used a broad definition of merit to try to secure the advantages of civil service protection.

This group lacked sufficient clout in both worlds. As civil servants, their career ladder did not offer the protection that operators and permanent clerical employees enjoyed. As analysts, they had to compete with others who possessed more cultural capital. Hence, their status as analysts provided few of the advantages it did for their provisional counterparts. They considered their job better than a clerical one (many had transferred from the clerical ladder), but the job provided neither the stability nor the clout it granted to permanent employees backed by a union. Hence both "self" and "other" comparisons were negative for this group.

Relative Deprivation, Resentment, and Dissatisfaction

The common thread in the self-evaluations of the four staff subgroups is the way inequality generated feelings of relative deprivation among its members. The theory of relative deprivation focuses on social comparisons in the distribution of rewards. This theory provides a key to understanding comparisons in PSA. In particular, it helps to explain how incongruencies of social status were transformed into a global sense of dissatisfaction.

This theory distinguishes two types of deprivation. The first is egoistic deprivation, when individuals compare themselves to similar others. Here individuals use a similar referent, and their concern is with their own individual status. The second is fraternal deprivation, when individuals identify with a group and compare that group to another. Here individuals use a dissimilar referent, and their concern is with the status of the group in which they are members (Folger 1987; Martin 1981). Scholars in this tradition suggest that experiencing egoistic deprivation may lead to *dissatisfaction*, while experiencing fraternal deprivation leads to *resentment*, that is, a sense of injustice shared with others like oneself (Kulik and Ambrose 1992; Martin 1981). Both attitudes are linked to issues of organizational justice, and both have profound effects on employee morale and organizational climate. There is a difference between them, however, which points to ways in which opportunity dynamics were played out in PSA.

The pattern of signs in the diagonal of self-self comparisons in Table 22 illustrates this. It shows that for some subgroups participation in a particular mode of employment (open or closed) coincided with their civil service schemata, whereas for other subgroups there was a discrepancy. The probability of a discrepancy depended on the degree of formalization of the rules in the ladder. Operators and permanent clerical employees fared well in the self-self comparisons of the diagonal. They gave no evidence of egoistic deprivation. The other three groups evaluated themselves differently. For them, the answer to how they fared in PSA, given who they were, was lukewarm at best for provisional clerical employees and negative for both analyst groups.

The lower the formalization, the higher the uncertainty, and therefore the higher the likelihood of both egoistic and fraternal deprivation. The discrepancy between participation in one mode of employment and an allegiance to another mode represented in fact an experience of egoistic deprivation. The three groups who experienced it were, understandably, the three groups significantly less satisfied than operators.

For provisional clerical employees the insecurity of their position generated both egoistic and fraternal deprivation. A comparison with permanent clerks produced some degree of egoistic deprivation, but not as much as analysts experienced. A comparison with operators yielded fraternal deprivation, since they were reminded of the disadvantages of the clerical ladder. Their only mild degree of egoistic deprivation may explain why they were not more dissatisfied than the analysts.

The dissatisfaction of provisional analysts took the form of egoistic deprivation resulting from uncertain prospects and high expectations within PSA. This group felt they could move fast at an individual level. But a public environment that reinforced civil service protection and bureaucratic procedures made them ambivalent about their advancement prospects. The definition of merit sanctioned by the system where they worked contradicted the definition of merit they brought with them upon entering. It negated the sense of professionalism based on credentials. Hence their egoistic deprivation.

The same sense of egoistic deprivation made operators a target of comparison, despite the differences in occupational and civil service status. The comparison was not of the type "How do I, as an analyst, fare vis-à-vis an operator?" It was instead "Why is it that I, with an analyst's skills, don't do as well as an operator?" Although subtle, the distinction is important because it resulted in egoistic rather than fraternal deprivation.

Provisional analysts experienced only feelings of egoistic deprivation. Permanent analysts, who made a variety of comparisons, experienced mixed deprivation. They felt fraternal deprivation because they considered themselves to be less protected than other permanent employees and less valued than their provisional counterparts. But they also experienced egoistic deprivation, because they defined themselves as professionals in a job that granted such status to others but not to them.

This analysis points to subtle but important differences in work reactions among the four groups who participated in open employment relationships. *Permanent clerical employees* did not report global dissatisfaction (compared to operators), but they were resentful about their low opportunity. *Provisional analysts* were more dissatisfied with their jobs than operators, but they were not resentful. After all, their personal opportunities were fine; they just wanted more. *Provisional clerical employees* and *permanent analysts*, the two groups with the lowest social status within their career ladders, were both dissatisfied and resentful.

The analyst group was, as a whole, the most dissatisfied, and permanent analysts expressed the most negative global feelings toward the job. Clerical employees were split, with provisional employees exhibiting significant differences compared to operators, while permanent employees did not. But the magnitude of the difference in satisfaction among provisionals was smaller than that of the two analyst groups. In other words, using operators as the relative standard, provisional clerical employees were somewhat less satisfied than their permanent counterparts but a bit more satisfied than analysts. In view of the fact that clerical employees experienced the lowest opportunities and that they were so resentful, this finding about a split in their global satisfaction deserves further elaboration.

The Contradictory Feelings of the Clerical Group

The sense of discrimination had a strong influence on job satisfaction for both clerical subgroups. Considerations of legitimacy about inconsistent staffing practices in a civil service context were a crucial concern. The inconsistent practices added to an already negative experience of being in a socially devalued ladder with low opportunity. Furthermore, the gender- and race-segregated nature of the ladder heightened the negative experience, making the inconsistencies even more intolerable.

Why were these two groups not the most dissatisfied? I have indicated above that the attitudes of provisionals can be linked to the discrepancy between their civil service schemata and their participation in an open mode of employment. The union protected most clerical permanent employees, thus ensuring some of the advantages of a closed employment relationship. The group strongly believed in the legitimacy of this protection. This explains why, within the two groups, the civil servant subgroups would be more satisfied.

But then, why did both groups exhibit such high levels of dissatisfaction with specific job dimensions, as reported in Chapter 7? One possible explanation is that most of the dissatisfaction tapped in the discrepancy scores came from the provisional clerks. After all, they did exhibit significant, although small, differences in satisfaction. But the percentages indicated that many permanent clerks also expressed job-specific dissatisfaction. Another possibility is that the entire clerical group appeared dissatisfied because the discrepancy scores did not differentiate between dissatisfaction and resentment. This, however, cannot be verified. Furthermore, this does not explain the fact that clerical provisionals were more satisfied than their analyst counterparts, who enjoyed positive opportunity features. The group's negative responses to opportunity-specific aspects of the job would suggest otherwise. Another explanation could be that the lack of external opportunities made clerical employees more cautious in expressing global dissatisfaction, both to protect their personal sense of respect and to protect their jobs. In this sense, they may have expressed themselves positively in their overall orientations, but more candidly when evaluating specific aspects of the job. The problem with this explanation is that it should also work for permanent analysts, but it doesn't. Hence something else was at work for clerical employees.

Della Fave's theory of self-evaluation provides powerful ammunition to interpret the links between clerical feelings and their position in PSA (Ritzman and Tomaskovic-Devey 1992; Della Fave 1980, 1986a). This theory explores how social systems legitimate and maintain the unequal distribution of primary resources typical of stratified contexts. Legitimation refers in this context to the acceptance of institutionalized inequality on the basis of reasonable justifications that are widely believed and sometimes taken for granted.

Della Fave uses a combination of insights from social psychology and sociology to understand how the "structure of the larger society becomes incorporated within the inner consciousness of the individual" (Della Fave 1980:956).[13] He uses these elements to explain the puzzling observation that even those who loose in the distribution may tend to grant legitimacy to the structure responsible for their disadvantages. The theory argues that legitimation is maintained in part through the role that major social institutions—such as occupations, work, and education—play in pressing individuals to define themselves within the status quo. When existing unequal distributions are successfully translated into societal norms, they become an integral part of one's self-identity.

The theory identifies the social psychological process through which perceptions of *what is* are transformed into notions of *what ought to be*. Individuals are socialized into evaluating themselves according to those notions. They use them to interpret and accept their position in the social order:

> Through the status attribution process, those possessing greater amounts of primary resources come to be seen as actually being superior. At this point, the principle of equity takes over, and people believe that those who appear to be superior deserve to be more richly rewarded. (Della Fave, 1980:962)

This proposition adds an interesting twist to the well-established applications of attribution theory in the organizational behavior literature. OB scholars accept the idea that the evaluation of performance is based not only on actual performance levels but also on the evaluator's *beliefs* about the *causes* of performance (Ilgen, Major, and Tower 1994). Della Fave's theory suggests that such beliefs mirror the stratified system and therefore ultimately help to reproduce and legitimate unequal resource distributions. Attributing superiority to those with greater wealth and power implies that those lower in the system will, when making comparisons, see themselves as relatively inferior. This evaluation will then suggest that they deserve to have less wealth and power. Self-evaluations thus tend to be congruent with the distribution of primary resources, a circular process in which self-images reinforce the very status quo that generated them in the first place.

Three concepts are especially helpful in understanding the reactions of clerical employees in PSA: self-evaluation, role-reification, and investment in subordination. Self-evaluation refers to the definition persons attribute to their own ability to accumulate wealth and power. Della Fave suggests that when self-evaluation is high or positive, it becomes a source of self-esteem. But if self-evaluation is low, the self must rely on alternate bases to build self-esteem. Performing well in the role that originally created the low self-evaluation allows the person to compensate by attributing social value to it. Thus people tend to invest their identities in aspects of the very roles that lead them to evaluate themselves as inferior. This close identification with the role results in a tacit acceptance of its place within the structure. It generates a psychological investment in defending it. These responses represent the processes of role-reification and investment in subordination, respectively (Della Fave 1986).

In Della Fave's model, then, unequal resource distribution produces unequal self-evaluations. If the self-evaluation is positive (based on advantages in the distribution process), then those advantages are viewed as logical rewards to the person's contributions, following the equity principle. Because self-evaluation and self-interests coincide, there is satisfaction with the situation and the status quo gets legitimated. Hence the rich believe they deserve to be rich, managers believe they deserve to make more money, PSA operators believe they deserve better opportunities. If the self-evaluation is negative, the person searches for compensatory standards of evaluation to improve self-esteem. One such standard consists of viewing the role that produced the negative self-evaluation in positive terms: "The day-to-day activities of members of subordinate classes are filled with strategic efforts to cope with the exigencies of their subordinate roles." Della Fave further states that "in doing so, they tend to reify the moral categories that define their own subordinate roles and, thereby, legitimate them" (Della Fave 1986a:482).

Clerical jobs provided the least opportunity for accumulation of wealth and power both at the societal level and within PSA. This generated a low self-evaluation among members of this ladder. In contrast, the civil service job in the clerical ladder represented a source of pride and social significance. Civil servants in this ladder therefore invested their work identities in the very role that led them to a lower self-evaluation: being "professional" clerical employees. By defending the legitimacy of the closed nature of their positions, the entire clerical experience itself was reified. Civil service conferred a sense of professionalism that the clerical status denied. Both permanent and provisional clerks resented their lower social status, but the permanent clerks had more psychological investment in defending the integrity of their subordinate jobs. That is in part also why provisional clerks wanted the permanent status so badly.

It is perhaps for this same reason that clerical civil servants were so protective of the system. Civil service enforcement gave them the possibility of feeling proud. It gave them respectability as civil servants who had valuable experiences to offer, despite their placement in an occupation with low social value. The system's definition of merit returned some of the dignity taken from them by their lack of credentials, by the paucity of opportunity in their ladder, and by their negative self-evaluation as low-status employees. This did not dissolve their resentment, but at least the resentment did not necessarily translate into a negative global reaction to the job. Given the societal ideology, which assigns lower social value to individuals without educational credentials, and given PSA's culture, which assigns lower social value to the clerical ladder, permanent clerical employees may have felt that their job outputs were proportional to the skills they brought and the tasks they performed. To that extent, they felt good about their job, at least in global terms.

Finally, this theory is also valuable in understanding the dissatisfaction of analysts. Della Fave asks under what conditions people question the legitimacy of unequal distributions. He claims that the dominant rule of distribution is questioned when a significant societal counternorm gives a subordinate group an alternative frame of reference for evaluating the status quo. The theory hypothesizes that delegitimation emerges when the distribution of primary resources and self-evaluations become incongruent. This was the case for analysts. Provisional analysts proposed a rule of equitable distribution within a system that promoted equality. Credentialism and rationalization in public administration gave them a positive self-evaluation. This made them question the status quo rather than accept a disadvantaged position in it. Additionally, permanent analysts were caught in a double loop of uncertainty. Their identities as analysts were based on two opposing rationales of legitimacy. One part of them went through the mental exercises described for permanent clerks, while the other part went through those described for provisional analysts. The result was a generalized discontent, expressed both as resentment *and* as global dissatisfaction.

The Structural and Institutional Impact of Opportunity on Work Attitudes

Both the qualitative and quantitative analysis of job satisfaction indicated that operators were the most satisfied of the three occupational groups. Likewise, both types of analysis indicated that clerical employees were much more dissatisfied with (and perhaps resentful of) specific job dimensions than the other two groups; they were also pessimistic about their prospects and negative about their jobs. But a multivariate modeling of job satisfaction did not capture this differ-ence for the permanent clerks. Further analysis suggested that this group's civil service schemata motivated the group to "invest" psychological energy in finding value in their work (whereas society found little). The combined reality of higher enforcement and lower opportunity resulted in images of opportunity that justified resentment toward PSA but not global job dissatisfaction.

The final answer to the question of how opportunity structures affected job satisfaction is not a simple one. Yet, identifiable patterns confirmed our expecta-tions about the role of inequality. The original occupational categories used to classify employees in the three ladders concealed the existence of an important distinction among employees in each group. Subgroups within those occupa-tional categories had different experiences both in the amount of opportunity and in the formalization of opportunity. *Amount* of opportunity refers to the actual chances employees had to gain access to organizational resources; *formali-zation* of opportunity refers to the existence of structured and predictable means for employees to take advantage of the opportunities offered. While both are structural factors, the latter is highly determined by the degree of enforcement of an institutional factor, civil service law.[14]

We can now put together the different pieces of the puzzle. The amount of opportunity employees had in the ladder covaried with the degree of employee satisfaction with specific aspects of the job. The degree of global satisfaction of employees, in contrast, seemed to be directly related to how formalized the terms

Table 23. Structural and institutional impacts of opportunity on work attitudes by career ladder

	Operator	Analyst	Clerical
A. Structural impact of opportunity on satisfaction			
Amount of opportunity	High	Medium	Low
Facet-specific satisfaction[a]	High	Medium	Low
B. Institutional impact of opportunity on satisfaction			
Formalization of opportunity	High	Low	Medium
Global satisfaction	High	Low	Medium

[a] "Facet-specific" refers to satisfaction with specific dimensions of the job. See the Appendix.

of employment were for each subgroup in the ladder. The pattern becomes obvious when the findings are arranged according to critical differences (Table 23). The higher the amount of opportunity in a ladder, the higher the satisfaction of employees with specific facets of the job and vice versa. These relationships result from the work arrangements defining how much opportunity a person experiences. On the other hand, when considering the global measures of satisfaction, the direction of the reported satisfaction seemed to be better associated with the degree of formalization of the ladders. The more formalized the opportunity in the ladder, the higher the global satisfaction. This finding confirms the positive correlation between formalization of procedures and satisfaction, which traditional studies of job satisfaction have found (Snizeck and Bullard 1983). But it also clarifies the internal logic of this relationship in the context of hierarchical stratified work systems. In PSA the degree of formalization created important contextual conditions directly linked to a global sense of discontent. These conditions were, first, an uncertainty about processes and outcomes and, second, discrepancies between the merit discourse and staffing practices. If the reasoning presented here is correct, it reinforces the idea that perceptions of justice play a critical role in shaping work attitudes. These linkages, of course, need to be further tested in future research.[15]

Conclusion

The work expectations and value judgements of PSA employees were linked both to their location in the job structure and to the values and standards of the employment model they used to make sense of the reward distribution. Ultimately, the incongruence between participation in a given employment mode (the actual experience of some employees) and belief in its legitimacy (their expectations) was the strongest factor in shaping affective reactions, both dissatisfaction and resentment. In this complex and contradictory work environment, a combination of several important factors influenced employees' cognitive maps: their location in career ladders, their civil service status, their personal stance with regard to the system's legitimacy, and their opinions about the employment contract. In turn, meanings derived from these maps guided employee interpretations of organizational life, their affective reactions, and their actions in the workplace.

Conclusions: Reactions to Stratification in the Workplace

Clerical employees, analysts, and operators worked hard to make something positive out of their jobs. They also reacted to the working environment in distinctive ways. Despite their differences, they all had needs, aspirations, and visions that they wanted to fulfil. Similarly, they wanted their co-workers, their supervisors, and the agency to treat them with dignity and respect.

But at the same time, PSA employees participated in labor market arrangements and specific conditions of employment, and these influenced the way they felt about work. The organization valued and treated separate subgroups of employees differently. Employees, working side by side—clerical and operator, analyst and clerical—were aware of these career ladder differences. Implicitly or explicitly, they understood that these differences had a real impact on their working conditions, on their employment contract, and, more concretely, on what they could expect in the way of advancement, remuneration, and personal growth in the agency.

Employees disliked unequal outcomes, but they accepted them. Inequality was consistent with wider societal beliefs about work and occupations. In this sense PSA, a "stratified system" embedded in a larger "system of stratification," distributed resources and rewards based on the same myths and beliefs that existed in the larger cultural ethos. These beliefs, translated and institutionalized inside the organization, provided the basis for meaning in daily interactions. When violations of their assumptions about justice and merit became salient, employees reacted.

Two opportunity factors strongly influenced the degree of satisfaction or dissatisfaction, resentment or contentment, that employees experienced in PSA. The first was the degree of *formalization* and the consequent *certainty* employees had with respect to their employment relationship. The second was the actual

197

availability of rewards and the consequent *amount of opportunity* that employees had with respect to promotion, compensation, and job challenge. Both factors were unequally distributed among groups of employees. This inequality colored the work experience of employees in all ladders. It affected PSA's organizational climate and general employee morale, because it directed employees' attentions to feelings of organizational justice.

Sensitivity toward issues of justice made comparative evaluations relevant. When these comparisons were negative, the discrepancy between employees' beliefs about merit and their experiences of inequality produced feelings of relative deprivation. Negative feelings about the job were either heightened or buffered dependent on whether the dominant employment mode in PSA was deemed legitmate or not. They were also influenced by discrepancies between ideological allegiance to that mode and actual participation in it.

These findings can be summarized briefly. First, employees whose employment relationship provided *high certainty* and much opportunity tended to report global satisfaction, job-specific satisfaction, and no deprivation. Employees whose employment relationship provided relative certainty and little opportunity tended to report global satisfaction but, at the same time, job-specific *dis*satisfaction and a strong sense of injustice. Second, employees whose employment relationship was based on *high uncertainty* reported lower levels of global and job-specific satisfaction, regardless of the amount of opportunity. Their resentment varied according to the amount of opportunity provided. Those for whom *rewards* were relatively available did not experience a sense of injustice, those with low opportunity, on the other hand, did experience a strong sense of injustice.

Hence, *formalization* of the employment relationship was associated with satisfaction, while *amount of opportunity* was associated with resentment. The reasons for these associations were context-specific. They had to do with how people felt about the legitimacy of the civil service system as the dominant mode of employment and whether they were able to use it to their advantage in PSA.

The Legitimation of Inequality

Theories of social closure help illustrate how the legitimation of inequality is linked to work attitudes. Closure occurs when one group monopolizes advantages by closing off opportunities to others. As the latter become outsiders, they are labeled as inferior and ineligible for group inclusion (Murphy 1988). Normally an identifiable mark will separate insiders from outsiders. Scholars from various traditions have illustrated how this type of social classification is linked to the monopolization of resources. For example, Bourdieu (1984) has investigated the role of aesthetics as a cultural form that ultimately contributes to justify the inclusion of some and the exclusion of others in the class structure. Williams

(1990) has documented how race and ethnicity became forms of social classification in the U.S. labor market as the country was being populated. And Collins (1979) has studied the role of cultural capital in turning jobs into sinecures over which people claimed proprietary rights. In the same way, it could be argued that organizational rewards and human resource management systems also produce institutionalized forms of social classification.

Most contemporary organizations are hierarchical orders. They are built under the premise that an inducement-contributions work contract represents a legitimate way to move people into action. The acceptance of this psychological contract as the solution to the problem of organizational cooperation is rooted in the belief that those who get the rewards deserve them. The opposite then becomes true, by attribution: those who do not get rewards must not have contributed, and those who get fewer rewards must have not contributed enough. Studies have found that experimentally manipulated rewards do create corresponding inequalities in expectations, so that people who are paid more are viewed as more competent and productive in accomplishing tasks.[1]

This social order can only exist if there is a mechanism to separate the deserving from the undeserving. Hence, while the structure of incentives is offered to all, the actual distribution of rewards is limited to some. In both "pyramids" and "webs" the most desired positions and best rewards are limited to a few "chosen" individuals. In the typical pyramid, these positions are at the upper level of the hierarchy. In the unusual case of the web, they tend to be located close to the center. As the number of desired positions decreases upwardly (or inwardly), access to other organizational commodities increases proportionally. The quality of jobs and the nature of work also tend to change in the same direction.

Employees participate in competitions to attain rewards at each level. They also compete for the most desired jobs at the top (or at the center). Personal success is identified with movement up the ladder, or into the center of the circle. Both types of arrangements produce tournaments with winners and losers. The continuity of this type of social order requires that participants believe in the legitimacy of the outcomes. Winners must feel that they deserve their advantages. Losers must feel they are not worthy of enjoying them. Otherwise, losers may try to change the situation using mechanisms as varied as exit or voice (Hirschman 1970).

Employees' perceptions of work are grounded in the social forces that sustain the stratified order they accept as legitimate. These include the accepted standards of distributive justice to interpret experience, regardless of whether one evaluates it positively or negatively. The ultimate consequence of accepting the competition, its rules, and its outcomes is legitimated organizational inequality. The tension between the acceptance of the status quo and the search for an alternative state of affairs represents a permanent feature of the experience of work.

In a sense, the case study of PSA is an excellent example of how people structure and use rules of closure to distribute resources in a particular organizational setting. There are two typical means for mobilizing power to enhance or defend a group's share of rewards or resources: exclusion and usurpation (Murphy 1988).[2] The meaning of exclusion is self-evident. Usurpation refers to the efforts of those excluded to try to take a bite out of the advantages awarded to the closed groups. It is precisely the potential of the excluded groups to react that provides the basis for social transformation. Change can be incremental or revolutionary. In the former case, groups just want a share of the pie. In the latter case a subversion of the status quo produces new distributive patterns and different notions of distributive justice.

The processes of exclusion and usurpation affect the social context from which feelings and attitudes emerge. Some of the conflicts and resentments described among PSA employees can be clearly framed within these dynamics. Clerical employees' and analysts' claims to a larger share of organizational resources illustrate the groups' interest in challenging the legitimacy of the operators' monopolization of resources. The clerical position represented a claim to a legitimate share of civil servants' privileges. The analysts' position advocated the legitimacy of a different code of inclusion, that of credentialism. The clerical and analyst definitions of merit represented, each, different criteria to decide who should be excluded and who should be included. Both were legitimate codes used by different social groups holding relative degrees of power.

Usurpation efforts in PSA, however, were only partial. Both analysts and clerical employees wanted a share of the resources rather than a total subversion of the system. The views of the two groups were not antagonistic, just different. Both clericals and analysts accepted the validity of the proportionality rule of inputs to outputs; both stressed the "equity" principle of justice in the distribution of goods and punishments. Hence both embraced a competitive approach to resource distribution, and both emphasized achieved rather than ascribed merit qualities.

There were, however, subtle differences in the assumptions of distributive justice used by each group. The open market view of employment, with its accompanying credentialist definition of merit, reflected a utilitarian notion of "justice as the greatest good." Provisional analysts and many PSA managers who espoused this view believed in the power of the market to select which individuals would be included and which excluded. This appeared "radical" in a system sanctioned by the merit ideology of civil service. In contrast, the closed market view, with its accompanying definition of merit based on experience, had at its basis the notion of "justice as fairness." Civil servants in general believed in the power of institutional mechanisms to correct the imperfections of the market. This was necessary because the market tended to "discriminate" against those who possessed important merit attributes not linked to a credential. In this sense, civil servants added values reflecting the justice principle of equality to their expectations of equity.

Social closure theory therefore helps give one a better grasp of the interdependence of the structural process of resource distribution and the institutional process of justification of outcomes. This can be visualized with two metaphors that describe opportunity in organizations. Employee prospects for promotion, compensation, and challenge are rooted in hierarchically ordered *chains of opportunity* (Murphy 1988:222).[3] But employees also participate in the creation, reproduction, and alteration of those chains by developing *images of opportunity*, which provide the basis for individual and collective action.

Personal choice is ultimately framed in terms of the dynamics set in motion within the chains. Interpretations of the outcomes of action, on the other hand, tend to be framed in terms of the logic provided by the images. Possessing different types of resources (diplomas, contacts, experience) can either increase or decrease the probability of winning the initial contest in the chain (i.e., being hired or promoted to a job). Winning then increases the probability of further wins by opening access to the networks and resources required to be competitive in the next contest. Some chains look like upward escalators while others resemble dead-end traps, and the probability of gaining access to resources varies from chain to chain:

> Winners accumulate not only rewards, but also resources which place them in an advantageous position to win future contests. Conversely, the lower the resources on entry, the lower the probability of winning. This in turn prevents one from acquiring the resources necessary for winning, or even for entering, subsequent contests. (Murphy 1988:222)[4]

Although the contest would appear open to all, it does not produce substantive equality. To this extent formally open contests are, despite their apparent openness, systems of closure. People must make sense of this contradiction somehow.

Chains of opportunity contribute to produce the ultimate contradiction individuals experience in hierarchical organizations. These chains constitute forms of "exclusion and yet inclusion, monopolization and yet competition for career opportunities" (Murphy 1988:223). The rules of exclusion and codes of closure become institutionalized over time to form part of the administrative systems that organizations accept as legitimate tools of control. Images of opportunity, which mirror the generalized norms and expectations of society, help legitimate these institutionalized practices. They are, however, only illusions. Nevertheless, these images have in their very nature the potential for change, since people are capable of imagining alternative futures.

Here are then the two sides of stratification that affect employees' work experience. On the one hand, a system creates a contest that is theoretically open to all but that uses different criteria for inclusion and dissimilar rules of distribution. These represent the chains of opportunity. On the other hand, a discourse defines employment models and human resource management systems as rational tools to attract, retain, and manage the "best and brightest" people in the organization. This represents the illusions of opportunity, sanctioned by an ideology espousing equal and fair chances in the distribution of rewards, based on merit.

Dominant definitions of merit place individuals either inside or outside the circle of the selected ones.[5] This classification machinery has become institutionalized in industrial societies under the designation of an open contest based on merit. In this context, people tend to define their inclusion as success and their exclusion as failure. The chains of opportunity therefore are invisible, but they are still very real. Employees experience their consequences on a daily base. The resulting contradictions are part of the cognitive baggage they use to make sense of reality.

The case of PSA also illustrates the dynamic process toward heterogeneity of work arrangements in an "industry" (public sector) that traditionally espoused the bureaucratic model. This is another instance of the process of "isomorphism" described by the new institutionalists (Powell and DiMaggio 1991). In this case, employment models used successfully in the private sector were being transferred into a public sector context. The accepted bureaucratic approach to employment (the closed model of the "merit system"), was being challenged by the presence of another type of relationship (the open model regulated by market forces). This shift is illustrated by managerial use of noninstitutionalized practices to expedite decisions without openly challenging the old structures. A concrete example is that of managers negotiating individual deals to bring provisional analysts into the position classification system.

At the micro level of interaction this was translated into different experiences for different groups in PSA. There were those who expected and got something out of the traditional arrangements (these were the operators and permanent clerks). There were those who hoped for some new arrangement but had to put up with the old (the analysts). There were others who expected equal treatment based on the traditional arrangements but who received unequal treatment when noninstitutionalized practices were applied (provisional clerical employees and permanent analysts).

The patterns of satisfaction, dissatisfaction, contentment, and resentment documented in the previous chapters were clearly linked to the cognitive dissonance produced. The gradual shift in employment models contributed to wider the gap between employees' expectations and experiences. The gap was reduced for those members of the group attached to the old paradigm and benefiting from it, but even for them it widened slowly as conditions inevitably changed. The gap was greatest for the group espousing the new paradigm, which had still not become institutionalized within the system. Some members of groups attached to the older perspective either saw their closed world eroding (a few operators) or felt relatively excluded (clerical employees). The former tried to cling to the legitimacy of their privileges by insisting on the validity of the dominant rules of exclusion. The latter felt that they were being taken advantage of and thus developed a strong sense of injustice. The newer group (analysts) felt frustrated and impatient and developed a strong sense of dissatisfaction with the status quo. The most powerless groups from each career ladder experienced both dissatisfaction and resentment.

Because of the demographic composition of the ladders, these patterned reactions of discontent became intertwined with conflicts between groups whose members belonged to recognizably different social categories (race, gender and civil service status). Operators felt uncomfortable when women and people of color entered their ladder. Employees in the race and sex typed clerical progression interpreted their lower opportunity as discrimination. In the more demographically balanced ladders, civil service status became the predominant "mark" of conflict. Independent of the criterion used, the potential conflicts had a clear impact on PSA's organizational climate.

Reward Systems as Forms of Social Classification

Social distinctions get translated inside organizations into individual and group distinctions through the reward system. At the same time, this system provides employees with organizational information about how they ought to act, given who they are, and how they fit within the larger collective effort. The structural basis of this organizational tool can be found in the job classifications and career progressions. Job classifications regulated within a human resource management system serve a rational function. "Objective" standards defined in job descriptions protect employees from their superiors' potentially arbitrary decisions. Universalistic rather than personalistic criteria become normative. But this logic produces another important social consequence. As its name suggests, job classifications distribute individuals through the organization, legitimating the existing division of labor, the allocation of resources, and ultimately the consequent distribution of power.

Since power gives individuals access to resources, the system creates a feedback loop that helps reproduce the chains of opportunity described earlier. People enter an organization and are placed in a position that relates them to others in very specific ways. Associated with the position is a specified level of authority, a particular level of compensation, specific work benefits, delimited chances to move up, and even particular working conditions that specify the context in which the employee will perform. These job attributes ultimately become the most important assets individuals will use in their effort to pursue future rewards.

Over time, organizational actors work out a set of agreements about what merit is and who is considered meritorious within the organization. In this process, some subgroups will succeed in imposing their definitions of merit, which will become the dominant values in the organization's culture. Part of becoming socialized into the organization consists of understanding these definitions and learning how to behave accordingly. Differences in opinion about the value of an educational credential versus long-term experience for job performance illustrate this point. Who is to say that a recent graduate from a prestigious management school is more meritorious and more deserving of certain prerogatives than an old-timer who has come up the ranks and has mastered the nuts and bolts of the trade? The new, credentialed manager will argue for the value of an educational degree. He or she will relate it to technical expertise and professionalism. The older, experienced manager will argue for the value of seniority, loyalty, and institutional memory. Both are right to some extent. But the power of those espousing each view, along with the organizational subculture in which the debate is posed, will determine which point of view will predominate. This will have consequences for the way rewards are distributed.

The dominant view will be shaped through the negotiation of meanings about organizational reality. Alternatives will be proposed by different actors, cliques, and coalitions. Resources such as information, status, and money will get distributed. Over time, a given definition of merit, espoused by the most powerful groups, will gain legitimacy. It will eventually dominate explanations about who gets what, how, and when. The reward system that sanctions this version of reality can be viewed as the institutionalized product of this dynamic process.

Hence the reward system is at the same time a source and an outcome of the organizational dynamics through which the processes of exclusion and monopolization take place. It is a *source* because, once employees perceive it as an objective reality out there, it serves the important symbolic function of legitimating the actual distribution of power. It presents as a fact the validity of criteria used to distribute resources. The reward system is, in this sense, a cultural artifact employees use to learn how to gain desired organizational resources, be they money, authority, positions, or benefits. As employees follow the cues that define appropriate behavior, the status quo gets legitimated and is reproduced. Acting as one of the most important instruments to distribute organizational resources, the reward system helps legitimate the view that a certain degree of organizational inequality is inevitable.

The reward system is also an *outcome* of the process of social closure. Despite its appearance as an objective system, the specific details about compensation and promotion result from competing claims to desired resources. As individuals and groups gain power to ensure that their claims are accepted as legitimate, parts of the reward system get reshaped accordingly (Cyert and March 1963). This ongoing process of negotiation is masked under the prevailing assumption that "merit" means the same thing for everyone. This suggests that the reward system itself is just the manifestation of the merit principle implemented in a given context.

Scholars of work attitudes and human resource specialists have not stressed the theoretical connection between the degree of structural inequality, the reward system, and people's feelings about their jobs. The reason for this blindness might be that inequality is assumed as a natural point of departure for organizational analysis. Issues of organizational justice are not addressed unless specific perceived injustices become apparent. Even in such cases, the general view is that such perceptions are only subjective understandings of temporary situations that can be corrected. Inequality is, however, a permanent condition of hierarchically stratified work systems.

From Occupational to Organizational Status

Occupational classifications may be one of the most direct—yet invisible—forms of alienation in modern societies. They reaffirm the illusion of merit and competence, while maintaining clear distinctions between different types of work. As individuals are placed in jobs according to their membership in occupational groups, status and perks associated with these groups create a hierarchy of work experiences. Occupations classify individuals based on firmly established categories. Credentials and other forms of certification become keys to unlock their carefully guarded entry doors (Starr 1982; Larson 1977).

The study of PSA suggests that two social realities are directly linked to occupational classifications: one is the acceptance of heterogeneous work arrangements inside organizations; the other is the existence of several different and yet equally legitimate definitions of merit and competence within the same organization. Which of those meanings becomes dominant gets resolved within particular organizations. Indeed, it is inside particular organizations that people accept differences in placement and treatment as valid, despite the feelings of ambivalence that may arise from experiencing disparities at a personal level. This confirms the value of focusing on specific organizational contexts to better understand the impact of occupational status on work attitudes. It also reaffirms the usefulness of shifting focus from occupational to career ladder membership to better understand employee reactions to work.

Viewing occupational membership exclusively as a personal attribute (or as proxy for the degree of mastery of a task) assumes an almost perfect correlation between occupational prestige at a societal level and job status at an organizational level. This is not always the case. Consider the example of PSA. There were two occupational groups with low prestige at a societal level (operators and clerical employees) and another with relatively high societal prestige (analysts).

Yet the opportunity packages offered to each group were not entirely consistent with these statuses. Moving down one level of analysis from the dynamics of occupational labor markets, to consider the dynamics of organizational labor markets was helpful to uncover information about specific work arrangements. This in turn helped disclose the organizationally defined meanings employees used to asses their jobs.

Moreover, factors associated with the job, such as salaries, assigned perks and benefits (from parking spaces to health insurance), authority, and potential for movement largely define the quality of life outside the work context. Focusing on abstract occupational labels may hide these connections.

The occupational statuses employees bring to the organization significantly affect work attitudes. But this is so less because they shape expectations of opportunity than because they affect employee placement within particular chains of opportunity. It is there that the contradictions between illusions and realities—between expectations and experiences—get played out. The common experience of participation in occupational groups represents therefore much more than a sharing of common educational backgrounds, similar preferences, similar professional values, or equivalent levels of skill or expertise. It represents the sharing of a particular structural context that defines the conditions of work and the reward system associated with them. Groups of employees thereby share similar chances of being excluded or included in circles of advantage within a given organization's power structure.

The Complexity of Work Attitudes

If scholars of work attitudes agree on anything, it is that characteristics associated with jobs clearly affect employees' evaluative reactions in the workplace. Less clear is how this happens. In fact, how it happens is a black box that various traditions in the social sciences have tried to understand.

What has been learned from empirical efforts to clarify this link is summarized in the diagram. An attitude such as job satisfaction is directly shaped by employee perceptions of their job. These in turn are affected by who the employees are (their individual characteristics) and where they are located in the organization (their specific jobs). The latter, finally, are a function of structural forces operating at the organizational level.

Researchers have emphasized different aspects of this model. One perspective has focused on individual attributes of employees. This view suggests that people with different characteristics (occupations, educational levels, ages, ethnic backgrounds, genders, and internal predispositions) perceive their jobs differently, and, this in turn affects satisfaction.[6] For example, a job with structured supervision may be perceived negatively by a professionally educated young employee

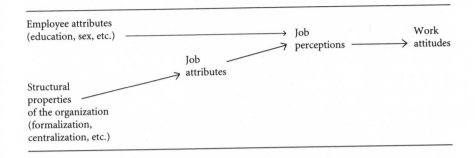

and positively by an older blue-collar worker. Job satisfaction would be influenced by the effect of this match or mismatch. The analytical assumption behind this reasoning is that employee job perceptions mediate the relationship between job attributes and satisfaction, and that personal characteristics directly influence employee perceptions about the job.[7]

Another line of research emphasizes properties of the job structure, such as formalization or centralization.[8] A good salary, for example, cannot be considered isolated from the broader systems that define the salary structure in the organization.[9] The analytical assumption behind this view is that job attributes, and perceptions of them, represent mediating factors in the relationship between objective structures and job satisfaction.

The emphasis on personal or structural components has practical relevance because it provides managers with guidelines to create different types of interventions in the workplace. Depending on the perspective used, managers may try to promote positive attitudes by developing personalized strategies (training, counseling, job matching efforts) or by changing the structures and systems that shape the work environment. The two perspectives agree on the direct link between job perceptions and job satisfaction. They disagree about the relative importance of the factors, individual or structural, that shape these perceptions. To some extent, the debate itself misses the interdependencies generated by the new complexity added when one views organizations as stratified work systems.[10]

We know that employees in PSA experienced their job from different structural contexts even within the same organization. We also know that employees who performed similar jobs had different employment contracts, each with its own differentiated reward structure. Hence, jobs that appeared to be of the same type were in fact different in important ways. This feature of PSA's job structure affected the objective nature of the job and how the employee perceived it. But it also affected which of the employee's personal characteristics were socially relevant in interpreting experiences on the job.

In PSA's hierarchical system, personal preferences and even particular charac-

teristics of employees were not simply subjective attributes of employees as individuals. For example, gender was important less as a personal characteristic
than as a social label with a particular meaning within a given cluster of jobs.
Once people sharing the same personal characteristic—gender—were clustered
in the same career ladder, this compositional reality defined the terms of interaction for workers there. This was the case with the three career ladders in PSA.
Hence, the gender, race, or even education of an employee had different effects
on how the employee perceived the job, according to the particular meaning of
that employee's personal traits within the career ladder. Other examples of this
were the different meanings education and experience had for provisionals and
civil servants in PSA, and the different meaning of being a male or a person of
color in the operator ladder compared to the clerical ladder.

This discussion suggests the need to stress an additional linkage in the model.
It is shown in the revised diagram as an arrow linking structural properties and
employee attributes. This linkage might be hard to operationalize, but it is nonetheless decisive for understanding work reactions.

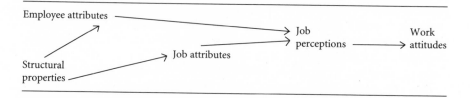

One strategy to ensure attention to the more subtle but critical aspects of work
is to focus on the proximate levels where the job gets defined structurally, and
from which employees assign meaning. One such level is that of the career ladder.
Once a shift is made from occupations to organizational career ladders, the
analysis can take advantage of the insights of scholars in the cognitive tradition
(Salancik and Pfeffer 1978; Lincoln 1985; Masters and Smith 1987). The switch
entails giving equal emphasis to the slots and to the interaction of people in them,
focusing on the patterns of relations operating in a given setting.

The portrait of the feelings of PSA employees created in the last five chapters
required constantly shifting attention from structure to individual action and
back to structure. It meant viewing the emerging cognitions within their structural source and conceiving them as realities embedded in the work experience.
The successful results of this exercise give credence to the notion of
"embeddedness" advanced by Granovetter:

> Actors do not behave or decide as atoms outside of a social context, nor do they
> adhere slavishly to a script written for them by the particular intersection of
> social categories they happen to occupy. Their attempts at purposive action are

instead embedded in concrete, ongoing systems of social relations. (Granovetter 1985b:9)

Granovetter reaffirms here the importance of establishing an adequate link between macro- and micro-level theories of action (Granovetter 1981). Doing so requires a detailed understanding of the proximate mechanisms in which social relations take place as people work in organized settings. However, it is critical to acknowledge that patterns of social relations emerge as "the result of a struggle over who will do what among people *whose very inequality* gives them different aims as to how they want the others to behave" (Collins 1975:316, emphasis added). This interaction of structure and action in the context of a stratified system opens a broader universe of meanings to the social scientist studying work attitudes.

Hence the role of cognition must be redefined in light of the reality of organizational stratification. Theories of justice in the social comparison tradition[11] suggest that evaluative judgements are generally based on reference group comparisons. They also result from mental simulations involving alternative imaginable scenarios (Folger 1987; Masters and Keil 1987; Martin 1981). Given situations of structured inequality typical of hierarchical organizations, comparisons represent a central focus of attention for understanding job perceptions, even when the research agenda is not justice related.

Justice itself should be viewed as an inevitable component of the work environment. Patterns of opportunity enacted directly through formalized reward systems necessarily produce the conditions that trigger feelings of justice. They thus increase the inherent potential for contradiction in the workplace. The volatility of contemporary conditions of work—in the public, private, and non-profit sectors alike—suggests that this contradiction will become more visible as contemporary organizations engage in practices that violate the rules of distributive justice that legitimate the system. General instances where feelings of justice may strongly affect employee work reactions in today's environment include:

- situations in which the formalization of employment rules varies across work groups, creating clear inconsistencies in treatment or discrepancies between discourses and practices
- situations where the organizational culture is shaped by clear ideological conflicts between actors, or where strong institutional forces such as unionization or corporatism exist
- situations where material and symbolic resources become scarce, thus intensifying the competition over them (e.g., plant closings, retrenchment, downsizing)
- situations of change that directly question or threaten the legitimacy of the domi-

nant rules of distribution (e.g., reengineering efforts, shifts in structural design, or efforts to change the culture, such as TQM)

Feelings of justice proved to be a potent means of understanding both work perceptions and attitudes in PSA. Mental maps or scenarios of comparative evaluation shaped these attitudes, and were in turn shaped by opportunity outcomes and outputs. Perceptions of justice were a filter through which employees reacted to job attributes and work experiences. As light was directed to previously ignored areas of attention, our diagram gained further complexity.

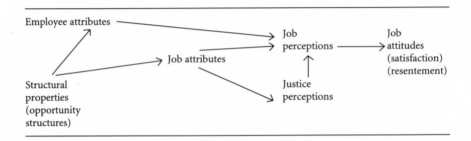

Personal dimensions as well as job attributes did contribute to shape work perceptions in PSA. They did so situationally and always filtered through feelings and cognitions drawn from a broader social context. This social context was greatly determined by two factors: a work organization based on stratification, and a heterogeneity of work arrangements. Both produced important differences in the processes and outcomes of resource distribution. These products, however, strongly contradicted the merit ideology underlying employee illusions of opportunity in the workplace. It was ultimately the meaning assigned to this complexity that shaped job satisfaction or dissatisfaction, resentment or contentment. Although complex and full of paradox, the emerging picture reflected accurately the characteristics of the contemporary organizations in which many of us work.

Implications and Challenges

Managers and scholars agree that important transformations are occurring in the contemporary workplace. The urgency to find different and innovative ways to organize work is clear. Management buzzwords include "flexibility," "empowerment," "autonomy," "circular management," and "concentrical structures." The pyramid is out, the circle and the web are in. The present search for more "organic" structures announces a new type of workplace. We are living at a time that future historians may designate as the period when bureaucracy died.

This is, at least, what most experts of work and organizations claim today. If bureaucracy was historically an important development of industrial society, its time, according to many, has passed. In a peculiar way, the contemporary era resembles the period when the modern bureaucracy was invented at the advent of industrialism. The contemporary shift from a manufacturing to a service-based economic system requires now, as it required then, a rethinking of the way organizational structures are designed and the way people are managed in them.

Today, rules covering hiring, training, promotion, job classification, and wage setting—in both union and non-union firms and for both white- and blue-collar workers—are in flux. Indeed, environmental pressures are forcing employers to reconsider the validity of employment arrangements that seemed to work well for the post-war labor market. Most human relations and human resource experimentation typical of today's work world must be viewed within this context. The basic transformations occurring now are characterized by transitions from bureaucratic or corporatist to market models of employment, or by attempts to keep the corporatist model viable (Osterman 1988; Pfeffer and Baron 1988; Aronowitz and DiFazio 1994).

Tensions are created when the macro forces of the economy are translated into formulas for managing the employment relationship. This is the context in which several different models of employment coexist within the same organization. The models create advantages and disadvantages for rational decision makers. They also have human consequences. The case study of PSA illustrates some of the consequences of mixing the models, especially when the resulting working conditions affect individuals possibly working side by side.

What was most innovative about bureaucratic arrangements, when they first emerged was precisely that bureaucracy solved problems of efficiency by directly addressing a critical human resources dilemma: the need to move from ascribed to achieved criteria in employment, thus making business decisions more attuned to the values of the times. This was in harmony with the new ideology of liberalism, which espoused the values of liberty, fraternity, and equality, and which promised to protect the integrity of the individual at all costs. For reasons too complex to discuss here, the solution to that imperative was the design of a hierarchical structure of work sustained by a clear separation between the person and the job. Bureaucracy solved the critical problem of protecting members of the organization from the potential arbitrariness inherent in decision making associated with the complexities of industrial work.

Today, the search for more efficient and effective ways to organize the workplace takes place in a different historical context. A popular argument behind this search is that bureaucratic work arrangements have become oppressive to all parties involved. For employees, they depersonalize the experience of work. This produces the much studied and dreaded existential condition of alienation. For managers, they interfere with the fast pace of modern decision making, thus representing a constant source of managerial frustration.

Yet the search for new work arrangements must still consider the fact that many of the human resources problems bureaucracy was designed to solve have not disappeared. What needs replacement in the present context is the anachronistic solution to the problems, not the concern with them. This is particularly true because the new organizational forms promise more discretion for all employees, from frontline workers to managers. A critical problem associated with this is the consequent growth of uncertainty and a reduction of predictability in work interactions. At a time of economic turbulence, with the threat of retrenchment and downsizing, a move toward more flexible work arrangements may also be a move away from the protection of the inherent dignity of employees and their right to a job and a decent standard of living. There is indeed a very fine line between responsible judgement and discretion on the one hand and arbitrariness and inconsistent behavior on the other. In this sense, the questions of distributive justice that framed the emergence of bureaucracy are equally critical in the emergence of a postbureaucratic paradigm. They cannot be absent from the search for new solutions that are historically more in keeping with postindustrial times and values.

Given the pervasiveness of heterogenous work arrangements in contemporary organizations, the human problem cannot be dismissed. It can be formulated as the generic question of how to ensure that individuals are treated with equity and equality, protecting their integrity as human beings regardless of their social condition and background. The problem is linked to the ultimate human resource management concern of how to preserve the inherent dignity of every single human being in the milieu where that person spends most of his or her productive life, that is, in the workplace. As many have already suggested, this is not just a moral but a practical concern linked to organizational survival.

For most of us who accept the inevitability of change in the workplace, this human resource management question can also be formulated in terms of how to make workplace transformations successful. This will require being sensitive to the needs and points of view of all parties involved. The pervasive effects of the cognitive discrepancies arising out of work today become even more relevant given the present shift toward more organic designs of organized collective actions. Moving toward more flexible structures may exacerbate many of the contradictions within today's workplace, as ingrained assumptions of distributive justice are violated.

Contemporary models of organizational change must therefore include considerations about how to address people's views of justice and deservedness. Managers will have to make efforts to define clearly the terms of the new psychological contracts. They will have to make sure that all parties involved—including themselves—understand the implications of the differences between the new and the old contracts. Furthermore, if it is true that jobs as we understand them today will disappear in the organizations of the future, managers and scholars need to consider very seriously how to deal with the present images of opportunity, which, after all, emerged and consolidated around the bureaucratic model of employment.

Even more importantly, as long as new work arrangements continue to be designed as zero-sum games where people must compete against each other for rewards, the stakes associated with uncertainty will be too high for employees to ignore. In the PSA example, as the agency sent mixed messages about merit to different occupational groups, employees spent a considerable amount of their energy and efforts pushing for the legitimacy of their own definitions. Accepted definitions of merit, after all, would have a direct impact on their share in the distribution of organizational rewards and resources. A critical question to address in the present transformation refers to the kind of mechanisms required to help develop the trust that all members of an organization need if they are not to be distracted by conditions of uncertainty and competition.

Finally, at a more pragmatic level, managers will have to pay closer attention to how they contribute to feelings of injustice among employees. They do so wherever a gap emerges between discourse and practice—a discourse that reflects management's best intentions to design more democratic, bottom-up, and inclusive organizations, and an actual human resource management practice that denies equal opportunity in the distribution of the resources necessary to make such democratic arrangements feasible.

The accomplishments and the satisfaction of operators in PSA do point to an important implication for action. They suggest that there are ways through which potentially bad jobs can be turned into good jobs, given the will to do so. I am not proposing here that operators should not have enjoyed the advantages they had in PSA. I am instead arguing that their advantages should not have happened at the expense of the sense of worth of other groups of employees within PSA. It may even be possible to consider structural designs and administrative systems that maximize equality among all employees in an organization. In PSA the inequalities not only had real consequences in excluding people from participation in the distribution of rewards, they also violated justice principles strongly reinforced by the ideology of merit. From this contradiction emerged resentments and dissatisfactions, and these fostered an atmosphere of conflict despite an appearance of cordiality.

Solutions to the dilemmas managers face to make organizations more flexible, efficient, and responsive also require acknowledging the dangers of choosing organizational designs that ignore the distributive problem bureaucracy tried to solve. Bringing issues of organizational justice to the forefront of the managerial agenda for change can only increase an employee's sense of organizational membership and commitment. Humanizing the system will be an important challenge to keep in mind as we reengineer, reinvent, restructure, or reform the workplace.

Methodological Issues

This study was based on fieldwork in an organization during the course of three years. The inquiry combined quantitative and qualitative approaches to data collection and analysis, including unobtrusive research on agency documents and records, participant observation, in-depth interviews with selected managers and employees, and a survey applied to a sample of employees from the three career ladders studied.

Sources of Data Collection

Work Site

Data from the work site were collected by three methods: participant observation for a period of three months in the role of analyst intern, face-to-face interviews with employees of different levels of the organization and from the three career ladders, and semi-structured interviews with other subjects linked to the agency's operations in the city (union representatives, a city labor relations representative, and previous management consultants to PSA).

Agency Documents and Records

The Action Form.   This is a personnel form reporting any instance when a person's employment situation changed in PSA (salary adjustments, transfers, title changes, promotions, separations, leaves of absence, disciplinary actions, etc.). Processed daily, they were filed every three months. Thus, they reported every possible movement performed in the agency throughout the year. I studied action forms filed in PSA during one randomly chosen month in 1986 and those filed for all titles of the three selected career ladders during a twelve-month period in 1985 and 1986. The objective was to acquire an understanding of the types of movements and salary changes employees experienced.

The Managerial Roster. This was a list that included demographic and organizational information for the total managerial population working in PSA at one point in time during 1986 (N = 180). The roster yielded a data set of the managerial population (15 variables and 175 cases).

Personnel Files. I had access to files for 410 employees (370 who answered my survey and another 39 selected male and female managers in the agency). These were used to construct work histories. The survey sample is described in the following section. The 39 managerial work histories give a profile of 22 percent of the total managerial group. They include 14 line and 24 staff managers. Their years of entry vary between 1939 to 1985. I did not have access to all managerial files. I used seniority and organizational level as the main categories to choose among available files whenever possible. These work histories were not randomly chosen and thus they are not a representative sample. Comparisons with the total managerial population indicate, however, that the collection includes a fairly varied group of managers by function and type. Because of these limitations, I have used the information from these cases only to illustrate patterns documented with other sources and to complement the more reliable information offered from the managerial roster and from the surveyed employees.

Miscellaneous Agency Documents. These included personnel employee rosters, equal employment opportunity reports, formal job descriptions for each job title in PSA, and job title lists with actual salary ranges for PSA.

Supplemental Documents. These included written reports from previous consultants, union manuals, archival material about union actions, newspaper articles about PSA, papers written by PSA managers, and PSA memoranda.

The Survey Instrument

The Questionnaire. This was a fifteen-page questionnaire on topics ranging from job satisfaction and related work attitudes to perceptions of opportunity and fairness, to demographic data.

The Sampling Frame. I used a systematic stratified random sample of nine hundred employees from the three occupational groups, drawing from job title and level in the career ladder. The sample was stratified for two reasons. First, the sample had to include enough employees who had entered the agency during the year previous to the study, so that time order issues could at least be partially addressed. (All new employees from the selected job titles were included in the sample.) Second, the sample had to include enough employees from each group to perform the analysis. Because of the small size of the analyst group I included the entire group rather than a sample.

Respondents were given several incentives to answer the survey: two follow-up letters, the union's endorsement of the survey, a managerial memorandum alerting supervisors to encourage responses, and a raffle with cash prices. The response rate was of 41 percent, yielding a final total of 370 usable questionnaires. This sample represents fairly well the subgroups studied in PSA with respect to gender, ethnic background, civil service status, and organizational level distributions. Table A.1 compares the sample and the actual populations.

Discussion of Quantitative Models

Data for the quantitative analysis about opportunity and satisfaction were drawn from the managerial roster, the work histories, and the survey. The most important models are briefly described below.

Table A.1. Comparison of sample and actual PSA population by sex, race, civil service status, and level (%)

	Operators			Clerical employees			Analysts		
	Sample	Population	Difference	Sample	Population	Difference	Sample	Population	Difference
Sex									
Male	99.3	99.5	−0.2	29	33	−4	62	66	−4
Female	0.7	0.5	0.2	71	67	4	38	34	4
Race									
White	77	76	1	47	43	4	76	61	15
Black	15	17	−2	40	46	−6	14	25	−10
Other	8	7	1	13	11	2	10	14	−4
Civil service status									
Permanent	97	100	−3	57	61	−4	40	33	7
Provisional	0	0	0	43	38	5	42	30	12
Noncompetitive	0	0	0	0	1	−1	18	37	−19
Don't know	3	0	3	—	—	—	—	—	—
Level									
Managerial	7	1	6	1	0	0	0	2	−2
Supervisory	35	15	20	16	13	3	20	20	0
Entry (old)	36	80	−44	50	74	−24	54	53	1
Entry (new)	22	4	18	33	12	21	25	24	1

Models to Study Opportunity

A Model of Managerial Earnings in PSA. This model predicted the annual salary, using 1986 dollars, by function and job title. The independent variables were:

- sex (male = 1, female = 0),
- race (white = 1, minority = 0)
- organizational unit where manager worked (dummy variables for administration, operations, other)
- seniority (number of years in the organization)
- time prior to most recent promotion (number of years before last promotion divided by seniority)
- managerial grade level (three dummy variables representing high, intermediate, and low levels)
- employee's work function (line managers = 1, staff managers = 0)

A Model of the Determinants of Opportunity Dimensions. The following models were specified to predict each opportunity dimension:

Log(ratio of salary increase) = b(seniority) + b1(education) + b2 (level) + b3 (career ladder) + b4 (promotion)

Log(promotion+1) = b(seniority squared) + b1 (education) + b2 (level) + b3 (career ladder)

Log(training+1) = b(natural log of seniority) + b1 (education) + b2 (career ladder * education)

where
- Promotion = the number of promotions attained, as reported in the personnel file
- Salary increase = the ratio of current to starting salary
- Training = the number of programs taken, as reported by the employee
- Seniority = number of years in the agency
- Education = number of years of education completed
- Level = entry, intermediate, supervisory, or managerial (Omitted category: Intermediate)
- Career ladder = operator, permanent clerical, provisional clerical, permanent analyst, or provisional analyst (omitted: operator)

Given the demographic composition of the ladders, race and sex variables were not included to avoid multicollinearity effects. It was assumed that these were attributes of career ladder participation.

The association between seniority and the dependent variables was curvilinear in the sample. Thus the dependent variables were transformed to the natural logs of the salary ratio, of the number of promotions, and of the training programs. In addition, the promotion model used the square of seniority, and the training model used the natural log of seniority. In the salary model, for all new employees the salary ratio was 1, and ln(1) = 0; in the promotion and training models, many entry-level employees may have 0 as a valid value; hence the variables were transformed to ln(Salary ratio +1), ln(promotion + 1), and ln(training +1). Finally, a better fit was ensured by imposing a restriction in the models, forcing the regression to go through the origin and suppressing the constant term.[1]

Models to Study Job Satisfaction

Measuring Employee Satisfaction. Facet-free measures (overall job satisfaction as reported by employees) and facet-specific measures (satisfaction with specific aspects of the job) were used following standard instruments from the literature (Miller 1980).

Facet-specific measures included social relations, promotion, job challenge, financial security, adequate resources (supervisory and other), and physical surroundings (comfort). Fourteen items included questions about these dimensions: whether the job offered chances to make friends; whether the co-workers were friendly and helpful; whether the job offered opportunity to develop one's own special abilities; whether it offered enough help and equipment to get the job done; whether the work was interesting; whether it offered good pay, fringe benefits, job security, good chances for promotion, and fairly handled promotions; whether it provided enough authority to do the work; whether the supervisor was competent in doing the job and successful in getting people to work together; and whether physical surroundings were pleasant.

Two different sets of questions elicited information about how important each dimension was to employees and how much of that dimension they felt they had in their present job. Following traditional procedures in the field, these two responses were compared to produce a discrepancy score, which indicated satisfaction or dissatisfaction with each job dimension. A discrepancy would indicate that the person was dissatisfied; no discrepancy would indicate the person was satisfied.

The Job Satisfaction Regression Models. The models assessed how much of the variation in global job satisfaction for each career group was connected to individual, organizational, and job factors, including "opportunity"-related aspects of the job, both objectively measured and subjectively reported. The *dependent variable* was global job satisfaction. This variable was measured by a job satisfaction score ranging from −12 (indicating dissatisfaction) to +12 (indicating satisfaction). The score was the result of adding the answers to four question-naire items that tapped the overall sense of satisfaction of employees. To each answer a value ranging from $+3$ to -3 was assigned.

The *independent and control variables* were four sets of variables representing the most important determinants of job satisfaction covered in the literature: individual and organizational variables, objective opportunity variables, subjective perception of opportunity, and perception of job characteristics.

Individual and organizational variables[2] and their measurement are shown in Table A.2.

"Objective" opportunity variables. These were constructed unobtrusively rather than relying on employees' perceptions. The patterns of mobility, earnings, and personal growth found in the work histories of the employees who answered the survey were used to develop three individual attainment variables for promotion, compensation, and job challenge. These variables indicate how each employee has done relative to the rest of the sample with respect to each dimension. They thus capture how employees have used the opportunities available in the ladder.

To construct the individual indicators I created a standard against which employees' attainment could be compared for each dimension of opportunity. The standard is the predicted value for the attained number of promotions, the ratio of salary increase from time of entry to present time, and the number of training programs taken. The assumption is that each of these could be success-fully explained as a function of five variables: seniority (years in the agency), education (years of education completed), level (position in the hierarchy: entry, intermediate, supervisory, or managerial), civil service status, and membership in a career ladder. The difference in the predicted value and the observed actual value for each employee—that is, the residual after regressing each opportunity

Table A.2. Individual and organizational variables

Variable	Type of variable	Range of variation
Race	binary	1 = minority; 0 = non-minority
Sex*	binary	1 = female; 0 = male
Civil service status*	binary	1 = provisional; 0 = permanent
Education	continuous	6 to 16 (years of school completed)
Seniority	continuous	1 to 46 (years working in the city)
Organizational level	dummy	Entry level
		Intermediate level
		Supervisory level
		Managerial level**

* For analyst and clerical ladders only.
** For operator ladder only.

variable on the mentioned independent variables—represents how each individual has done relative to the rest: average, above average, or below average. The following steps were used to construct the final scores for each dimension of opportunity:

1. Consider as raw indicators of *opportunity for compensation*: ratio of salary increase from entry to present time ($R = S/S_0$, where R = ratio, S = present salary, and S_0=salary at time 0); *opportunity for promotion*: number of promotions that the employee has experienced (P); *opportunity for job challenge*: number of training programs in which employee has participated (T).

2. Run regression models to obtain predicted scores for each raw indicator. Use as predictors seniority, education, level, and career membership, specifying civil service status. Specify each model (see equations in the Appendix section "A Model of the Determinants of Opportunity Dimensions," page 218).

3. Create a final opportunity indicator for each dimension by computing the residual for each model:

Salary increase = $\hat{R} - R$ (Opportunity for salary increment)

Promotion = $\hat{P} - P$ (Opportunity for promotion)

Training = $\hat{T} - T$ (Opportunity for personal growth)

These measures capture how well each employee has done in his or her attainment of these dimensions of opportunity compared to others—that is, attainment above or below the average opportunity an employee is expected to have, given his or her seniority, education, level, civil service, and career ladder membership.

The three resulting variables used in the job satisfaction model tapped each dimension of opportunity studied: promotion (number of promotions), salary increase (increments in salary from entry to present position), and training (amount received in PSA). Each variable ranges from negative to positive numbers, where 0 indicates an average opportunity, a negative value indicates fewer opportunities than the average, and a positive value indicates more opportunities than the average in the sample. The actual ranges are as follows:

Variable	Lowest	Highest
Promotion	−0.886	2.993
Training	−0.854	6.200
Salary increase	0.472	2.105

"Subjective" perceptions of opportunity were measured by means of two self-reported variables, discrimination and opportunities outside the agency. They were coded for the model as follows:

Variable	Type of variable	Range of variation
Discrimination	Binary	1 = has felt discrimination 0 = has not felt discrimination
Outside opportunity	Binary	1 = easy to find an outside job 0 = hard to find

Perceptions of the job were assessed by means of six variables, using the same dimensions described in the Appendix section "Measuring Employee Satisfaction." For each dimension employees reported how much of it they felt they had in their present job, regardless of how much they valued or desired the aspect. These are therefore different from the discrepancy scores described in the facet-specific measures of satisfaction. Indexes for the six indicators were created by adding scores for items that loaded in a factor analysis. The results of this analysis replicated Quinn and Sheppard's results (1978). The variables were coded for the model as shown:

Variable	Type of variable	Range of variation
Job learning	Binary	1 = job has opportunities to learn 0 = job does not have opportunities
Comfort	Binary	1 = job is pleasant 0 = job is not pleasant
Social relations	Continuous	0 = not true at all; 6 = very true
Advancement	Continuous	0 = not true at all; 6 = very true
Adequate resources	Continuous	0 = not true at all; 9 = very true
Financial security	Continuous	0 = not true at all; 9 = very true

The Model for the Entire Sample

The model specification uses the same variables of the previous models, with the following changes:

1. The individual and organizational variables, as well as the objective opportunity measures and the subjective sense of outside opportunity, were excluded. The assumption was that these variables were either subsumed in membership in the ladder (for example, sex composition and opportunity measures) or are in fact not important (for example, hierarchical level or tenure).[3]
2. The model included an objective measure of the complexity of the job in addition to career ladder membership and job perceptions. This is a binary variable where 1 = low complexity and 0 = high complexity.[4]

3. Employees were divided into five categories: operators (all are permanent), permanent clerical employees, permanent analysts, provisional clerical employees, and provisional analysts. Operators represented the omitted category.

A separate model of job satisfaction was used to test the contextual effect of education. This model replaced the variables representing each subgroup (permanent analysts, provisional analysts, permanent clerical employees, provisional clerical employees) by four categories constructed by multiplying the dummy for each subgroup by their education, as done when creating interaction terms. It did not include separate terms for education and career ladder. Thus, rather than testing for interaction effects, it tested for significant differences in the effect of education on the satisfaction of the staff groups vis-à-vis the operators. It also explored possible differences in the slopes of each subgroup given the specific dynamics of their experience.

These interaction parameters might be biased because of the exclusion of the first-order dummy variables. They might, in fact, be a proxy for either education or career ladder. The goal was not to focus on interaction effects, however, but to illustrate the importance of education despite its lack of significance in the previous models. Hence this model tests a less complex, yet still interesting hypothesis: that the effect of education on satisfaction varies by career ladder for the staff groups. I am aware that the decision to use this model does not represent the best methodological solution to the problem. The larger conceptual and methodological problem requires further attention before firmer conclusions about the combined effect of education and career ladder, over and above the independent effect of each, can be reached. Such an analysis lies beyond the scope of this project. The present exercise served the global purpose of providing some checks on an intuitive proposition about the PSA environment: that education is still important, despite its lack of statistical significance.

Notes

Chapter 1. Introduction: The Promise of Opportunity and the Experience of Inequality

1. In all fairness, this model is too simple. Rather than linear, the causality is circular, as work attitudes may trigger employees' acceptance or rejection of existing opportunity structures, thus helping legitimate or transform them. Furthermore, the arrows can go in both directions, because in particular contexts, work attitudes may affect perceptions of justice and these may motivate individuals to change the structures. I have kept the simplified version for clarity's sake.

2. Two critical internal documents were the lists of existing job titles with their salary ranges and the equal employment opportunity report for the agency.

3. The following analytical questions guided this part of the inquiry: Which factors most influenced job satisfaction of PSA employees? Did the same factors affect the satisfaction of employees in different career ladders? How important were job-related opportunity perceptions in shaping satisfaction or dissatisfaction with the job? And finally, were the differences in satisfaction among groups associated with differences in their opportunity structures, and if so, in what ways? The Appendix describes the measurement of employee satisfaction and other variables in the models.

4. It is important to clarify that the components of the quantitative models do not represent a departure from the job satisfaction research tradition. The goal of the analysis was not to develop new analytical models but to apply a different perspective to existing research issues. The novelty of the present inquiry consists in its concern with pervasive organizational inequality. The reasoning was that the same variables already treated in traditional models can provide new insights, once areas previously ignored are brought to light.

5. In 1985 government employment represented about 16 percent of the total U.S. labor force. Of these, about three-quarters were state and local employees (DiPrete 1989).

6. For an excellent review of the literature on internal labor markets (ILMs) see Althauser 1987. I provide a definition of ILMs in Chapter 5 and a discussion of its application to PSA in Chapter 3.

7. In his discussion of equality and justice Deutsch (1985) differentiates healthy distinctions (which recognize and value individual differences) from invidious or unacceptable distinctions (which label and rank individuals). He defines the latter as those which (1) promote generalized or irrelevant feelings of superiority or inferiority (e.g., assuming that a beautiful person is superior as a person); (2) promote generalized or irrelevant status differences (e.g., assuming that a manager deserves a higher standard of living than a factory worker); (3) promote generalized or irrelevant superordinate-subordinate relations (e.g., assuming that a private must shine the captain's shoes); (4) promote the view that the legitimate needs and interests of some people are less important than those of other people (e.g., assuming less consideration of someone's needs because of sex, race, age, national or family origin, religious preference, political affiliation, occupation, physical handicap, or lack of special talents).

8. Two types of competition affecting the employment relationship have become exacerbated in the present societal context. From the point of view of employees, the competition for jobs or the opportunity to participate in redefined work processes increases as the workplace is transformed. This is true not only among new or prospective job seekers but also among those who until recently may have felt safe in a stable job. Increasingly they see their job security threatened. From the point of view of employers, the competition to attract and retain employees with the right type of skills and attitudes is also increasing. This is a result of both demographic changes, and changes in skill requirements in the transition to service and information economies.

Chapter 2. Exploring the Nature and the Impact of the Gap

1. Research on work attitudes has usually concentrated on two important questions: (1) what factors affect or shape employee attitudes? and (2) how do attitudes affect employee performance and other organizational outcomes (productivity, commitment, turnover, citizenship) associated with it? Answers to the first question are useful to design successful managerial strategies to direct employee behavior in a positive way. The second question is relevant to determine whether managers should pay attention to employee attitudes in promoting higher levels of organizational performance. In today's turbulent environment, answers to both questions have acquired a renewed importance.

2. This approach to organizational stratification is based on a reformulation of some basic assumptions used by the status attainment and human capital research traditions to explain the outcomes of stratified systems. For details on this discussion see Pfeffer 1977, and Bielby and Baron 1980. The new stratification research tradition presents the "organization of work" as the link between social structure and individual attainment. In this view, the firm is the missing link between the macro and the micro dimensions of inequality.

3. Examples of stratification research traditions that consider these levels include the theory of segmented and dual labor markets, the vacancy chains approach, the organizational demography approach, and traditional schools of the sociology of stratification, of organizations, and of labor. All these have in common an emphasis on structure. They differ, however, in the specific variables proposed at each structural level and in the importance given to each. Overall, few attempts have been successful in interrelating the variables in a coherent theoretical framework (Spaeth 1984). As a consequence, these traditions differ greatly in methodology.

4. Although scholars have not agreed on a label for this form of organization, they characterize it as a unique combination of bureaucracy and paternalism, best described by the term *welfare corporatism* (Lincoln and Kalleberg 1990).

5. Even the highly paid "contingent" white-collar employee is at a disadvantage by virtue of lack of a stable income and exclusion from benefits such as health insurance.

6. Kluegel and Smith document that the same individuals who accept this ideology are in fact aware of existing inequalities and often doubt whether it is fair. Half the respondents in their study, for example, reported that they received less income than they felt they deserved. A large number of respondents evaluated the average incomes of low-paid and high-paid occupations as unfair relative to the contribution that people in these occupations made to society. Finally, most were aware that some causes of poverty were beyond the control of the poor.

7. The authors explore the conditions under which these challenges either overthrow the dominant ideology or are deflected. They identify several possible reasons why people accept the dominant ideology, including the absence of a strong counterideology in American society. Even more important, in these authors' estimate, is the effect of cognitive mechanisms in attitude and belief formation. These include treating contradictory evidence as exceptions (limits to generalization), compartmentalizing information and beliefs into separate schemas (nonintegration of beliefs), and ignoring the contradictions to minimize distress (motivational reasons).

8. One feels entitled to something if one has met the appropriate preconditions for obtaining it. A sense of entitlement evokes feelings of justice or injustice when one compares oneself to others (Lerner, Miller, and Holmes 1976).

9. The other 4 percent and 6 percent answered "do not know."

10. Faith in the market's capacity to distribute social goods is illustrated by answers about the fairness of the U.S. free enterprise system in national surveys conducted in 1959 and 1977. Eighty-two percent of respondents held that this system is "fair and wise," 65 percent that it "gives everyone a fair chance," and 63 percent that it is a "fair and efficient system" (McClosky and Zaller 1984).

11. This definition characterizes distributive justice in terms of fairness and represents the approach that views justice as "liberal equality" (Taylor 1991).

12. Verba and Orren argue, for example, that tolerance for economic inequality is not a universal phenomenon in this country. Yet they also indicate that opposition to economic inequality tends to manifest itself as support for "a floor under incomes to eliminate extreme poverty" in contrast to "ceiling on income to limit extreme wealth" (1985:19).

13. For example, more than 85 percent of the public in a 1984 poll characterized America as an open society and believed that what is achieved in life no longer depends on family background but on abilities and education (Lane 1986).

14. Perhaps for the same reason there are clear disagreements about what justice really means. Even though the term is frequently used in a "universal" sense, and its definition is taken for granted, the notion of justice is very ambiguous. For example, philosophers make a distinction between the *formal* and the *material* principles of justice. The first defines the broad domain of justice as "giving each his or her due." Most people agree with this general proposition. The second, on the other hand, specifies the conditions that must be met if justice is to exist. It refers to the actual content of what is just. These conditions are to some extent a function of processes of negotiation among subgroups with different claims over the legitimacy of their fair share, as well as different degrees of power to enforce these claims (Greenberg and Cohen 1982; Homans 1974; Blau 1964).

15. In this sense, bureaucracy represents a form of domination, albeit one more bearable than its predecessors. The main difference between more traditional and more modern bureaucratic designs is perhaps that the latter's formal authority relations and practices have become instruments to regulate individual behavior and to legitimate unequal distributions of organizational resources. This new form of discipline relies heavily on individually internalized values rather than on physical force or other forms of external coercion typical of traditional authority (Ferguson 1984; Edwards 1979).

16. While the traditional bureaucracies of the precapitalist era were far more authoritarian and controlling of the ruled than protective of their rights, their original mind-set did not totally disappear from the modern bureaucracy. That the bureaucratic form (which reached its full development with capitalism and the modern regulatory state) has within itself an inherent contradiction is partly due to its origins in the monarchism of the late feudal period. Bureaucracy's intellectual roots can be traced to the ancient Chinese dynasties as well as the large scale organizations of the Russian czars (Ferguson 1984). The new, more organic forms, which reject some of the basic bureaucratic traits, have nonetheless inherited many assumptions from this dynamic transformation.

17. Some cognitive psychologists add the possibility that employees may accommodate psychologically to these contradictions by compartmentalizing them in separate schemes, which their minds never interconnect. This allows people to endorse contradictory beliefs and to maintain unchallenged the contradiction between beliefs and experience (see Kluegel and Smith 1986 for a review of this perspective). I argue that as the transparency of justice violations grows, so does the probability that the barriers between schemes will disappear.

Chapter 3. The Organizational Setting

1. To maintain confidentiality, the nature of PSA's prime mandate, or "critical task" will not be revealed. Information lost by this decision is partially counterbalanced by the "thick description" of work life at PSA, which provides an accurate portrait of the nature of this organization.

2. These were distributed among the eight occupational categories designated to analyze equal employment opportunity requirements, as follows: officials/administrators 22 percent, professionals 26 percent, technicians 15 percent, protective services 1 percent, paraprofessionals 4 percent, office clerical 5 percent, skilled craft 19 percent, and service maintenance 8 percent. Employees from the targeted ladders—analysts, clerical employees, and operators—belong to the professional, office clerical, the skilled craft/service maintenance categories respectively. Managers and supervisors of the three groups belong to the officials/administrator category.

3. These structures exemplify the notion of a "perfect Internal Labor Market" in the context of public sector employment (Doeringer and Piore 1971; Sorensen and Tuma 1981; Althauser 1987).

4. For the purpose of this discussion the difference between the two groups can be equated with the classic organizational distinction between line and staff, based on task distributions and authority lines (Blau and Scott 1963).

5. According to the mayor's management report for the year 1986–87, the total city work force was 225,238. PSA and the three other agencies nearly identical to PSA had a work force of 69,718, or 31 percent of the total. The four similar agencies had a work force

of 110,624, or 49 percent. All the other agencies together accounted for 44,896 workers, or 20 percent.

6. Source: Report by a PSA consultant.

7. Some operator managers with blue-collar origins acquired a college education as they moved up, even though it was not technically required for the job.

8. Source: Agency computer runs for a 1986 point in time, with a total PSA work force count of 12,884 employees.

9. These jobs contributed toward the standardization of the work processes (e.g., work study analysts), of the outputs (e.g., planners, budget analysts, and accountants), as well as of the skills needed to turn inputs into outputs (e.g., staff analysts, trainers, recruiters, etc.).

10. Their position ceilings, that is, numbers of incumbents assigned to them by the city, varied from 1 to 7,000 individuals assigned within each title. Single-incumbent or specific titles in PSA represented 32 percent of all titles. Examples included landscape architect, head nurse, and heads of units or offices. Generic titles represented general tasks and functions for positions substantially similar in character, responsibilities, and qualification requirements. The jobs in the operator, analyst, and clerical career ladders were generic and included both managerial and nonmanagerial titles. Some examples of managerial generic titles were administrative manager (clerical) and administrative staff analyst (analyst). Nonmanagerial titles included staff analyst, office associate, and supervisors for other titles.

11. Until the 1960s civil service was defined as a public personnel system guided by merit principles and administered by a semi-autonomous board, the civil service commission. With the decline of these commissions, some authors refer to this system as "the civil service merit system" (Fox 1993).

12. Some scholars attribute the creation of these titles to a desire to make professional appointments without the constraint of civil service examinations. The argument is that people with "demonstrated" talent should not be bothered with tests and delays. A more formal explanation is that an organization needs to hire individuals who are able to establish links with targeted communities, whether or not they can pass standardized tests. Indeed one of the noncompetitive titles is community liaison (Rich 1982).

13. To decide whether or not to include a job title I worked out definitions of "analysts," "clerical employees," and "operators" that would reflect PSA's culture. This helped identify the job titles and their actual links in the job sequences from entry ports to managerial ceilings. My procedure involved asking personnel staff to indicate in what job titles each type of employee tended to be located formally and informally; confirming the formal relationships in PSA's official documents on position classification; asking selected managers about the typical informal movement of employees in each of the three groups; and analyzing records of daily and monthly staffing actions in PSA. (I looked at daily changes in the employment situation of PSA employees during two randomly chosen months, and I also looked at monthly summaries of such changes for twelve consecutive months.)

14. The same structure existed for the city planner, statistician and project coordinator ladders.

15. These data were gathered in the 1989 survey on local personnel practices of the International City/County Management Association (ICMA). The study surveyed 979 cities with populations over 10,000 and 268 counties with populations over 25,000.

16. Klinger and Nalbandian mention four. They are individual rights (protection from capricious and arbitrary employment decisions), administrative efficiency (the technocratic imperative to do the task adequately), political responsiveness (effective response to and representation of the public interest), and social equity (responsibility to provide equal access and fair treatment to all social groups, with particular emphasis on those that have been historically denied such rights). Fox (1993) provides a more comprehensive inventory: efficiency, effectiveness, economy, equity, representativeness, responsiveness, accountability, civil rights and liberties, procedural fairness, and equal protection. Interestingly enough, he reminds us that the existence of the first three values is linked to the civil service reform movement of the nineteenth century, while the rest are more recent values emerging under what is called democratic constitutionalism.

17. In theory these standards are protected by the existence of a centralized personnel entity external to the bureaucracy where civil servants work. This agency is usually a personnel department, a civil service commission, or in some cases a combination of both. Originally, at the federal level the Civil Service Commission was responsible for the administration of the civil service rules. In 1978 this charge was transferred to the Office of Personnel Management, and the commission was replaced by the Merit Systems Protection Board, which had an exclusively watchdog role. Local governments have followed the same model, slowly replacing independent civil service commissions with professional personnel departments. Fox's study of local personnel practices reports that 44.1 percent of the cities in the survey had a personnel department, while only 2 percent had independent civil service commissions; 41.4 percent of them had a combination of both.

18. Fox compiled these using the federal government standards proposed for local government personnel practices.

19. Much has been written about the origins of the civil service in the United States, and it is not the purpose of this section to summarize this extensive literature. For the best historical source see Van Riper (1958).

20. The 1883 passage of the Pendleton Act at the federal level created the momentum for the introduction of merit systems in cities like Albany, Buffalo, and New York City in 1884, 1885, and 1888 respectively, and later in Chicago and Seattle in 1895 and 1896. Coverage of these systems was limited to a few occupational groups, and it only involved features such as competitive entrance exams, job security, protection against political reprisal, and the existence of an independent Civil Service Commission. The introduction of the Social Security Act of 1935 provided another important federal impetus for the adoption of merit principles at the local level. To ensure the efficient implementation of the new welfare programs introduced by the government, Congress required in 1939 the adoption of merit-based personnel standards for employees in state and local agencies administering the new federal programs. By the mid-sixties, many local governments had implemented formal merit systems, and the use of merit principles was common in public agencies (Fox 1993).

21. Public managers adopted different strategies toward unions as these appeared in various regions. Union leaders reacted either by fighting or by supporting the passage of formal merit systems (Fox 1993).

22. Fox bases this argument on the observation that strong unions apparently coincide with weak civil service systems and that powerless unions (or no unions) coincide with strong civil service systems.

23. The argument here is that in many jurisdictions public unionization and collective bargaining grew out of civil service associations and other groups of employees struggling to have their say about the conditions of employment.

Chapter 4. Processes: Moving Up, Getting Paid, and Learning from Work

1. The names of all employees have been changed to protect confidentiality. In some cases male employees have been given female names and vice versa.

2. To identify patterns in the three ladders and to ascertain the routes to success at PSA I studied 409 work histories. Formal and informal interviews, as well as data from direct observation and from agency documents, complemented this information.

3. For example, although I have made a modest attempt at measuring probabilities for promotion and search statistical differences in earnings, the use of formal Markov or semi-Markov models is beyond the scope of this project. I have also attempted to construct career histories of the employees studied, but I make no claim to have performed formal career-line or event-history analyses.

4. Although the organizational stratification and job satisfaction literatures have given some consideration to these dimensions, they usually treat them separately rather than as a set reflecting the multidimensional nature of opportunity. Treating them integrally represents another important contribution of this book.

5. The analysis of the managerial group confirmed the difference in the number of transfers between line and staff employees. Of those studied, line managers moved very frequently around PSA before they became managers. They were transferred many times to different work sites in the Operations Unit, mostly in the field. There were also transfers from the field to headquarters. This helped them acquire a more varied experience and the exposure necessary for future promotional advances. In contrast, staff managers had fewer transfers reported throughout their careers, and they usually specialized in very specific areas. Most of them worked outside the Operations Unit before and after becoming managers.

6. Only in a few instances did operators deviate from the civil service path. In those cases the abnormality was usually corrected within a month.

7. I was not able to find work histories of analyst managers comparable to those of Managers A and B.

8. Only 15 percent of the 20 administrative staff analysts, 7 percent of the 29 administrative managers, and 2 percent of the 52 managers in miscellaneous titles were permanent employees, according to PSA's managerial employment roster.

9. It could be argued that a 70 percent rate of internal recruitment for staff managers was satisfactory as a promotion policy. Yet this number includes managers who had held at least two positions in PSA. It represents a conservative estimate, since some of the managers counted might not have developed their careers in PSA.

10. The accident consisted in being in the right job when a city-wide effort to consolidate titles allowed this employee to move into a more favorable job.

11. To establish if there were any particular attributes to explain his success, I compared his career to those of other managers who had entered PSA during the same period (the mid-1950s). The only apparent difference was that he had skipped two levels of the managerial ladder, perhaps aided by his high visibility.

12. Other statistics confirmed the lower prospects of career success for staff employ-

ees: 81 percent of the hires in nonmanagerial positions in the agency came from civil service lists, and thus moved following its rules. The combination of this figure and those for managers implies that the actual prospects of career success for the many nonmanagerial staff employees were few.

13. Clerical employees who were aware of this would try to change from the clerical to the analytical ladder to improve their status. For example, one such employee moved up the clerical ladder to the position of permanent supervisor. He then took the staff analyst civil service exam and changed titles, with no salary increase. Five years later, he was promoted to associate staff analyst with a salary increase of $1,500. While this was not a typical route, it illustrates the possibility of pursuing change without breaking the formal rules of the system.

14. During the last period of this investigation a new law was passed to protect provisionals from such arbitrary dismissals.

15. Examples of these practices at the federal level can be found in the so-called Malek Manual, a document prepared by the White House personnel office during Nixon's presidency. It instructed managers about ways to manipulate the system. An excerpt from this document is reprinted in Thompson 1991: 58–81.

16. For an in-depth analysis of the consequences of these practices for personnel, see Ospina 1992a and 1992b.

17. Women managers from Fortune 500 corporations reported this to be the case in focus groups conducted by the research firm Catalyst (source: personal conversation with Marcia Brumit Kropf, vice-president of research advisory services for Catalyst, 1995).

18. While 79 percent of the operators and 63 percent of the clerical employees had participated in training programs, only 45 percent of the analysts had. Those who had not participated were asked why. Sixty-five percent reported that programs had not been offered, 20 percent reported having had no information about them, and 15 percent reported having chosen not to participate. Even though the differences across groups were not significant, it is worth mentioning that 27 percent of the clerical employees reported having no information about the programs as the reason for not participating, compared to 16 percent of the analysts and operators.

19. Later the agency won an award as well as open public recognition for these innovative efforts.

20. PSA's Personnel Department spent much time devising ways to document these efforts without breaking the law. This generated a lot of additional paper work and procedures, which otherwise would have been unnecessary.

Chapter 5. Outcomes and Outputs: The Consequences of Patterned Opportunity

1. Sources for this analysis include the report for 1986 from PSA's Equal Employment Opportunity Office, personnel documents such as computer rosters listing all titles in the agency with the corresponding salary ranges for 1986, and the formal job descriptions for each job title in PSA.

2. The job descriptions examined in this study included both generic ones, used by all city agencies, and ones specific to PSA.

3. In this analysis I calculated the midpoint for the official salary range assigned to each entry-level title. I then used the midpoint to rank all titles within a scale of $5,000

intervals, considering the lowest and the highest possible salaries among all entry-level jobs (Figures 1, 2, and 3 in Chapter 3 help visualize salary midpoints and ranges for the jobs in each ladder). The midpoints represent a conservative estimate because in reality, most clerical employees and analysts started closer to the bottom of the range and got increases only after their first year.

4. For this analysis I used the midpoints of the managerial salary ranges from level I to level VIII in each ladder. To check the results, I repeated the exercise using raw starting salaries for the managerial entry level in each title. The ranking did not change.

5. Peterson-Hardt and Pearlman quantified these factors to produce a job requirement score. This score can be used to compare advancement requirements across ladders. The points used to code each requirement in the job descriptions were as follows. *Educational requirements*: none mentioned, 0; literacy, 1; high school diploma, 2; associate or technical degree, 3; bachelors degree, 4; masters, 5; specialized masters, 6; doctorate, 7. *Experience length*: none or less than 1 yr, 0; one year, 1; two years, 2; three years, 3; four years, 4; five or more years, 5. *Experience content*: none or unspecialized, 0; specialized skill or experience, 1. *Accessibility by former GS employment*: none mentioned, 0; yes, 1. *Exam requirements*: none, 0; yes, 1. Adding the points in each category provides a final score that ranges from 0 to 15. The higher the score the harder the job requirements to enter that title and thus the lower the opportunity. The final scores for the three ladders were as follows: *Entry titles*: operator, 2; analyst, 7; clerical, 5 and 2 (two entry titles). *Supervisory titles*: operator, 4 and 3 (two levels); analyst, 9; clerical, 8. *Managerial titles*: operator, 6; analyst, 8; clerical, 8.

6. Consistent with Peterson-Hardt and Pearlman's approach, I subtracted the ceiling job requirement score from the entry score in each ladder. If the difference was of 2 points or more, then the ladder would be considered harder to climb because the increase in requirements would be steeper. A difference of 0 or only 1 point would indicate an easier movement.

7. The difference between entry and managerial requirements was 7 points for the clerical ladder (hardest to climb), 4 points for the operator ladder, and 2 points for the analyst ladder.

8. Peterson-Hardt and Pearlman call this the level of possible mobility (LPM) for each ladder. They use the following coding scheme for the analysis:

		Mobility level	
Entry level	*Low*	*Medium*	*High*
Low	Low	High	High
Medium	Low	High	High
High	Low	High	High

Applying this scheme to the PSA case, the entry level was medium and the mobility level was medium for the operator ladder; thus its LPM was high. For the clerical ladder, the LPM was low for both the shop clerk route (entry level = medium, mobility level = low) and the office aide route (entry level = low, mobility level = low). For the analyst ladder, using the staff analyst progression, the LPM was low (entry level = high, but mobility level = low).

9. Some would argue that the histories of managers are not helpful unless they are compared to those of employees who either did not make it into management or left PSA

after reaching management—what Kelsall (1955) calls "wastage" in the system. Since this information is not available, the present discussion offers only a partial view.

10. Information about the managerial group came from PSA's management employment roster, which included characteristics for all 180 managers employed in the agency during 1986. I eliminated from the analysis five managers who held exempt positions, including the commissioner and deputy commissioners of the agency.

11. DiPrete (1989) suggests that a similar process was responsible for the gradual creation of the boundary between clerical and administrative jobs in the federal system.

12. Of the 176 managers in PSA, 101 were staff and 75 were line. Together, analysts and clerical titles constituted 29 percent of the staff managerial titles at the time of the study.

13. The average tenure for line managers was twenty-six years and their average number of years prior to their last promotion (possibly to the managerial level) was twenty-two. Comparable figures for staff managers are not useful, since the lower limit of the range for this group is zero. The five oldest civilian managers, however, had an average of thirty-six years of tenure, so sixteen years or more is a fairly conservative standard.

14. It is harder to estimate the pattern of the 29 percent who fell in the middle (managers with tenures of between eleven and fifteen years), but the extremes illustrate the point clearly enough.

15. A regression model was used to predict the salary of PSA managers. The data set was the managerial employment roster, which included information about the 175 managers representing the 1986 managerial population of PSA. The model included tenure, race/ethnic group, sex, organizational unit where the manager worked, the number of years in the organization, the amount of time prior to the most recent promotion, the managerial grade level, and the manager's function (line or staff). Methodological details are reported in the Appendix.

16. Education was not included in the managerial roster and thus was absent from the analysis. This omission reduces the explanatory value of the findings. It does not totally invalidate them, however, because there is aggregate information about the distribution of education among staff and line employees. Indeed, line managers had higher average earnings than staff managers despite the fact that the latter were on the average more highly educated.

17. The model explained 74 percent of the variation in the yearly salary of the managers. Indeed, introducing the organizational *function* of the employee (line or staff) into the model increased its explanatory power by 7 percent.

18. These figures resulted from further differentiating among clerical and analyst jobs, by replacing the *function* variable with a *job title* variable. This variable included four categories: managers in the operator career ladder (the same as the line category in the function variable), managers in administrative titles coming from the clerical career ladder, managers in administrative titles coming from the analyst or computer career ladders, and all other managers.

19. The net difference between clerical and analyst job titles was $1,093 in favor of the analysts, but this figure was not statistically significant. This suggests that the strongest difference in opportunity was between operators on the one hand and clerks and analysts on the other.

20. The hiring of women in the operator ladder started during the year of this study, when twenty women became entry-level operators. Many years must pass before they reach the higher levels of the hierarchy.

21. This could reflect a loosening of civil service enforcement to promote PSA's affirmative action efforts. It could also be a sign that women and people of color had fewer opportunities to succeed using the traditional civil service system.

22. The rest had either provisional status (89 percent) or noncompetitive status (5 percent).

23. The methodological details of this exercise appear in the Appendix.

24. Because the dependent variable was transformed by the natural logarithm, the magnitudes of the parameters cannot be easily interpreted. Of more interest, however, are the direction and the significance of the relationship between the number of promotions and participation in career ladders.

25. The intermediate clerical rate included promotions that occurred after a lawsuit described in Chapter 6. This event greatly inflated the rate of mobility during the period when data were collected.

26. A ratio of 2, for example, means that the salary of the employee had doubled since entry. The minimum value of the ratio was 1, when the present salary equaled the initial salary, as was the case for new employees.

27. Of those who did not participate in programs, 15 percent reported in the survey that they had chosen not to do so.

Chapter 6. Power and the Distribution of Rewards

1. The main sources for the analysis in this chapter were in-depth interviews with selected PSA employees and managers, with organizational consultants for PSA, and with union representatives of the different occupational groups. I also used written information from official PSA documents, from union documents, and from the consultants' reports.

2. Equity payments refer to an additional lump sum provided to certain occupational groups to make their salaries competitive with external market conditions.

3. This observation appears in the consultant's 1986 report. Referring to the lower status of operators as blue-collar workers, the consultant made this comment: "In contrast to their invisibility in the community, operators are highly visible to each other. They grant each other the recognition and the status they are denied by the community." Even though there may be other ways to interpret these signs of solidarity, they support the general notion that the group was highly cohesive within PSA.

4. Evidence of this trend is the growth of graduate schools of public administration, policy analysis, urban planning, health administration, and public affairs. These schools supply professionals ready to take on the challenge of managing complex operations in the public sector. Further evidence includes the increasing importance of graduate degrees in public administration, greater utilization of a scientific approach, the development of a core literature, accreditation activities by the National Association of Schools of Public Administration and Public Affairs (NASPAA), subfield specializations, and the development of a code of ethics by the American Society of Public Administration (ASPA).

5. Other blue-collar workers likewise participated in highly enforced civil service progressions, with clear-cut job descriptions and career paths, and their salary increases, too, were based on union contracts.

6. From a personnel point of view, a simplified description of the process of using a civil service list has three basic steps: scheduling and giving the test, establishing lists based

on test results, and calling people to their positions in order of ranking. Civil servants do not have control over the pace of these steps, which in turn affects the rate of upward movement.

7. The organization has now gained official union recognition.

Chapter 7. Perceptions of Opportunity (1): Realities and Myths

1. This distinction has been a concern of scholars studying the structural determinants of behavior since the early seventies (Herman and Hulin 1972; Kalleberg 1975; Mustari 1992). It has emerged again in the nineties in epistemological and ontological debates about the socially constructed component of organizational reality. For examples of the contemporary discussion of the social construction of reality in the management context, see the July 1992 issue of the *Academy of Management Review* (vol. 17, no. 3), which was entirely devoted to new intellectual currents in organization and management theory. For an earlier discussion see Burrel and Morgan (1979).

2. The elusive nature of cognition and perception demands the use of a qualitative approach in Part III. Although survey data supply useful quantitative information about employees' perceptions and feelings about opportunity, much of the argument presented here is the result of systematic analysis of qualitative data based on participant observation and in-depth interviews.

3. This represents the typical measure of dissatisfaction used in the need-satisfaction school.

4. The discrepancy scores were constructed by comparing the answers employees gave to these two questions. In the first question they reported how important the indicators for the dimensions were (whether very important, somewhat important, not too important, or not important at all). In the second question (in a different section of the questionnaire) they reported whether it was true that their job provided these dimensions (whether very true, somewhat true, not very true, or not true at all).

5. The scoring also took into account the direction of the differences between preference and experience, so that only those responses that indicated something was wanted but not received were considered indicators of dissatisfaction. Scores were assigned using the criteria presented in the following matrix. A score of 1 indicates a discrepancy (dissatisfaction); a 0 indicates no discrepancy (satisfaction); a — indicates inverted discrepancy (neutrality).

	Importance for the employee			
Offered by job	Very important	Fairly important	Somewhat important	Not at all important
Very true	0	—	—	—
Somewhat true	1	0	—	—
Not very true	1	1	0	—
Not true at all	1	1	1	0

6. Fourteen different job dimensions were originally analyzed. The results indicated that operators were more satisfied than both analysts and clerical employees with more

aspects of their jobs. The two groups who participated in the open employment mode generally had the highest percentages of dissatisfaction for most dimensions of the job. Moreover, when a relatively large number of operators also reported dissatisfaction with a particular aspect of the job, the percentages for the two other groups were even higher for the same aspect. Hence, even in those cases when dissatisfaction was generalized, fewer operators felt it.

7. In the original scale a 1 indicated very poor chances for promotion and a 10 indicated excellent chances. In Table 6, low chances include those who rated their chances as 1, 2, or 3; high chances include ratings of 8, 9, or 10.

8. About one-third of analysts and one-fifth of the clerical employees believed this.

9. The miscellaneous category includes reported reasons that did not yield any particular pattern.

10. This committee was a city-wide organization designed to provide support to women in city government. A delegate from each agency, appointed by the commissioner, represented the agency's female work force in a larger forum where activities were organized and problems discussed. The delegate was in turn responsible for organizing agency-level activities and group discussions on the topics of interest.

11. Each group recommended very specific topics for these training programs. Analysts asked for systems training, for financial, budgetary, and fiscal procedures, for statistics, labor relations, and equal employment opportunity procedures, as well as construction law, personnel procedures, occupational health issues, environmental protection, and handling of departmental forms and codes. Clerical employees recommended job-related classes in stenography, real estate, insurance, business law, data entry, programing, wordprocessing, handling of departmental forms and codes, and retirement, pension, and personnel procedures. Operators recommended driving courses, more training in equipment use, and physical fitness.

12. Unfortunately, I did not include any particular questions about this in the survey, so I rely here on documents written by operator managers and on what the literature tells us about the impact of this type of participatory mechanism on employees' sense of personal growth.

Chapter 8. Perceptions of Opportunity (2): Conflicting Definitions of Merit and the Meaning of Work

1. Almost half of the operators in the survey liked the way promotions were handled and said nothing needed to be changed, compared to about one-fifth of the analysts and clerical employees.

2. This information is contained in a union manual. The legal coverage of provisional employee rights has since increased. Presently they are covered under the same laws as their permanent counterparts.

3. This view proposes that civil service systems have failed to create professionals because they fail to provide incentives for good performance (Savas and Ginsburg 1973; Wilson 1989; Kelman 1990).

4. DiPrete also mentioned growth, organizational demography, and external labor market dynamics as forces that shaped these ladders.

5. DiPrete called the narrow position the "professional" perspective and the broad position the "non-professional" perspective.

Chapter 9. The Power of Comparisons: Perceptions of Justice and the Organizational Climate

1. This refers to the notion of "referential comparison" (Greenberg and Cohen 1982).

2. This is a direct application of the process Masters and Keil document in their 1987 work.

3. Tomaskovic-Devey also mentions C. Wright Mills' use of the term as early as 1956.

4. Here Murphy is summarizing Collins' (1979) general argument about the political economy of culture.

5. Kanter developed this argument first for women (1977). Later she extended the argument to include any other individual placed in a situation of tokenism in *A Tale of O* (Kanter and Stein 1994).

6. Empirical evidence seems to support this last argument. Tomaskovic-Devey (1993), for example, found that black employees in his sample were more closely supervised than white employees, not only because of the characteristics of their jobs but also because they were black.

7. The distribution by career ladder was operators 14 percent, analysts 28 percent, and clerical employees 35 percent.

8. For example, one mentioned in an interview his concern with the staff absenteeism rate for the previous year, which was unacceptably high compared to the city standard.

9. Törnblom and Jonsson (1985) identify three different sub-rules that can be legitimately used to apply the contribution principle of equity. Each defines merit differently: merit as contribution-of-effort, merit as contribution-of-ability, or merit as contribution-of-productivity.

10. Taylor identifies two dominant versions of justice: justice as the greatest good and justice as fairness. The two views are conceptually rooted in very different philosophical assumptions about why moral principles are worth following. Justice as fairness is derived from a deontological approach to normative ethics. It assumes universal laws of morality to which people have a duty independent of any payoffs. Justice as the greatest good is linked to a consequentialist approach. It assumes that moral laws must be obeyed because of the particular human and social benefits that are derived from doing so (Taylor 1991).

11. This situation is not an anomaly. The literature on justice documents different sub-rules that can define an egalitarian allocation of resources. *Equality of treatment* implies that everyone receives the same treatment; *equality of opportunity* implies that everyone has the same chance to receive the same share; and *equality of results* implies that everyone winds up with the same rewards in the long run, even if there is unequal treatment in the process (Törnblom and Jonsson 1985). Oppenheim (1980) further distinguishes between equal benefits, equal chance, equal access, equal satisfaction of basic needs, and equal opportunity. In the United States there is a strong preference for the principles of equality of treatment and equality of opportunity over those that promote equality of results (Lane 1986; Gans 1974; Deutsch 1985). The dominance of this narrow definition of equality in U.S. society is evidenced by the strong emphasis on formal political equality, while at the same time the culture shows a lack of attention to economic equality. To this extent, dominant concepts of distributive justice in the United States have seldom been directed toward equality of condition (Lane 1986).

12. Deutsch (1985) argues that issues of justice or injustice only come up in relation to others who are perceived to be inside or potentially inside one's own moral community. The narrower the group's conception of community, the narrower the scope of situations

and people to which justice must be extended. If one takes all humankind as one's community, the scope of one's concept of justice will obviously be much wider than if one takes a small group as the basic reference.

Chapter 10. Job Satisfaction

1. For example, the most global question asked employees how satisfied they were with their job, all in all. A substantial majority of employees from the three groups reported being either "very satisfied" or "somewhat satisfied," as opposed to being "not too satisfied" or "not at all satisfied." On the other hand, when employees were asked to report their feelings about fourteen different job-related dimensions, a broader sense of dissatisfaction with particular aspects of the job emerged. Indexes of satisfaction and dissatisfaction for each job attribute revealed much more complex, much more ambivalent, and much less positive judgements about jobs.

2. Primary data for the analysis and findings reported here came from responses to survey questions. In-depth interviews and direct observations conducted during fieldwork helped interpret the findings.

3. Except for measures of "objective"opportunity, these represent the relevant individual, organizational, and job-related factors traditionally associated with job satisfaction in the literature. Parameter estimates for the models are presented in Table 18 and the variables are described in Table 19.

4. The comparison of parameters across models in this section is only an heuristic exercise to gain information about the links between groups. These parameters are in reality the result of three totally independent models with their consequent unique internal statistical logics. Slight differences in model specification as well as differences in sample size affect the magnitude of the numbers and their levels of significance. Rather than a rigorous technique to measure differences in magnitude overall, the comparison establishes differences in the direction of the relationships and the relative importance that different variables have for each group.

5. The figures for operators are based on the findings of a multivariate analysis performed *exclusively* for the operator group. The analysis evaluates the factors that resulted in differences in satisfaction within this career ladder only. The same applies to the other two ladders, the clerical and the analyst. (Table 18 shows the results for all three).

6. Several respondents in my survey sample waited for ten years before they were appointed to the job.

7. Another factor related to pay was not statistically significant but was strong enough to be worth mentioning. This was the measure of the salary increments that employees had received from entry until the present (controlling for inflation). This measure was included in the analysis as a complement to the subjective measure of financial security reported by employees themselves. The magnitude of the coefficient for this variable does suggest that the larger the increments, the higher the satisfaction. Although methodologically it is not possible to accept this finding as reliable, substantively its strength confirms the finding that perceived financial security was strongly connected to the operators' level of satisfaction.

8. This is similar to the notion Williams (1990) develops for the larger social system in the United States, with respect to the socially constructed and structurally based nature of race and ethnicity.

9. Zaleznick, Christensen, and Roethlisberger (1958) reported this psychological reaction in their study of job satisfaction.

10. In contrast, only 8 percent of the clerical employees and 9 percent of the operators gave a similar answer.

11. Compared to 11 percent of the operators and 16 percent of the clerical employees.

12. This was documented in the multivariate analysis of factors affecting managerial salaries presented in Chapter 5.

13. In the stratification literature as well, one finds no extensive study of this link. Sometimes the topic appears in discussions of the broader negative effects of organizational inequality.

14. Tomaskovic-Devey claims this is so because blacks are subject to systematic discrimination in their access to jobs requiring more skill, but they tend to share employment with at least some white workers.

15. "Goodness of fit" has become a critical feature in the work of dominant scholars in the field, including the Michigan group under the leadership of J. R. P. French and the Job Descriptive Index group under the leadership of P. C. Smith (Dawis 1992).

16. For excellent discussions of this debate see Porter and Lawler 1965, James and Jones 1976, Herman and Hulin 1972, Oldman and Hackman 1981, and Mustari 1992.

Chapter 11. Relative Deprivation, Self-Evaluation, and Work Attitudes

1. The findings of the model were robust. They accounted for 50 percent of the variation in job satisfaction among the employees sampled. A description of the model is presented in the Appendix.

2. The job-related factors used in this model differ from the measures used in the analysis of job dissatisfaction presented in Chapter 7. There the comparisons were based on *discrepancy scores*, which were in and of themselves indicators of raw dissatisfaction. The multivariate analysis described here uses a global measure of satisfaction. It measures employees' responses to the question of whether a specific job dimension existed in their job, regardless of how important they considered it and regardless of whether actually having it was possible. Inasmuch as the distinction can be made, these were measures of employees' factual perceptions of the job dimension. See the Appendix for a description of these measures.

3. Individual and organizational variables traditionally included in job satisfaction models were either subsumed in the variable "membership in the ladder" (for example, sex composition and opportunity measures) or found to be unimportant during earlier stages of the analysis (for example, organizational level or seniority). The model did include an additional measure to control for the complexity of the job, using the criteria developed in the *Dictionary of Occupational Titles* (Department of Labor 1977a). For a discussion of the model specification decisions, refer to the Appendix.

4. Because previous information indicated that operators were the most satisfied group, they became the standard of comparison.

5. The statistical test for the probability that both clerical groups together (provisional and permanent) had lower satisfaction scores than the operators was not significant at or below the traditional 5 percent (.08).

6. In a first iteration of the analysis, the comparisons showed that there was a statistically significant difference between the satisfaction of operators and the satisfaction of

those in the open employment setting. The analysis also confirmed that the operators were indeed *more satisfied* than the others. The statistical test for the probability that analysts and clerical employees together had lower satisfaction scores than the operators was significant at a .03 level.

7. This ranking holds only relative to the operators. When I changed the omitted category in the model to compare the staff subgroups, the least satisfied group was still the permanent analyst, but the differences between provisional analysts and provisional clerical employees were not significant.

8. Zero-order correlations between education, provisional status, and the interaction between education and this status would be very high and yield unreliable results, were these to be placed in the same multivariate equation.

9. The full test of this proposition would require specifying a model with a set of interaction terms representing the differential effects that each group's education had on the satisfaction of employees. But precisely because of the patterned demographic composition of each career ladder, all terms required to make the equation technically correct would result in a high degree of multicollinearity. This could be solved in a technical way by using sophisticated mathematical strategies. But including both types of variables simultaneously would in fact be conceptually redundant and thus not desirable.

10. In order to reflect the previous assumption in the model, the equation has no separate term for education. Thus, mathematically, the omitted category (operators) had a slope of 0. By using this simple model I aim to show only that the effect of education on satisfaction varies by career ladder for the staff groups. For a description of the model and its variables, refer to the Appendix.

11. This is suggested by the significant differences between the omitted category (operators) and each subgroup except for the permanent clerical group.

12. This is why I have placed the negative sign in the provisional analyst/operator cell in parenthesis.

13. In particular, Della Fave uses Mead's theory of the self, Berger and Luckman's notion of reification, social psychology's notion of status attribution, the proportionality principle of justice theories, relative deprivation notions of equity theory, and the notions of legitimation and social action from critical theory (including Gramsci's notion of cultural hegemony).

14. This difference stresses even more the pervasive effect of the civil service on the job satisfaction of PSA employees. Ironically, while many studies of job satisfaction have taken place in public settings, civil service has seldom been considered a critical factor. It has been treated instead as a background variable. The absence of statistical significance in formal regression models may have motivated researchers to discard it from the discussion. A well-rounded theory of employee motivation in the public sector requires exploring the subtle but strong effect of this ideology.

15. Further research is all the more necessary because the traditional literature has yielded inconsistent evidence about the relationship between formalization and job satisfaction (Mustari 1992).

Chapter 12. Conclusions: Reactions to Stratification in the Workplace

1. The power of attribution in helping reproduce stratified orders has been consistently tested in experiments. In one example, subjects equal in abilities were randomly

assigned to manager titles with high-skill tasks or clerical titles with low-skill, repetitive tasks. Those with manager titles were consistently rated higher performers than those with clerical titles. For a review of these empirical tests, see Ritzman and Tomaskovic-Devey (1992). The example presented here was drawn from their discussion. For a full discussion of attribution theory within the organizational behavior tradition, see Weiner 1986.

2. Murphy attributes this distinction to F. Parkin and further develops it using A. Gidden's notion of considering exclusion/usurpation as a "duality" rather than a "dichotomy."

3. Murphy alludes here to White 1970.

4. Notice how analogous this description is to Rosenbaum's (1983) "tournament model" and to H. White's (1970) view of mobility in organizations.

5. In his insightful discussion of the differences between achieved and ascribed criteria for selection, Murphy reminds us that the substance of social exclusion might have changed over time but the reality of exclusion remains unchanged in modern bureaucracies. While in earlier social systems the monopolization of resources and the exclusion of individuals from organizations were determined by particularistic processes connected to birth and rank, in contemporary societies processes of closure have become more stochastic. This means that who wins and who succeeds is not determined so much by particularistic attributes as by chance. Nevertheless, the outcome is the same: some are included and others excluded. Instances of occupational and job segregation, however, remind us that the shift to a probabilistic process of closure is by no means complete.

6. For example, Weiss and Adler (1984) classify personality variables used in the study of organizational behavior as either cognitive, motivational, or a combination of both. The first category includes how individuals process information or how they perceive the world around them. These include cognitive style variables such as reflectivity/impulsivity, dogmatism, and locus of control, as well as perceptual personality constructs such as field dependence/independence. The motivational category includes individual differences in how behavior is energized and maintained. It includes factors such as needs, motives, and values as well as drive-related variables such as trait anxiety.

7. Moreover, the approach would expect that individuals with certain characteristics would tend to select organizations with certain characteristics, reducing the potential for a mismatch. Such expectations form part of the attraction-selection framework.

8. Oldham and Hackman 1981, Herman and Hulin 1972, Kalleberg and Griffin 1978, Mustari 1992, Rousseau 1978, Pierce 1979, and Brass 1981 represent selected examples of this perspective, labeled in the literature as the 'new structuralists.' Two schools in particular specify these links: the job modification framework and the attraction-selection framework.

9. This represents the job modification framework.

10. An example illustrates how the discussion gains by broadening the view. Mustari (1992) examined how "occupational grouping" moderates the relationship between organizational structure and job satisfaction. She found that occupation influenced the magnitude and the direction of the effect of certain organizational structural characteristics on satisfaction. For example, centralization correlated with the job satisfaction of white-collar middle managers and blue-collar nonmanagement workers, but the direction was positive for the former and negative for the latter. Mustari's explanation suggested that increasing the centralization of decision-making increases the motivating potential score of management positions while it decreases the same score for nonmanagement line positions. She concluded that centratization increases the autonomy and task significance

of management *at the expense* of the line. This relational analysis certainly adds to our knowledge of the black box. Yet the analysis still ignores the fact that such variations are a direct function of heterogeneous work arrangements. In fact, white-collar middle managers and blue-collar nonmanagement workers take part in two completely separated opportunity structures! This explains why occupational grouping had a different impact on the relationship between structure and satisfaction for each group in her sample.

11. In particular, relative deprivation and the referent cognitions model.

Appendix: Methodological Issues

1. These technological manipulations were justified because the conceptual interest behind the exercise was less to find actual parameters than to explore the strengths and direction of the relationships between the variables.

2. Employee's age, salary, organizational unit, and geographical location were not included in the model because they were highly correlated with other variables. Age was highly correlated with seniority. Organizational unit and geographical location overlapped considerably with membership in ladder and were a function of it. Salary was highly correlated with seniority and level. Since the latter are determinants of salary, I decided to include them in the model and exclude salary. Monetary renumeration is indirectly included in the objective measure of salary increase and the subjective measure of financial security.

3. I ran the regression including all the variables to make sure that this assumption was correct. While the significant parameters did not change, none of the excluded variables showed any significance or substantive size. Taking them out of the model had no substantive effect on the results. It could still be argued, however, that the career ladder variable is a proxy for education and that the parameters thus represent education as well as other career ladder effects. I am aware of this possibility, and I discuss the conceptual implications in Chapter 11.

4. The measures of complexity developed in the *Dictionary of Occupational Titles* (Department of Labor 1977a) were highly correlated among each other and with the career ladder. Hence the three measures of complexity with respect to data, people, and things were converted into a categorical high-low variable with a score to 0 for low and 1 for high. Then the three measures were added. The criterion for creating the binary was that if a person held a job in which two out of the three complexity measures were high, then this indicated high complexity. If the job had one or no complexity measures then this indicated low complexity.

References

Abraham, K., and J. Medoff. 1983. *Length of Service and the Operation of Internal Labor Markets*. Working Paper 1394-83, MIT Sloan School of Management.

Abrahamson, Mark, and Lee Sigleman. 1987. "Occupational Segregation in Metropolitan Areas." *American Sociological Review* 52(5):588-597.

Abrams, Philip. 1982. *Historical Sociology*. Ithaca: Cornell University Press.

Aktouf, Omar. 1992. "Management and Theories of Organizations in the 1990's: Toward a Critical Radical Humanism?" *Academy of Management Review* 17(3):407-431.

Allan, P., and S. Rosenberg. 1986. "An Assessment of Merit Pay Administration under NYC's Managerial Performance Evaluation System: Three Years of Experience." *Public Personnel Management* 15:297-309.

Allison, Graham T. 1971. *Essence of Decision: Explaining the Cuban Missile Crisis*. Boston: Little, Brown.

Althauser, Robert P. 1987. "Internal Labor Markets in USA: A Thematic Review." Paper presented at the annual meeting of the American Sociological Association, April, at Chicago.

Althauser, Robert P., and Arne L. Kalleberg. 1981. "Firms, Occupations, and the Structure of Labor Markets: A Conceptual Analysis." In *Sociological Perspectives on Labor Markets*, ed. Ivar Berg. New York: Academic Press.

Argyriades, Demetrios. 1991. "Bureaucracy and Debureaucratization." In *Handbook of Comparative and Development Public Administration*, ed. Ali Farazmand, pp. 567-585. New York: Marcel Dekker.

Aronowitz, Stanley, and William DiFazio. 1994. *The Jobless Future: Sci-Tech and the Dogma of Work*. Minneapolis: University of Minnesota Press.

Babbie, Earl R. 1983. *The Practice of Social Research*. 3d ed. Belmont, Calif.: Wadsworth Publishing.

Baird, Lloyd S., Craig E. Schneier, and Richard W. Beatty, eds. 1988. *The Strategic Human Resource Management Sourcebook*. Amherst: Human Resource Development Press.

Baron, James N. 1984. "Organizational Perspectives on Stratification." *Annual Review of Sociology* 10:37.

Baron, James N., and William T. Bielby. 1980. "Bringing the Firms Back In: Stratification, Segmentation, and the Organization of Work." *American Sociological Review* 45(5):737–765.

———. 1984. "The Organization of Work in a Segmented Economy." *American Sociological Review* 49(4):454–473.

———. 1985. "Organizational Barriers to Gender Equality: Sex Segregation of Jobs and Opportunities." In *Gender and the Life Course*, ed. Alice Rossi. New York: Aldine.

Baron, James N., Alison Davis–Blake, and William T. Bielby. 1986. "The Structure of Opportunity: How Promotion Ladders Vary within and among Organizations." *Administrative Science Quarterly* 31(2):248–273.

Baron, James N., Frank R. Dobbin, and P. Devereaux Jennings. 1986. "War and Peace: The Evolution of Modern Personnel Administration in United States Industry." *American Journal of Sociology* 92:350–383.

Baron, James N., Brian S. Mittman, and Andre E. Newman. 1991. "Targets of Opportunity: Organizational and Environmental Determinants of Gender Integration within the California Civil Service, 1979–1985." *American Journal of Sociology* 96(6):1362–1401.

Baron, James N., and Andrew E. Newman. 1990. "For What It's Worth: Organization, Occupations, and the Value of Work Done by Women and Nonwhites." *American Sociological Review* 55:155–175.

Bartuneck, Jean, and Michael K. Moch. 1987. "First Order, Second Order, and Third Order Change and Organizational Development Interventions: A Cognitive Approach." *Journal of Applied Behavioral Science* 23(4):483–500.

Barzelay, Michael. 1992. *Breaking Through Bureaucracy: A New Vision for Managing in Government*. Berkeley: University of California Press.

Bateson, Mary Catherine. 1989. *Composing a Life*. New York: Atlantic Monthly Press.

Beck, E. M., Patrick M. Horan, and Charles M. Tolbert, II. 1978. "Stratification in a Dual Economy: A Sectoral Model of Earnings Determination." *American Sociological Review* 43(5):704–720.

Bedau, Hugo Adam. 1971. *Justice and Equality*. Englewood Cliffs, N.J.: Prentice-Hall.

Beer, Michael, Bert Spector, Paul R. Lawrence, D. Quinn Mills, and Richard E. Walton. 1985. *Human Resource Management: A General Manager's Perspective*. New York: The Free Press.

Bell, Daniel. 1973. *The Coming of Post–Industrial Society: A Venture in Social Forecasting*. New York: Basic Books.

Benveniste, Guy. 1987. *Professionalizing the Organization: Reducing Bureaucracy to Enhance Effectiveness*. San Francisco: Jossey–Bass.

Berg, Ivar E. 1970. *Education and Jobs: The Great Training Robbery*. New York: Praeger Publishers.

———, ed. 1981. *Sociological Perspectives in Labor Markets*. New York: Academic Press.

Berg, Ivar E., Marcia Freedman, and Michael Freeman. 1978. *Managers and Work Reform: A Limited Engagement*. New York: The Free Press.

Berg, Thomas R. 1991. "The Importance of Equity Perception and Job Satisfaction in Predicting Employee Intent to Stay at Television Stations." In *Group and Organization Studies* 16(3):268–284.

Berger, Joseph, Morris Zelditch, Jr., B. Anderson, and B. B. Cohen. 1972. "Structural Aspects of Distributive Justice: A Status Value Formulation." In *Sociological Theories in Progress*, vol. 2, ed. Joseph Berger, Morris Zelditch, Jr., and B. Anderson. Boston: Houghton Mifflin.

Berger, Peter L., and Thomas Luckmann. 1967. *The Social Construction of Reality: A Treatise in the Sociology of Knowledge.* Garden City, N.Y.: Anchor Books.

Berheide, Catherine White, Cynthia H. Chertos, Lois V. Haignere, and Ronnie T. Steinberg. 1986. *Minorities and Pay Equity in New York State Government Employment.* Albany: Center for Women in Government.

Berwick, Donald M. 1989. "Continuous Improvement as an Ideal in Health Care." *New England Journal of Medicine,* January, pp. 53–56.

Bielby, William T. 1981. "Models of Status Attainment." *Research in Social Stratification and Mobility* 1:3–26. Greenwich, Conn.: JAI Press, Inc.

Bierhoff, Hans W., Ronald L. Cohen, and Jerald Greenberg, eds. 1986. *Justice in Social Relations.* New York: Plenum Press.

Bies, Robert J. 1987. "The Predicament of Injustice." In *Research in Organization Behavior,* vol. 9, ed. Barry M. Staw and L. L. Cummings. Greenwich, Conn.: JAI Press.

Blackburn J., and W. Bruce. 1989. "Rethinking Concepts of Job Satisfaction: The Case of Nebraska Municipal Clerks." *Review of Public Personnel Administration* 10:11–28.

Blalock, Hubert M. 1960. *Social Statistics.* New York: McGraw-Hill.

Blau, Peter M. 1963. *The Dynamics of Bureaucracy: A Study of Interpersonal Relations in Two Government Agencies.* 2d ed. Chicago: University of Chicago Press.

——. 1964. *Exchange and Power in Social Life.* New York: J. Wiley.

——. 1974. "Parameters of Social Structure." *American Sociological Review* 39(5):615–635.

Blau, Peter M., and Otis Dudley Duncan. 1967. *The American Occupational Structure.* New York: The Free Press.

Blau, Peter M., and W. Richard Scott. 1963. *Formal Organizations: A Comparative Approach.* London: Routledge Kegan Paul.

Blauner, R. 1966. "Work Satisfaction and Industrial Trends in Modern Society." In *Class, Status and Power,* ed. R. Bendix and S. M. Lipset. New York: The Free Press.

Bluedorn, Allen C. 1982. "The Theories of Turnover: Causes, Effect and Meaning." In *Research in the Sociology of Organizations,* ed. Samuel Bacharach, 1:75–128. Greenwich, C.T.: JAI Press.

Borjas, C. 1980. "Wage Determination in the Federal Government: The Role of Constituents and Bureaucrats." *Journal of Political Economy* 88:1110–1147.

Bottini, Maria, Cynthia H. Chertos, and Lois Haignere. N.d. *Initiating Pay Equity: A Guide for Assessing Your Workplace.* Albany: Center for Women in Government.

Boudon, R. 1971. *The Uses of Structuralism.* London: Heinemann.

Bourdieu, Pierre. 1984. *Distinction: A Social Critique of the Judgement of Taste.* Cambridge: Harvard University Press.

Bowles, Samuel, and Herbert Gintis. 1976. *Schooling in Capitalist America: Educational Reform and the Contradictions of Economic Life.* New York: Basic Books.

Bozeman, Barry, and Jeffrey D. Straussman. 1990. *Public Management Strategies: Guidelines for Managerial Effectiveness.* San Francisco: Jossey-Bass.

Brant, Richard B., ed. 1962. *Social Justice.* Englewood Cliffs, N.J.: Prentice-Hall.

Brass, Daniel J. 1981. "Structural Relationships, Job Characteristics, and Worker Satisfaction." *Administrative Science Quarterly* 26(3):331–348.

Brecher, Charles. 1972. *Upgrading Blue-Collar and Service Workers.* Baltimore: Johns Hopkins University Press.

Brecher, Charles, and Raymond D. Horton, eds. 1986. *Setting Municipal Priorities: American Cities and the New York Experience.* New York: New York University Press.

Bridges, W., and W. Villemez. 1982. "On the Institutionalization of Job Security: Internal Labor Markets and Their Corporate Environments." University of Illinois at Chicago. Duplicated.

Brock, Jonathan. 1984. *Managing People in Public Agencies: Personnel and Labor Relations.* Boston: Little, Brown.

Brody, David. 1980. *Workers in Industrial America: Essays on the Twentieth-Century Struggle.* New York: Oxford University Press.

Brown, Richard, and Stanford M. Lyman. 1978. *Structure, Consciousness, and History.* Cambridge: Cambridge University Press.

Burnstein, P. 1985. *Discrimination, Jobs, and Politics: The Struggle for Equal Employment Opportunity in the United States since the New Deal.* Chicago: University of Chicago Press.

Buroway, M. 1977. "Social Structure, Homogenization, and the Process of Status Attainment in the U.S. and Great Britain." *American Journal of Sociology* 82(5):1031–1042.

Campbell, Angus, Philipe Converse, and Willard L. Rodgers. 1976. *The Quality of American Life: Perceptions, Evaluations, and Satisfactions.* New York: Russell Sage Foundation.

Center for Women in Government. 1991. "Number of Women in Government Increasing." *Women in Public Service.* Summer:1(1).

Center for Women in Government. 1991–1992. "Women Face Barriers in Top Management." *Women in Public Service.* Winter:1(2).

Center for Women in Government. 1992. "Women Still Stuck in Low-Level Jobs." *Women in Public Service.* Fall:1(3).

Chapa, Jorge. 1992. "Creating and Improving Linkages between the Tops and Bottoms: Moving Ideas Upward from the Non-professional and Paraprofessional Ranks of Government." Paper presented at the Organizational and Innovation Conference, 18–20 September, at the Humphrey Institute of Public Affairs, University of Minnesota.

Cohen, Ronald, L. 1986. "Power and Justice in Intergroup Relations." In *Justice in Social Relations*, ed. H. W. Bierhoff et al. New York: Pelham Press.

Cohen, Ronald L., and Jerald Greenberg. 1982. "The Justice Concept of Social Psychology." In *Equity and Justice in Social Behavior*, ed. Jerald Greenberg and Ronald L. Cohen. New York: Academic Press.

Collins, Randall. 1975. *Conflict Sociology: Toward an Explanatory Science.* New York: Academic Press.

———. 1979. *The Credential Society.* New York: Academic Press.

Cook, Karen S. 1986. "Distributive Justice: A Psychological Perspective." *Administrative Science Quarterly* 31:677–679.

Cook, Karen S. and Karen A. Hegtvedt. 1983. "Distributive Justice, Equity, and Equality." *Annual Review of Sociology* 9:217–241.

———. 1986. "Justice and Power." In *Justice in Social Relations*, ed. H. W. Bierhoff, et al. New York: Pelham Press.

Coser, Lewis A. 1975. "Presidential Address: Two Methods in Search of a Substance." *American Sociological Review* 40:691–700.

———. 1976. "Reply to My Critics." *American Sociologist* 11(1):33–38.

Cotton, John. 1993. *Employee Involvement: Methods for Improving Performance and Work Attitudes.* Newbury Park, Calif.: Sage Publications.

Cox, Taylor, Jr. 1990. "The Multicultural Organization." Unpublished transcript, October 17. School of Business, University of Michigan, Ann Arbor.

——. 1993. *Cultural Diversity in Organizations: Theory, Research, and Practice.* San Francisco: Berett-Koehler.

Cox, Taylor, Jr., and S. Blake. 1991. "Managing Cultural Diversity: Implications for Organizational Competitiveness." *Academy of Management Executive* 5(3):45–56.

Cox, Taylor, Jr., and Stella M. Nkomo. 1986. "Differential Performance Appraisal Criteria: A Field Study of Black and White Managers." *Group and Organization Studies* 11:101–119.

Cranny, C. J., Patricia Cain Smith, and Eugene Stone. 1992. *Job Satisfaction: How People Feel about Their Jobs and How It Affects Their Performance.* New York: Lexington Books.

Cropanzano, Russell. 1993. *Justice in the Workplace: Approaching Fairness in Human Resource Management.* Hillsdale: Lawrence Erlbaum Associates.

Crosby, Faye. 1984. "Relative Deprivation in Organization Settings." In *Research in Organization Behaviour*, vol. 6, ed. Barry M. Staw and L. L. Cummings. Greenwich, Conn.: JAI Press.

Crosby, Faye, and A. Miren Gonzalez-Intal. 1984. "Relative Deprivation and Equity Theories: Felt Injustice and the Undeserved Benefits of Others." In *The Sense of Injustice: Social Psychological Perspectives*, ed. Robert Folger. New York: Plenum Press.

Cyert, Richard M., and James G. March. 1963. *A Behavioral Theory of the Firm.* Englewood Cliffs, N.J.: Prentice Hall.

Daley, Dennis M. 1990a. "Humanistic Management and Organizational Success: The Effect of Job and Work Environment Characteristics on Organizational Effectiveness, Public Responsiveness, and Job Satisfaction." *Public Personnel Management* 15:131–142.

——. 1990b. "The Organization of the Personnel Function: The New Patronage and Decentralization." In *Public Personnel Administration: Problems and Prospects*, 2d ed., ed. Steven W. Hays and Richard C. Kearney. Englewood Cliffs, N.J.: Prentice Hall.

Dalton, Melville. 1959. *Men Who Manage: Fusions of Feeling and Theory in Administration.* New York: Wiley.

Dawis, Rene. 1992. "Person-Environment Fit and Job Satisfaction." In *Job Satisfaction: How People Feel about Their Jobs and How It Affects Their Performance*, ed. C. J. Cranny, Patricia Cain Smith, and Eugene Stone. New York: Lexington Books.

Della Fave, L. Richard. 1980. "The Meek Shall Not Inherit the Earth: Self-Evaluation and the Legitimacy of Stratification." *American Sociological Review* 45:955–971.

——. 1986a. "Toward an Explication of the Legitimation Process." *Social Forces* 65(2):476–500.

——. 1986b. "The Dialectics of Legitimation and Counternorms." *Sociological Perspectives* 29(4):435–460.

DeNisi, A. S., and K. J. Williams. 1988. "Cognitive Approaches to Performance Appraisal." In *Research in Personnel and Human Resource Management*, vol. 6, ed. K. M. Rowland and G. R. Ferris. Greenwich, Conn.: JAI Press.

Denzin, Norman K. 1978. *The Research Act: A Theoretical Introduction to Sociological Methods.* 2d ed. Englewood Cliffs, N.J.: Prentice Hall.

Department of Commerce. 1988. *Statistical Abstract of the United States, 1988.* 108th ed. Washington, D.C.: Bureau of the Census.

Department of Labor. 1972. *Handbook for Analyzing Jobs.* Washington, D.C.: U.S. Government Printing Office.

——. 1977a. *Dictionary of Occupational Titles*, 4th ed. Washington, D.C.: Government Printing Office.

——. 1977b. *The Survey of Working Conditions*. Washington, D.C.: U.S. Government Printing Office.

——. 1989. Women's Bureau. *Facts on Working Women*, no. 89–4. Washington, D.C.: Government Printing Office.

——. 1991. *A Report on the Glass Ceiling Initiative*. Washington, D.C.: U.S. Government Printing Office.

——. 1992. *Pipelines of Progress: An Update on the Glass Ceiling Initiative*. Washington, D.C.: U.S. Government Printing Office.

Deutsch, Morton. 1985. *Distributive Justice: A Social Psychological Perspective*. New Haven: Yale University Press.

DiPrete, Thomas A. 1983. "Status Boundaries, Labor Markets, and the Structure of Mobility: A Case Study in the U.S. Federal Government." Paper presented at the Annual Meeting of the American Sociological Association, Detroit.

——. 1987. "Horizontal and Vertical Mobility in Organizations." *Administrative Science Quarterly* 32(3):422–444.

——. 1989. *The Bureaucratic Labor Market: The Case of the Federal Civil Service*. New York: Plenum Press.

DiPrete, Thomas A., and Soule T. Whitman. 1988. "Gender and Promotion in Segmented Job Ladder Systems." *American Sociological Review* 53(1):26–40.

Doeringer, Peter B., and Michael J. Piore. 1971. *Internal Labor Markets and Manpower Analysis*. Lexington, Mass.: Heath.

Dubin, Robert, Joseph E. Champoux, and Lyman W. Porter. 1975. "Central Life Interests and Organizational Commitment of Blue-Collar and Clerical Workers." *Administrative Science Quarterly* 20(3):411–22.

Dyer, G., and A. Wilkins. 1991. "Better Stories, Not Better Constructs, to Generate Better Theory: A Rejoinder to Eisenhardt." *The Academy of Management Review* 16:613–619.

Edwards, Richard C. 1979. *Contested Terrain: The Transformation of the Workplace in the Twentieth Century*. New York: Basic Books.

Elbaun, Bernard. 1984. "The Making and Shaping of Job and Pay Structures in the Iron and Steel Industry." In *Internal Labor Markets*, ed. Paul Osterman. Cambridge: MIT Press.

Featherman, David L. 1976. "Coser's . . . 'In Search of a Substance.'" *American Sociologist* 11(1):21–27.

Featherman, David L., and R. Hausser. 1978. *Opportunity and Change*. New York: Academic Press.

Ferguson, Kathy E. 1984. *The Feminist Case against Bureaucracy*. Philadelphia: Temple University Press.

Fernandez, John P. 1981. *Racism and Sexism in Corporate Life: Changing Values in American Business*. Lexington, Mass.: Lexington Books.

Fitzsimmons, James A., and Robert S. Sullivan. 1982. *Service Operations Management*. New York: McGraw-Hill.

Folger, Robert. 1984. "Emerging Issues in the Social Psychology of Justice." In *The Sense of Injustice: Social Psychological Perspectives*, ed. Robert Folger. New York: Plenum Press.

——. 1987. "Reformulating the Preconditions of Resentment: A Referent Cognition Model." In *Social Comparison, Social Justice, and Relative Deprivation*, ed. John C.

Masters and William P. Smith. Hillsdale, N.J.: Lawrence Erlbaum Associates.

——. 1993. "Reactions to Mistreatment at Work." In *Social Psychology in Organizations: Advances in Theory and Research*. ed. J. Keith Murnighan. Englewood Cliffs, N.J.: Prentice Hall.

Folger, Robert, and Jerald Greenberg. 1985. "Procedural Justice." In *Research in Personnel and Human Resource Management*, vol. 3, ed. Kendrith Martin Rowland and Gerald R. Ferris. Greenwich, Conn.: JAI Press.

Fox, Siegrun F. 1993. "Professional Norms and Actual Practices in Local Personnel Administration." *Review of Public Personnel Administration* 13 (Spring):5–28.

Frankena, W. 1962. "The Concept of Social Justice." In *Social Justice*, ed. Richard B. Brant. Englewood Cliffs, N.J.: Prentice Hall.

Freedman, Marcia K. 1969. *The Process of Work Establishment*. New York: Columbia University Press.

Freedman, Marcia, and Gretchen Maclachlan. 1976. *Labor Markets: Segments and Shelters*. Lanham, Md.: Rowman & Littlefield.

Freeman, Richard B. 1980. "The Exit-Voice Tradeoff in the Labor Market: Unionism, Job Tenure, Quits, and Separations." *Quarterly Journal of Economics* 94(6):643–676.

Freeman, Richard B., and J. Medoff. 1979. "The Two Facts of Unionism." *Public Interest* 57(1):69–93.

Fryxell, G. E., and M. E, Gordon. 1989. "Workplace Justice and Job Satisfaction as Predictors of Satisfaction with Union and Management." *Academy of Management Journal* 32:851–866.

Gabris, Gerald T., and Kenneth Mitchell. 1988. "The Impact of Merit Raise Scores on Employee Attitudes: The Matthew Effect of Performance Appraisal." *Public Personnel Management* 17(4):369–402.

Gallup, George, Jr. 1989. *The Gallup Poll: Public Opinion 1989*. Wilmington: Scholarly Resources.

Gans, Herbert. 1974. "The Equality Revolution." In *More Equality*, ed. Herbert Gans. New York: Vintage Books.

Garfinkel, Harold. 1967. *Studies in Ethnomethodology*. Englewood Cliffs, N.J.: Prentice Hall.

Garvin, David A. 1988. *Managing Quality: The Strategic and Competitive Edge*. New York: The Free Press.

Gatewood, R., and W. Rockmore. 1988. "Combining Organizational Manpower and Career Development Needs: An Operational Human Resource Planning Model." In *The Strategic Human Resource Management Source Book*, ed. L. Baird et al. Amherst, Mass.: Human Resources Development Press.

Gibson, F., and L. E. Teasley. 1973. "The Humanistic Model of Organizational Motivation: A Review of Research Support." *Public Administration Review* 33:89–96.

Giddens, Anthony. 1984. *The Constitution of Society: Outline of the Theory of Structuration*. Berkeley: University of California Press.

Goffman, Erving. 1961. *Asylums: Essays on the Social Situation of Mental Patients and Other Inmates*. Garden City, N.Y.: Anchor Books.

Gold, Michael Evan. 1983. *A Dialogue on Comparable Worth*. Ithaca: ILR Press.

Golembiewski, R. 1962. "Civil Service and Managing Work." *American Political Science Review* 56:961–974.

Goodman, P. 1977. "Social Comparison Processes in Organizations." In *New Directions in Organizational Behavior*, ed. Barry Staw and G. Salancik. Chicago: St. Clair.

Gordon, David, Richard Edwards, and Michael Reich. 1982. *Segmented Work, Divided Workers: The Historical Transformation of Labor in the United States.* Cambridge: Cambridge University Press.

Gottfried, Frances. 1984. "The Myth of Meritocracy: A Study of Challenges to Municipal Civil Service Systems." Ph.D. diss., New York University.

——. 1988. *The Merit System and Municipal Civil Service: A Fostering of Social Inequality.* Westport, Conn.: Greenwood Press, Inc.

Graham, Cole Blease, and Steven W. Hays. 1986. *Managing the Public Organization.* Washington, D.C.: Congressional Quarterly Press.

Grandjean, Burke D. 1981. "History and Career in a Bureaucratic Labor Market." *American Journal of Sociology* 86(5):1057–1092.

Grandjean, Burke D., and Patricia A. Taylor. 1980. "Job Satisfaction among Female Clerical Workers: 'Status Panic' or the Opportunity Structure of Office Work." *Sociology of Work and Occupations* 7(1):33–53.

Granovetter, Mark. 1981. "Toward a Sociological Theory of Income Differences." In *Sociological Perspectives in Labor Markets*, ed. Ivar Berg. New York: Academic Press.

——. 1985a. "The Direct Impact of Labor Processes on Inequality." Working paper, part 2, Sociology Department, State University of New York at Stony Brook.

——. 1985b. "Economic Action and Social Structure: A Theory of Embeddedness." Working paper no. 850301, Sociology Department, State University of New York at Stony Brook.

——. 1985c. "Labor Mobility, Internal Markets and Job Matching: A Comparison of the Sociological and the Economic Approaches." Sociology Department, SUNY at Stony Brook.

Greenbaum, Thomas L. 1988. *The Practical Handbook and Guide to Focus Group Research.* Lexington, Mass.: Lexington Books.

Greenberg, D. B., S. Strasser, L. L. Cummings, and R. B. Dunham. 1989. "The Impact of Personal Control on Performance and Satisfaction." *Organizational Behaviour and Human Decisions Process* 43:29–51.

Greenberg, Jerald. 1986. "The Distributive Justice of Organizational Performance Evaluations." In *Justice in Social Realtions*, ed. H. W. Bierhoff et al. New York: Plenum Press.

——. 1987. "Taxonomy of Organizational Justice Theories." *Academy of Management Review* 12(1):9–22.

Greenberg, Jerald, and Ronald L. Cohen. 1982. *Equity and Justice in Social Behaviour.* New York: Academic Press.

——. 1990. "Looking Fair vs. Being Fair: Managing Impressions of Organizational Justice." In *Research in Organizational Behavior*, vol. 12, ed. Barry M. Staw and L. L. Cummings. Greenwich, Conn.: JAI Press.

Grinker, William, D. Cooke, and A. Kirsch. 1970. *Climbing the Job Ladder: A Study of Employee Advancement in Eleven Industries.* New York: E. F. Shelley.

Grodin, J., D. Wollett, and A. Reginald, Jr. 1979. *Collective Bargaining and Public Employment.* Washington, D.C.: Bureau of National Affairs.

Gruenberg, Barry. 1980. "The Happy Worker: An Analysis of Educational and Occupational Differences in Determinants of Job Satisfaction." *American Journal of Sociology* 86(2):247–271.

Haberfeld, Yitchak. 1992. "Employee Discrimination: An Organizational Model." *The Academy of Management Journal* 35(March):161–180.

Habermas, Jürgen. 1973. *Legitimation Crisis*. Boston: Beacon Press.

Hackman, J. Richard, and E. Lawler. 1971. "Employee Reactions to Job Characteristics." *Journal of Applied Psychology* 55:259–86

Hackman, J. Richard, and Greg Oldham. 1980. *Work Redesign*. Reading, Mass.: Addision-Wesley.

Halaby, Charles N. 1978. "Bureaucratic Promotion Criteria." *Administrative Science Quarterly* 23:466–484.

Hale, Mary M., and Rita M. Kelly, eds. 1989. *Gender, Bureaucracy, and Democracy: Careers and Equal Opportunity in the Public Sector*. New York: Greenwood Press.

Halle, David. 1984. *America's Working Man: Work, Home, and Politics among Blue-Collar Property Owners*. Chicago: University of Chicago Press.

Hamper, Ben. 1991. *Rivethead: Tales from the Assembly Line*. New York: Warner Books.

Harmon, Michael, and Richard T. Mayer. 1986. *Organization Theory for Public Administration*. Boston: Little, Brown.

Hatfield, Elaine, and Susan Sprecher. 1984. "Equity Theory and Behaviour in Organizations." *Research in the Sociology of Organizations* 3:95–124.

Hauser, Robert M., W. M. Beck, Patrick M. Horan, and Charles M. Tolbert, II. 1980. "On Stratification in a Dual Economy." *American Sociological Review* 45(4):702–712.

Hauser, Robert M., and David L. Featherman. 1977. *The Process of Stratification: Trends and Analyses*. New York: Academic Press.

Hays, Steven W., and T. Zane Reeves. 1984. *Personnel Management in the Public Sector*. Boston: Allyn and Bacon.

Helgesen, Sally. 1990. "The Pyramid and the Web." *New York Times*, 27 May.

Heneman, Herbert G. III. 1985. "Pay Satisfaction." In *Research in Personnel and Human Resource Management*, vol. 3, ed. K. Rowland and G. Ferris. Greenwich, Conn.: JAI Press.

Henning, B., and M. Love. 1984. "Know Your Rights." *Local 1180 CWA*. New York: Communication Workers of America.

Herman, J., and C. Hulin. 1972. "Studying Organizational Attitudes from Individual and Organizational Frames of Reference." *Organizational Behavior and Human Performance* 8:84–108.

Higgins, E. Tory, and John A. Bargh. 1987. "Social Cognition and Social Perception." *Annual Review of Psychology* 38:369–425.

Hill, Linda, and Nancy Kamprath. 1991. "Beyond the Myth of the Perfect Mentor: Building a Network of Developmental Relationships." Teaching note 9-491-096, Harvard Business School.

Hirschman, Albert. 1970. *Exit, Voice, and Loyalty: Responses to Decline in Firms, Organizations, and States*. Cambridge: Harvard University Press.

Hodson, Randy, and Robert L. Kaufman. 1982. "Economic Dualism: A Critical Review." *American Sociological Review* 47(6):727–739.

Homans, George C. 1974. *Social Behavior, Its Elementary Forms*, rev. ed. New York: Harcourt, Brace, Jovanovich.

——. 1976. "Commentary." In *Advances in Experimental Social Psychology*, vol. 9, ed. L. BerKowitz and E. Walster, 231–244. New York: Academic Press.

Hopkins, Anne H. 1983. *Work and Job Satisfaction in the Public Sector*. Totowa, N.J.: Rowman and Allanheld.

Horan, Patrick M. 1978. "Is Status Attainment Atheoretical?" *American Sociological Review* 43(4):534–541.

Ibarra, Herminia. 1993. "Personal Networks of Women and Minorities in Management: A Conceptual Framework." *Academy of Management Review* 18:56–87.

Ilgen, Daniel, Debra Major, and Spencer Tower. 1994. The Cognitive Revolution in Organizational Behavior. In *Organizational Behavior: The State of the Science*, ed. Jerald Greenberg. Hillsdale, N.J.: Lawrence Earlbaum Associates.

Jacoby, S. 1984. "The Development of Internal Labor Markets in American Manufacturing Firms." In *Internal Labor Markets*, ed. Paul Osterman. Cambridge: MIT Press.

Jackson, Bruce. 1987. *Fieldwork*. Urbana: University of Illinois Press.

James, L., and A. Jones. 1976. "Organizational Structure: A Review of Structural Dimensions and Their Conceptual Relationship with Individual Attitudes and Behavior." *Organizational Behavior and Human Performance* 16:74–113.

Jasso, Guillermina. 1980. "A New Theory of Distributive Justice." *American Sociological Review* 45(1):3–32.

Johnson, Terry, Christopher Dandeker, and Clive Ashworth. 1984. *The Structure of Social Theory: Dilemmas, Strategies, and Projects*. New York: St. Martin's.

Johnston, William B., and Arnold E. Packer. 1987. *Workforce 2000: Work and Workers for the 21st Century*. Indianapolis: Hudson Institute.

Jovanovic, Boyan. 1984. *Job Matching and the Theory of Turnover*. New York: Garland.

Kalleberg, Arne L. 1974. "A Causal Approach to the Measurement of Job Satisfaction." Working Paper 74-2, Center of Demography and Ecology, University of Wisconsin, Madison.

———. 1975. *Work Values, Job Rewards, and Job Satisfaction: A Theory of the Quality of Work Experience*. Ph.D. diss. University of Wisconsin.

Kalleberg, Arne L., and Larry J. Griffin. 1978. "Positional Sources of Inequality in Job Satisfaction." *Sociology of Work and Occupations* 5(4):371–401.

———. 1980. "Class, Occupation, and Inequality in Job Rewards." *American Journal of Sociology* 85(4):731–68.

Kanter, Rosabeth Moss. 1976. "The Impact of Hierarchical Structures on the Work Behavior of Women and Men." *Social Problems* 23:415–30.

———. 1977. *Men and Women of the Corporation*. New York: Basic Books.

———. 1984. "Variations in Managerial Career Structures in High Technology Firms: The Impact of Organizational Characteristics on ILM Patterns." In *Internal Labor Markets*, ed. Paul Osterman. Cambridge: MIT Press.

———. 1987. "Men and Women of the Corporation Revisited." *Management Review* 76:14–16.

Kanter, Rosabeth Moss, and Barry Stein. 1994. *A Tale of O*, rev. ed. Cambridge, Mass.: Goodmeasure Inc. Videotape.

Karabel, Jerome, and A. H. Halsey. 1977. "Educational Research: A Review and Interpretation." In *Power and Ideology in Education*, ed. Jerome Karabel and A. H. Halsey. New York: Oxford University Press.

Katzell, Raymond, and David Yankelovich. 1985. *Work, Productivity, and Job Satisfaction: An Evaluation of Policy-Related Research*. New York: The Psychological Corporation.

Kearney, Richard C., and Chandan Sinha. 1988. "Professionalism and Bureaucratic Responsiveness: Conflict or Compatibility?" *Public Administration Review* 48(1):571–579.

Kelly, Michael P. 1980. *White-Collar Proletariat: The Industrial Behavior of British Civil Servants*. London: Routledge and Kegan Paul.

Kelman, Steven. 1987. *Making Public Policy: A Hopeful View of American Government.* New York: Basic Books.

——. 1990. "The Renewal of the Public Sector." *The American Prospect*, Summer, 51–57.

Kelsall, Roger Keith. 1955. *Higher Civil Servants in Britain: From 1870 to the Present Day.* London: Routledge and Kegan Paul.

Kerr, J., and J. W. Slocum. 1987. "Managing Corporate Culture Through Reward Systems." *Academy of Management Executive* 1(2):99–107.

Kilborn, Peter T. 1995. "For Many in Work Force, Glass Ceiling Still Exists." *New York Times*, 16 March.

Kim, Pan Suk, and Gregory B. Lewis 1994. "Asian Americans in the Public Service: Success, Diversity, and Discrimination." *Public Administration Review.* 54(3):285–290.

Klinger, Donald E. 1990. "Variables Affecting the Design of State and Local Personnel Systems." In *Public Personnel Administration: Problems and Prospects*, 2d ed., ed. Steven W. Hays and Richard C. Kearney. Englewood Cliffs, N.J.: Prentice Hall.

Klinger, Donald E., and John Nalbandian. 1985. *Public Personnel Management. Contexts and Strategies*, 2d ed. Englewood Claffs, N.J.: Prentice-Hall.

Kluegel, James, and Eliot R. Smith. 1986. *Beliefs about Inequality: Americans' Views of What Is and What Ought to Be.* New York: Aldine

Knoke, David, and Christine Wright-Isak. 1982. "Individual Motives and Organizational Incentive Systems." *Research in the Sociology of Organizations* 1:209–254.

Koch, James. L., and Richard M. Steers. 1978. "Job Attachment, Satisfaction, and Turnover among Public Sector Employees." *Journal of Vocational Behavior* 12(1):119–128.

Kohn, Melvin L., and Carmi Schooler. 1980. "Job Conditions and Intellectual Flexibility: A Longitudinal Assessment of Their Reciprocal Effects." In *Factor Analysis and Measurement in Social Research*, ed. E. F. Borgatta and D. Jackson. Beverly Hills: Sage.

——. 1983. *Work and Personality: An Inquiry into the Impact of Social Stratification.* Norwood, N.J.: Ablex Publishing.

Kratz, Harry. 1974. "Are Merit and Equity Compatible?" *Public Administration Review*, 34:434–440.

Krausz, Moshe. 1978. "A New Approach to Studying Worker Job Preferences." *Industrial Relations* 17(1):91–95.

Kulik, Carol T., and Maureen Ambrose. 1992. "Personnel and Situational Determinism of Referent Choice." *Academy of Management Review* 17(2):212–237.

Kulik, Carol T., E. Allan Lind, Maureen L. Ambrose, and Robert J. MacCoun. 1992. "Understanding Gender Differences in Procedural Justice." Paper presented at 1992 meeting of Academy of Management, Las Vegas.

Lane, Larry M., and James F. Wolf. 1991. *The Human Resource Crisis in the Public Sector: Rebuilding the Capacity to Govern.* Westport, Conn.: Quorum Books.

Lane, Robert E. 1986. "Market Justice, Political Justice." *American Political Science Review* 80:397–402.

——. 1991. *The Market Experience.* Cambridge: Cambridge University Press.

Larson, Magali. S. 1977. *The Rise of Professionalism: A Sociological Analysis.* Berkeley: University of California Press.

LaSalle, Robert, and Linda Bakst. 1987. *Statistics on Women and Minorities in Public Employment.* Albany: Center for Women in Government.

Lawler, Edward, III. 1977. "Satisfaction and Behavior." In *Perspectives on Behavior in Organizations*, ed. Richard Hackman et al. New York: McGraw Hill.

254

References

——. 1983. "The Strategic Design of Rewards Systems." In *Motivation and Work Behaviour*, 4th ed. New York: McGraw Hill.

Lefkowitz, J., ed. 1985. *The Evolving Process: Collective Negotiations in Public Employment.* Fort Washington, Pa.: Labor Relations Press.

Lepper, Mary. 1983. "Affirmative Action: A Tool for Effective Personnel Management." In *Public Personnel Administration: Problems and Prospects*, ed. Steven W. Hays and Richard C. Kearney. Englewood Cliffs, N.J.: Prentice Hall.

Lerner, Melvin, Dab Miller, and John Holmes. 1976. "Deserving and the Emergence of Forms of Justice." In *Advances in Experimental Social Psychology*, vol. 9, ed. L. Berkowitz and E. Walster, 133–162. New York: Academic Press.

Levine, C., and G. Wolohojian. 1983. "Retrenchment and Human Resources Management: Combatting the Discount Effects of Uncertainty." In *Public Personnel Administration: Problems and Prospects*, ed. Steven W. Hays and Richard C. Kearney, 175–189. Englewood Cliffs, N.J.: Prentice Hall.

Levine, John M., and Richard L. Moreland. 1987. "Social Comparison and Outcome Evaluation in Group Contexts." In *Social Comparison, Social Justice, and Relative Deprivation*, ed. John C. Masters and William P. Smith. Hillsdale, N.J.: Lawrence Erlbaum Associates.

Levine, Marvin J., and Eugene C. Hagburg, eds. 1979. *Labor Relations and the Public Sector: Readings, Cases, and Experimental Exercises.* Salt Lake City: Brighton Publishing Co.

Lewis, Gregory B. 1994. "Women, Occupation, and Federal Agencies: Occupational Mix and Interagency Difference in Sexual Inequality in Federal White-Collar Employment." *Public Administration Review* 54(3):271–275.

Lincoln, James R. 1982. "Intra- (and Inter-) Organizational Networks." In *Research in the Sociology of Organizations*, vol. 1 ed. Samuel Bacharach, Greenwich, Conn.: JAI Press, Inc.

Lincoln, James R., and Arne L. Kalleberg. 1990. *Culture, Control, and Commitment: A Study of Work Organization and Work Attitudes in the United States and Japan.* Cambridge: Cambridge University Press.

Lincoln, Yvonna. 1985. "The Substance of the Emergent Paradigm: Implications for Researchers." In *Organizational Theory and Inquiry: The Paradigm Revolution*, ed. Yvonna Lincoln. Newbury Park Calif.: Sage Publications.

Litchman, C., and R. Hunt. 1971. "Personality and Organization Theory: A Review of Some Conceptual Literature." *Psychological Bulletin* 76:271–94.

Locke, E. 1976. "The Nature and Causes of Job Satisfaction." In the *Handbook of Industrial and Organizational Psychology*, ed. M. Dunnette. Chicago: Rand McNally.

Loden, Marilyn, and Judy B. Rosener. 1991. *Workforce America!: Managing Employee Diversity as a Vital Resource.* Homewood, Ill.: Business One Irwin.

Lopez Amparano, Julie. 1992. "Study Says Women Face Glass Walls As Well As Ceilings." *Wall Street Journal.* 3 March.

Maccoby, Michael. 1988. *Why Work? Leading the New Generation.* New York: Simon & Schuster.

Mahoney, T. A. 1975. "Justice and Equity: A Recurring Theme in Compensation." *Personnel* 52:60–66.

Malcomson, James M. 1984. "Work Incentives, Hierarchy, and Internal Labor Markets." *Journal of Political Economy* 92(3):486–507.

Markham, S. E. 1988. "Pay-for-performance Dilemma Revisited: Empirical Example of the Importance of Group Effect." *Journal of Applied Psychology* 73:178–180.

Markham, William T., Scott J. South, Charles M. Bonjean, and Judy Corder. 1985. "Gender and Opportunity in the Federal Bureaucracy." *American Journal of Sociology* 91(1):129–150.

Marsden, Peter, and Nan Lin, eds. 1982. *Social Structure and Network Analysis*. Beverly Hills: Sage Publications.

Martin, Joanne. 1981. "Relative Deprivation: A Theory of Distributive Injustice for an Era of Shrinking Resources." In *Research in Organization Behaviour*, vol. 3, ed. Barry M. Staw and L. L. Cummings. Greenwich, C.T.: JAI Press.

———. 1986. "When Expectation and Justice Do Not Coincide." In *Justice in Social Relations*, ed. H. W. Bierhoff et al. New York: Plenum Press.

Martin, Joanne, and Joseph Harder. 1988. "Bread and Roses: Justice and the Distribution of Financial and Socio-Emotional Rewards in Organizations." Research paper 1010, Stanford University Graduate School of Business, Stanford.

Marx, Karl. 1975. *Capital: A Critique of Political Economy*. New York: International Publishers.

Masters, J. C., and L. J. Keil. 1987. "Generic Comparison in Human Judgement and Behavior." In *Social Comparison, Social Justice, and Relative Deprivation: Theoretical, Empirical, and Policy Perspectives*, ed. John P. Masters and William P. Smith. Hillsdale, N.J.: Lawrence Erlbaum Associates.

Masters, John C., and William P. Smith, eds. 1987. *Social Comparison, Social Justice, and Relative Deprivation: Theoretical, Empirical, and Policy Perspectives*. Hillsdale, N.J.: Lawrence Erlbaum Associates.

Mayer, William G. 1992. *The Changing American Mind: How and Why American Public Opinion Changed between 1960 and 1988*. Ann Arbor: University of Michigan Press.

Mayor's Office of Operations. 1986. *Mayor's Management Report*. By Edward I. Koch. New York.

McClintock, Charles G., and Linda J. Keil. 1982. "Equity and Social Exchange." In *Equity and Justice in Social Behavior*, ed. Jerald Greenberg and Ronald L. Cohen. New York: Academic Press.

McClosky, Herbert, and John Zaller. 1984. *The American Ethos: Public Attitudes toward Capitalism and Democracy*. Cambridge: Harvard University Press.

McFarlin, Dean, and Paul Sweeney. 1992. "Distributive and Procedural Justice as Predictors of Satisfaction with Personal and Organizational Outcomes." *Academy of Management Journal* 35:626–637.

McGregor, Eugene B. 1988. "The Public Sector Human Resource Puzzle: Strategic Management of a Strategic Resource." *Public Administration Review* 48(6):941–950.

———. 1991. *Strategic Management of Human Knowledge, Skills, and Abilities*. San Francisco: Jossey-Bass.

McKinney's Consolidated Laws of New York. 1983. *Civil Service Law*, book 9. St. Paul, Minn.: West Publishing.

McNair, R. H., and L. Pollane. "Citizen Participation in Public Bureaucracies: Foul Weather Friends." *Administration and Society* 14:507–524.

Mendl, J. R. 1989. "Managing to be Fair: An Exploration of Value Motives and Leadership." *American Sociological Review* 34:252–276.

Merit Systems Protection Board. 1992. *A Question of Equity: Women and the Glass Ceiling in the Federal Government.* Washington, D.C.: U.S. Government Printing Office.

Merton, Robert K. 1968. *Social Theory and Social Structure.* New York: The Free Press.

Meyer, John W., and Brian Roman. 1977. "Institutional Organizations: Formal Structure as Myth and Ceremony." *American Journal of Sociology* 83(2):340–363.

Meyer, John, and Richard Scott. 1983. *Organization Environments: Ritual and Rationality.* Beverly Hills: Sage Publications.

Meyer, C. Kenneth, and C. Brown. 1989. *Practicing Public Management: A Casebook,* 2d ed. New York: St. Martin's.

Meyer, Marshall W., and M. Craig Brown. 1977. "The Process of Bureaucratization." *American Journal of Sociology* 83(2):364–385.

Milcovich, G., et al. 1983. "Human Resource Management Planning." In *Human Resource Management in the 1980's,* ed. S. Carroll and R. Schuller. Washington, D.C.: Bureau of National Affairs.

Miller, A., D. Treiman, P. Cain, and P. Roos, eds. 1980. *Work, Jobs, and Occupations: A Critical Review of the D.O.T.* Washington, D.C.: National Academy Press.

Miller, E., Schon Beechler, Bhal Bhatt, and Raghu Nath. 1988. "The Relationship between Global Strategy and the Human Resource Management Function." In *The Strategic Human Resource Management Sourcebook,* ed. L, Baird et al. Amherst, Mass.: Human Resource Development Press.

Miller, Joanne. 1980. "Individual and Occupational Determinants of Job Satisfaction: A Focus on Gender Differences." *Sociology of Work and Occupations* 7(3):337–366.

Mills, C. Wright. 1959. *The Sociological Imagination.* New York: Oxford University Press.

Mintzberg, Henry. 1979. *The Structuring of Organizations: A Synthesis of the Research.* Englewood Cliffs, N.J.: Prentice Hall.

———. 1989. *Mintzberg on Management: Inside Our Strange World of Organizations.* New York: Free Press.

Mitchell, Terence R. 1979. "Organizational Behavior." *Annual Review of Psychology* 30:243–281.

Moch, M. 1979. "A Relational Structure of Formal Organizations: Employee Location in the Work Group and Clique Structure and Satisfaction with Interpersonal Relationships." Paper presented at the Annual Meeting of the American Sociological Association, Boston.

Moore, Carl M. 1986. *Group Techniques for Idea Building.* Beverly Hills: Sage Publications.

Moore, Perry. 1988. *Public Personnel Management. A Contingency Approach.* Lexington, Mass.: Lexington Books.

Morgan, Gareth. 1986. *Images of Organization.* Beverly Hills: Sage Publications.

Morrison, Ann M., Randall P. White, Ellen Van Velsor, and the Center for Creative Leadership. *Breaking the Glass Ceiling: Can Women Reach the Top of America's Largest Corporations?* Reading, Mass.: Addison-Wesley.

Morrison, Ann M., and M. A. Von Glinow. 1990. "Women and Minorities in Management." *American Psychologist* 45:200–208.

Morton, D. C., and D. R. Watson. 1974. "Compensatory Education and Contemporary Liberalism in the U.S.: A Sociological Review." In *Sociology of Education,* ed. W. Cave and M. Chesler. New York: Macmillan.

Mosher, F., and R. Stillman. 1977. "Introduction: The Professions in Government." *Public Administration Review* 37(6):631–633.

Muchinsky, P. 1987. *Psychology Applied to Work: An Introduction to Industrial and Organizational Psychology.* Chicago: Dorsey.

Murnighan, J. Keith., ed. 1993. *Social Psychology in Organizations.* Englewood Cliffs, N.J.: Prentice-Hall.

Murphy, Raymond. 1988. *Social Closure: The Theory of Monopolization and Exclusion.* Oxford: Clarendon.

Mustari, Elisa. 1992. "Organizational Structure and Job Satisfaction: a LISREL Causal Analysis of Proposed Mediators and a Moderator." Paper presented in the Academy of Management meetings, Las Vegas.

Nadler, David A., and Edward Lawler. 1977. "Motivation: A Diagnostic Approach." In *Perspectives on Behavior in Organizations,* ed. J. R. Hackman, E. Lawler III, and L. Porter. New York: McGraw Hill.

National Association of Public Administrators. 1991. *Modernizing Federal Classification: An Opportunity for Excellence.* Washington, D.C.: National Academy of Public Administration.

Okun, Arthur. 1975. *Equality and Efficiency, The Big Trade-Off.* Washington, D.C.: Brookings Institute.

Oldham, Greg, and J. Richard Hackman. 1981. "Relationships Between Organizational Structure and Employee Reactions: Comparing Alternative Frameworks." *Administrative Science Quarterly* 26(1):66–83.

Oldham, Greg, Carol Kulik, Maureen Ambrose, Lee Stepina, and Julianne Brand. 1986. "Relations between Job Facet Comparisons and Employee Reactions." *Organizational Behaviour and Human Decision Process* 38:28–47.

Ondrack, Daniel A., and Martin G. Evans. 1986. "Job Enrichment and Job Satisfaction in Quality of Working Life and Nonquality of Working Life Work Sites." *Human Relations* 39(9):871–889.

Oppenheim, Felix E. 1980. "Egalitarian Rules of Distribution." *Ethics* 90:164–179.

Organ, D. W. 1990. "The Motivational Basis of Organizational Citizenship Behaviour." In *Research in Organization Behaviour,* vol. 12, ed. Barry M. Staw and L. L. Cummings. Greenwich, Conn.: JAI Press.

Ospina, Sonia. 1989. "Opportunity and Satisfaction: A Structural Approach to the Study of Work Attitudes." Ph.D. diss., Department of Sociology, State University of New York at Stony Brook.

——. 1991. "Opportunity and Satisfaction: A Structural Approach to the Study of Job Attitudes." *Business and Economic Review* 4(2):69–90.

——. 1992a. "Expediency Management in Public Service: A Dead-End Search for Managerial Discretion." *Public Productivity and Management Review* 15(4):405–421.

——. 1992b. "When Managers Don't Plan. Structural Consequences of Non-Strategic Public Personnel Management." *Review of Public Personnel Administration* 12(2):52–67.

Osterman, P. 1980. *Getting Started: The Youth Labor Market.* Cambridge: MIT Press.

——. 1984a. "Introduction: The Nature and Importance of Internal Labor Markets." In *Internal Labor Markets,* ed. Paul Osterman. Cambridge: MIT Press.

——. 1984b. "White-Collar Internal Labor Markets." In *Internal Labor Markets,* ed. Paul Osterman. Cambridge: MIT Press.

——. 1988. *Employment Futures: Reorganization, Dislocation, and Public Policy.* New York: Oxford University Press.

References

Ouchi, William. 1980. "Markets, Bureaucracies, and Clans." *Administrative Science Quarterly* 25:129–141.

Page, Paul. 1994. "African-Americans in Executive Branch Agencies." *Review of Public Personnel Administration* 14:24–51.

Parker, Mike. 1986. *Inside the Circle: A Union Guide to Quality of Work Life.* Boston: South End Press.

Payne, R., S. Fineman, and T. Wall. 1976. "Organizational Climate and Job Satisfaction: A Conceptual Synthesis." *Organizational Behavior and Human Performance* 16:45–62.

Pennings, J. 1979. "Work Value Systems of White-Collar Workers." *Administrative Science Quarterly* 15:397–405.

Perrow, Charles. 1986. *Complex Organizations: A Critical Essay*, 3d ed. New York: Random House.

Peterson-Hardt, Sandra, and Nancy Pearlman. 1979. *Sex-Segregated Career Ladders in New York State Government: A Structural Analysis of Inequality in Employment.* Albany: Center for Women and Government, State University of New York.

Pfeffer, Jeffrey. 1977. "Toward an Examination of Stratification in Organizations." *Administrative Science Quarterly* 22(4):553–567.

——. 1981. *Power in Organizations.* Marshfield, Mass.: Pitman.

——. 1983. "Organizational Demography." In *Research in Organizational Behavior*, vol. 5, ed. L. Cummings and Barry M. Staw. Greenwich, Conn.: JAI Press.

——. 1992. *Managing with Power: Politics and Influence in Organizations.* Boston: Harvard Business School.

Pfeffer, Jeffrey, and James N. Baron. 1988. "Taking the Workers Back Out: Recent Trends in the Structuring of Employment." In *Research in Organization Behaviour*, vol. 10, ed. Barry M. Staw and L. L. Cummings. Greenwich, Conn.: JAI Press.

Pfeffer, Jeffrey, and N. Langton. 1988. "Wage Inequality and the Organization of Work: The Case of Academic Departments." *Administratively Science Quarterly* 33:588–606.

Pfeffer, Jeffrey, and Joyce D. Ross. 1980. "Do Wage and Status Attainment Differ by Industry Sector?" Graduate School of Business, Stanford University. Duplicated.

Pierce, J. L. 1979. "Employee Affective Responses to Work Unit Structure and Job Design: A Test of an Intervening Variable. *Journal of Management* 5:193–212.

Porter, L. W., and E. Lawler. 1965. "Properties of Organizational Structure in Relationship to Job Attitudes and Behavior." *Psychological Bulletin* 64:23–51.

Portigal, A. 1976. *Towards the measurement of Work Satisfaction.* OECD, Paris.

Powell, Gary N. 1993. *Women and Men in Management.* Newbury: Sage Publications.

Powell, Walter W. and Paul J. DiMaggio, eds. 1991. *The New Institutionalism in Organizational Analysis.* Chicago: University of Chicago Press.

Presley-Noble, Barbara. 1992. "And Now, the 'Sticky Floor.'" *New York Times.* 22 November.

Price, James L. 1972. *Handbook of Organizational Measurement.* Lexington, Mass.: D. C. Heath.

——. 1977. *The Study of Turnover.* Iowa City: Iowa University Press.

Pritchard, Robert D., Marvin D. Dunnette, and Dale O. Jorgenson. 1972. "Effects of Perceptions of Equity and Inequity on Worker Satisfaction and Performance." *Journal of Applied Psychology* 56:75–94.

Quinn, R., and L. Shepard. 1974. *The 1972–73 Quality of Employment Survey.* Ann Arbor: Institute of Social Research, University of Michigan.

——. 1978. *The 1977 Quality of Employment Survey*. Ann Arbor: Institute of Social Research, University of Michigan.

Ratner, R. S. 1981. *Barriers to Advancement: Promotion of Women and Minorities into Managerial Positions in New York State Government*. Albany: Center for Women in Government, SUNY.

Reis, Harry T. 1984. "The Multidimensionality of Justice." In *The Sense of Injustice: Social Psychological Perspectives*, ed. Robert Folger. New York: Plenum.

Reskin, Barbara F. 1984. *Sex Segregation in the Workplace: Trends, Explanations, Remedies*. Washington, D.C.: National Academy Press.

Reskin, Barbara F., and Heidi I. Hartman, eds. 1986. *Women's Work, Men's Work: Sex Segregation on the Job*. Washington, D.C.: National Academy Press.

Rich, Wilbur C. 1982. *The Politics of Urban Personnel Policy: Reformers, Politicians, and Bureaucrats*. Port Washington, N.Y.: Kennikat Press.

Ripley, Randall B., and Grace A. Franklin. 1982. *Bureaucracy and Policy Implementation*. Homewood, Ill.: Dorsey Press.

Ritzman, Rosemary L., and Donald Tomaskovic-Devey, 1992. "Life Chances and Support for Equality and Equity as Normative and Counternormative Distribution Rules." *Social Forces* 70(3):745–763.

Robinson, R., and J. Kelley. 1979. "Class as Conceived by Marx and Dahrendorf: Effects on Income Inequality and Politics in the U.S. and Great Britain." *American Sociological Review* 44:38–58.

Robinson, John, Robert, Athanasiou, and Kendra Head. 1969. *Measures of Occupational Attitudes and Occupational Characteristics*. Ann Arbor: Survey Research Center, University of Michigan.

Roos, Patricia A., and Barbara F. Reskin. 1984. "Institutional Factors Contributing to Sex Segregation in the Workplace." In *Sex Segregation in the Workplace: Trends, Explanations, Remedies*. Washington, D.C.: National Academy Press.

Rosenbaum, James E. 1984. *Career Mobility in a Corporate Hierarchy*. Orlando, Fla.: Academic Press.

Rosenberg, M. 1968. *The Logic of Survey Analysis*. New York: Basic Books.

Ross, Joyce D. 1990. "Developments in Recruitment and Selection." In *Public Personnel Administration*. 2d ed., ed. S. Hays and R. Kearney. Englewood Cliffs, N.J.: Prentice Hall.

Rousseau, Denise M. 1978. "Characteristics of Departments, Positions, and Individuals: Contexts for Attitudes and Behavior. *Administrative Science Quarterly* 23:521–540.

——. 1989. "Psychological and Implied Contracts in Organizations." *Employee Responsibilities and Rights Journal* 2(2):121–139.

Rubin, Lilian B. 1976. *Worlds of Pain: Life in the Working-Class Family*. New York: Basic Books, Inc.

Runciman, Walter Garrison. 1966. *Relative Deprivation and Social Justice*. Berkeley: University of California Press.

Salaman, Graeme. 1979. *Work Organizations, Resistance, and Control*. New York: Longman.

Salancik, Gerald, and Jeffrey Pfeffer. 1977. "An Examination of Need-Satisfaction Models of Job Attitudes and Task Design." *Administrative Science Quarterly* 22(3):427–456.

——. 1978. "A Social Information Processing Approach to Job Attitudes and Task Design." *Administrative Science Quarterly* 23(2):224–253.

Saltzstein, Alan. 1990. "Personnel Management in the Local Government Setting." In *Public Personnel Administration: Problems and Prospects*, 2d ed., ed. Steven W. Hays and Richard C. Kearney. Englewood Cliffs, N.J.: Prentice Hall.

Sampson, Edward E. 1983. *Justice and the Critique of Pure Psychology*. New York: Plenum Press.

———. 1986. "Justice Ideology and Social Legitimation." In *Justice in Social Relations*, ed. H. W. Bierhoff et al. New York: Plenum.

Savas, E. S., and Sigmund Ginsburg. 1973. "The Civil Service: A Meritless System?" *The Public Interest*, no. 32:70–85.

Schneider, B., S. Gunnarson, and J. Wheeler. 1992. "The Role of Opportunity in the Conceptualization and Measurement of Job Satisfaction." In *Job Satisfaction: How People Feel about Their Jobs and How it Affect Their Performance*, ed. C. J. Cranny, P. Crain Smith, and E. Stone. New York: Lexington Books.

Schoderbeck P. P., and Satish P. Deshpande. 1993. "Performance and Nonperformance Factors in Pay Allocations Made by Managers." *Journal of Psychology* 127(4):391–398.

Schuler, Randall. 1988. "Personnel and Human Resource Management Choices and Organizational Strategy." In *The Strategic Human Resource Management Sourcebook*, ed. L. Baird et al. Amherst, Mass.: Human Resources Development Press.

———. 1992. *Managing Human Resources*, 4th ed. New York: West.

Shafritz, Jay M., Albert C. Hyde, and David H. Rosenbloom. 1986. *Personnel Management in Government*, 3d ed. New York: Marcel Dekker.

Sheppard, Blair H., Roy J. Lewicki, and John W. Minton. 1992. *Organizational Justice: The Search for Fairness in the Workplace*. New York: Lexington Books.

Sheppard, Harold L., and Neal Q. Herrick. 1972. *Where Have All the Robots Gone? Worker Dissatisfaction in the Seventies*. New York: Free Press.

Smith, Patricia Cain, Lorne M. Kendall, and Charles L. Hulin. 1969. *The Measurement of Satisfaction in Work and Retirement: a Strategy for the Study of Attitudes*. Chicago: Rand McNally.

Smith, Thelma. E., ed. 1973. *Guide to the Municipal Government of the City of New York*. New York: Meilen Press.

Snizek, W., and J. Bullard. 1983. "Perceptions of Bureaucracy and Changing Job Satisfaction: A Longitudinal Analysis." *Organizational Behavior and Human Performance* 32:275–287.

Sorensen, Aage B. 1974. "A Model of Occupational Careers." *American Journal of Sociology* 80(1):44–57.

Sorensen, Aage B., and Arne L. Kalleberg. 1981. "An Outline of a Theory of the Matching of Persons to Jobs." In *Sociological Perspectives of Labor Markets*, ed. Ivar Berg. New York: Academic Press.

Sorensen, Aage B., and Nancy Brown Tuma. 1981. "Labor Market Structures and Job Mobility." In *Research in Social Stratification and Mobility*, vol. 1. Greenwich, Conn.: JAI Press.

Sorokin, Pitirim A. 1943. *Sociocultural Causality, Space, Time: A Study of Referential Principles of Sociology and Social Science*. Durham, N.C.: Duke University Press.

Spaeth, Joel L. 1984. "Structural Contexts and the Stratification of Work." In *Research in Social Stratification and Mobility*, vol. 3. Greenwich, Conn.: JAI Press.

Spero, Sterling D., and John M. Capozzola. 1973. *The Urban Community and its Unionized Bureaucracies: Pressure Politics in Local Government Labor Relations*. New York: Dunellen.

Spilerman, Seymour. 1977. "Careers, Labor Market Structure, and Socioeconomic Achievement." *American Journal of Sociology* 83(3):551–593.

Spring, Joel. 1985. *American Education*, 3d ed. New York: Longman.

Sprouse, M., ed. 1992. *Sabotage in the American Workplace: Anecdotes of Dissatisfaction, Mischief, and Revenge*. San Francisco: Pressure Drop Press.

Stafford, Walter. 1989. *Employment Segmentation in New York City Agencies*. New York: Community Service Society of New York.

Starr, Paul. 1982. *The Social Transformation of American Medicine: The Rise of a Sovereign Profession and the Making of a Vast Industry*. New York: Basic Books.

Staw, Barry M. 1974. "Attitudinal and Behavioral Consequences of Changing a Major Organizational Reward: A Natural Field Experiment." *Journal of Personality and Social Psychology* 29:742–51.

Staw, Barry M., Nancy E. Bell, and John A. Clausen. 1986. "The Dispositional Approach to Job Attitudes: A Lifetime Longitudinal Test." *Administrative Science Quarterly* 31(1):56–77.

———. 1986. "Organizational Psychology and the Pursuit of the Happy/Productive Worker." *California Management Review* 28:40–53.

Stein, L. 1987. "Merit Systems and Political Influence: The Case of Local Government." *Public Administration Review* 47(3):263–271.

Stewart, Judith. 1982. "Changing Structure and Social Composition of Occupations in Organizations." In *Research in the Sociology of Organizations*, vol. 1, ed. Samuel Bacharach. Greenwich, Conn.: JAI Press.

Stewman, Shelby, 1975. "An Application of a Job Vacancy Chain Model to a Civil Service Internal Labor Market." *Journal of Mathematical Sociology* 4(1):37–59.

Stewman, Shelby, and Suresh Konda. 1983. "Careers and Organizational Labor Markets: Demographic Models of Organizational Behavior." *American Journal of Sociology* 88(4):637–685.

Stone, Eugene. 1992. "A Critical Analysis of Social Information Processing Models of Job Perceptions and Job Attitudes." In *Job Satisfaction: How People Feel about Their Jobs and How it Affects Their Performance*, ed. C. J. Cranny, Patricia Cain Smith and Eugene Stone. New York: Lexington Books.

Sylvia, Ronald D., and Kenneth C. Meyer. 1990. "An Organizational Perspective on Training and Development in the Public Sector." In *Public Personnel Administration: Problems and Prospects*, 2d ed., ed. Steven W. Hays and Richard C. Kearny. Englewood Cliffs, N.J.: Prentice Hall.

Taylor, Bron Raymond. 1991. *Affirmative Action at Work: Law Politics and Ethics*. Pittsburgh: University of Pittsburgh Press.

Terkel, Studs. 1974. *Working People Talk about What They Do All Day and How They Feel about What They Do*. New York: Pantheon Books.

Thomas, J., and D. Heisel. 1983. "The Modernization of Recruitment and Selection in Local Governments." In *Public Personnel Administration*. ed. Steven W. Hays and Richard C. Kearney. Englewood Cliffs, N.J.: Prentice Hall.

Thompson, Frank J. 1990. "The Politics of Public Personnel Administration." In *Public Personnel Administration: Problems and Prospects*, 2d ed., ed. Steven W. Hays and Richard C. Kearney. Englewood Cliffs, N.J.: Prentice Hall.

———. 1991. *Classics of Public Personnel Policy*, 2d ed. Pacific Grove, Calif.: Brooks-Cole.

Tolbert, Pamela S., and Lynne G. Zucker. 1983. "Institutional Sources of Change in the

Formal Structure of Organizations: The Diffusion of the Civil Service Reform, 1880–1935." *Administrative Science Quarterly* 28(1):22–39.

Tomaskovic-Devey, Donald. 1993. *Gender and Racial Inequality at Work: The Sources and Consequences of Job Segregation.* Ithaca: ILR Press.

Törnblom, Kjell Y., and Dan R. Jonsson. 1985. "Subrules of the Equality and Contribution Principles: Their Perceived Fairness in Distribution and Retribution." *Social Psychology Quarterly* 48:3, 249–261.

Treas, Judith, and Andrea R. Tyree. 1979. "Prestige versus Socioeconomic Status in the Attainment Process of American Men and Women." *Social Science Research* 8(3):201–221.

Treiman, Donald J. 1970. "Industrialization and Social Stratification." *Sociological Inquiry* 40:207–234.

———. 1976. "A Comment on Professor Lewis Coser's Presidential Address." *American Sociologist* 11:27–33.

———. 1977a. *Occupational Prestige in Comparative Perspective.* New York: Academic Press.

———. 1977b. "Toward Methods for Quantitative Sociology: A Reply to Burawoy." *American Journal of Sociology* 82:1042–1056.

Treiman, Donald J., and Kermit Terrel. 1975. "The Process of Status Attainment in the United States and Great Britain." *American Journal of Sociology* 81(3):563–583.

Tuma, Nancy Brown. 1976. "Rewards, Resources, and the Rate of Mobility: A Nonstationary Multivariate Stochastic Model." *American Journal of Sociology* 41(2):338–360.

Turner, Arthur N., and Paul R. Lawrence. 1965. *Industrial Jobs and the Worker.* Boston: Division of Research, Graduate School of Business Administration, Harvard University.

Turner, Jonathan H. 1991. *The Structure of Sociological Theory,* 5th ed. Belmont, Calif.: Wadsworth.

Tyack, David B. 1974. *The One Best System: A History of American Urban Education.* Cambridge: Harvard University Press.

Tyler, Tom R. 1984. "Justice in the Political Arena." In *The Sense of Injustice: Social Psychological Perspectives,* ed. Robert Folger. New York: Plenum.

Urban Research Center. 1987. "Wage Discrimination and Occupational Segregation in New York City's Municipal Work Force: Time for a Change." Research paper, Graduate School of Public Administration, New York University. New York.

Van Riper, Paul P. 1958. *History of the United States Civil Service.* Evanston, Ill.: Row, Peterson.

Verba, Sidney, and Gary R. Orren. 1985. *Equality in America. The View from the Top.* Cambridge: Harvard University Press.

Vitalo, R., and S. Harrison. 1988. "What Happens When Organizational Policy and Human Resource Strategy Are Not Integrated: A Case Study of Failed Human Resource Planning." In *The Strategic Human Resource Management Sourcebook,* ed. L. Baird et al. Amherst, Mass.: Human Resources Development Press.

Vlastos, G. 1962. "Justice and Equality." In *Social Justice,* ed. Richard B. Brant. Englewood Cliffs, N.J.: Prentice-Hall.

Voydanoff, Patricia. 1978. "The Relationship between Perceived Job Characteristics and Job Satisfaction among Occupational Status Groups." *Sociology of Work and Occupations* 5(2):179–192.

Vroom, Victor H. 1964. *Work and Motivation*. New York: John Wiley and Sons.

Walker, J. 1988. "Linking Human Resources Planning and Strategic Planning." In *The Strategic Human Resource Management Sourcebook*, ed. L. Baird et al. Amherst, Mass.: Human Resources Development Press.

Wallace, Michael, and Arne L. Kalleberg. 1981. "Economic Organization of Firms and Labor Market Consequences: Toward a Specification of Dual Economy Theory," in *Sociological Perspectives on Labor Markets*, ed. Ivar Berg. New York: Academic Press.

Wallerstein, Immanuel. 1988. "The Ideological Tensions of Capitalism: Universalism versus Racism and Sexism'. In *Racism, Sexism, and the World-System*, ed. Joan Smith, Jane Collins, Terence Hopkins, and Akbar Muhammad. New York: Greenwood Press.

Walster, Elaine, Ellen Berscheid, and G. William Walster. 1973. "New Directions in Equity Research." *Journal of Personality and Social Psychology* 25:151–176.

Wanous, J. P., and E. E. Lawler III. 1972. "Measurement and Meaning of Job Satisfaction." *Journal of Applied Psychology* 56:95–105.

Weaver, C. 1980. "Job Satisfaction in the United States in the 1970s." *Journal of Applied Psychology* 65:364–367.

Weber, Max. 1978. *Economy and Society: An Outline of Interpretive Sociology*. Vol. 2. Berkeley: University of California Press.

Weiner, Bernard. 1986. *An Attributional Theory of Motivation and Emotion*. New York: Springer-Verlag.

Weiss, Harold M., and Seymour Adler. 1984. "Personality and Organizational Behaviour." In *Research in Organization Behaviour*, vol. 6, ed. Barry M. Staw and L. L. Cummings. Greenwich, Conn.: JAI Press.

White, Harrison C. 1970. *Chains of Opportunity: System Models of Mobility in Organizations*. Cambridge: Harvard University Press.

Whyte, William H. 1965. *The Organization Man*. New York: Simon and Schuster.

Williams, Richard E. 1990. *Hierarchical Structures and Social Value: The Creation of Black and Irish Identities in the United States*. Cambridge: Cambridge University Press.

Williamson, Oliver E. 1975. *Markets and Hierarchies, Analysis and Antitrust Implications: A Study in the Economics of Internal Organizations*. New York: The Free Press.

Wilson, James Q. 1989. *Bureaucracy: What Government Agencies Do and Why They Do It*. New York: Basic Books.

Wise, L. R. 1990. "The Civil Service as a Vehicle for Social Equity." Paper presented at the Symposium for Public Administration Research, April, at Los Angeles.

Wright, Erik Olin, and Luca Perrone. 1977. "Marxist Class Categories in Income Inequality." *American Sociological Review* 42(1):32–55.

Yankelovich, D. 1983. *Putting the Work Ethic to Work: A Public Agenda Report on Restoring America's Competitive Edge*. New York: The Public Agenda Foundation.

Young, Michael D. 1958. *The Rise of the Meritocracy 1870-2033: An Essay on Education and Equality*. London: Thames and Hudson.

———, ed. 1971. *Knowledge and Control: New Directions for the Sociology of Education*. London: Collier-Macmillan.

Zagoria, Sam, ed. 1972. *Public Workers and Public Unions*. Englewood Cliffs, N.J.: Prentice-Hall.

Zaleznik, Abraham, C. R. Christensen, and F. J. Roethlisberger. 1958. *The Motivation, Productivity and Satisfaction of Workers*. Boston: Division of Social Research, Graduate School of Business Administration, Harvard University.

Zanna, M. P., J. M. Olson, and C. P. Herman, eds. 1987. *Social Influence: The Ontario Symposium*, vol 5. Hillsdale, N.J.: Erlbaum Press.

Zeitz, Gerald. 1983. "Structural and Individual Determinants of Organizational Morale and Satisfaction." *Social Forces* 61(4):1088–1108.

Zerubavel, Eviatar. 1980. "If Simmel Were a Fieldworker: On Formal Sociological Theory and Analytical Field Research." *Symbolic Interaction* 3(2):25–32.

Zucker, Lynne G., and Carolyn Rosenstein. 1981. "Taxonomies of Institutional Structure: Dual Economy Reconsidered." *American Sociological Review* 46(6):869–884.

Zussman, Robert. 1985. *Mechanics of the Middle Class*. Berkeley: University of California Press.

Subject Index